D0908156

HOMO
QUAERENS

HOMO QUAERENS

THE SEEKER AND THE SOUGHT

Method Become Ontology

Leonard Charles Feldstein

New York
Fordham University Press
1978

© Copyright 1978 by FORDHAM UNIVERSITY PRESS
All rights reserved.
LC 76–18464
ISBN 0–8232–1019–7

Printed in the United States of America

For
LORI *and* JONATHAN
my beloved children
who ever renew the elemental wonder of life;
for me, they are the living embodiment of reverence and purity, when

There was a time when meadow, grove and stream
The earth, and every common sight,
To me did seem
Apparelled in celestial light,
The glory and the freshness of a dream.

—Wordsworth, "Intimations of Immortality"

CONTENTS

PREFACE

In these pages, I initiate inquiry, to be continued in subsequent books, into the generic traits of persons from a philosophic point of view. The foundations of the scheme which I set forth and the texture of the ideas which interweave its elements derive from many sources. Those to whom my indebtedness is overwhelming, whose influences pervade the entire work, and, indeed, inspire both choice and mode of development of the focal categories, are Spinoza and Whitehead, metaphysicians of immense intellectual breadth. Moreover, the great systems of Kant and Hegel are especially germane for any comprehensive treatment of the person. An effective theory requires that the tradition for which they are such notable spokesmen be wedded to the impressionistic but equally profound human insights of the Existentialists. I am particularly indebted to Kierkegaard, Nietzsche, Buber, Heidegger, and Marcel. Too, the immortal poets are often wiser than those whose wisdom is explicitly set forth as philosophy. I must renew my reflections again and again by consulting, in particular, the authors of Job, Isaiah, and the Psalms, Aeschylus, Dante, Shakespeare, Donne, Keats, Wordsworth, Yeats, Hopkins, Rilke, and so many others. In addition, I weave into the ideal image of man implied by the metaphysicians and the poets factors within Freud's and Jung's accounts of a *pathology* of the person; for attention to the negative, inhibiting, and destructive forces inhering in man may clarify and deepen that image, and exhibit its limits. Finally, the concept of man to be presented here has been greatly influenced by the writings and teachings of Erich Fromm, and by the personal impact upon me of his wisdom, humaneness, and aliveness. My specific obligations to these thinkers as well as to others—primarily (apart from those who have founded the heritage upon which all who treat such matters stand in perpetual gratitude) Thorman Boman, Justus Buchler, Henry Bugbee, John Dewey, H. F. Hallett, C. G. Carus, Ernst Cassirer, Georg Groddeck, John MacMurray, Pierre Teilhard de Chardin, Maurice Merleau-Ponty, Charles Sanders Peirce, Jean-Paul Sartre, Ernest Schachtel, Paul Tillich, Charles Williams, to mention just a few—will be incorporated in the detailed tracing of the principal themes.

This book is a statement of personal faith. As a philosopher, I try to secure the foundations of my inquiry, not in my private passions alone, but in the unturbulent waters of objectivity. But, when all is said and done, I can do no more than to commune again with those few with whom I have shared these experiences, and to set forth how I perceive what it is which has joined me to them. I write from the reminiscence of what in a human life is too seldom experienced: the joy and peace which stems from days long past when in childhood every person is truly alive, and from those meetings of zest doomed to fade, moments of eternity which rest in images of sacred memory, fleeting moments of which it has been written

> Thus have I had thee, as a dream doth flatter,
> In sleep a king, but, waking, no such matter.[1]

And I write from that knowledge of disappointment and sadness, of loneliness and self-deception, which in the life of any man must be weighed with those times of joy and peace. And if what I write has the quality of expressing an unattainable ideal, I take refuge, and commend my readers to do likewise, in Spinoza.

> I wish to direct all science to one end and aim, so that we may attend to the supreme human perfection . . . and, therefore, whatsoever in the sciences does not serve to promote our object will have to be rejected as useless. . . . All our actions and thoughts must be directed to this one end.[2]

Wherein this "supreme human perfection" consists is the object of my search. This is the question to which I address myself: What imparts to each life that special quality of clarity, purpose, and wholeness which will never in all human existence be duplicated? What by the finitude of man one seeks in vain in oneself I strive to illuminate as a *philosophic* issue: to penetrate the mystery of a life, to disclose its essence, and to discern the principles whereby in continual self–re-creation it may achieve a more perfect unity and serenity. In this way, I create as symbol what one seldom realizes as fact. I seek to disclose the character of the quest for integrity as it will recur without end from man to man. But when one makes this quest one's own life purpose, one must also resign oneself to Spinoza's thought that "noble things are as difficult as they are rare."[3]

Yet, as I proceed through this work, I shall endeavor to transmute my strictly personal experiences into a form which, I hope, will acquire increasing universality in aiding to bring about a cohering of the commonality of experience among humankind in general. And so, in the pages to follow, in what I here deem quite private reflections (owing to the fact that, after all, I am but a particular person setting forth a theory about *all* persons; hence, the book is pervaded by my idiosyncratic experiences), I aim toward a statement of my themes in a way which is explicitly objective even if, for the most part, always immanently personal.

Bearing this approach in mind, I stress a matter which requires special mention in this Preface. For it hovers about these pages, and those of the books to follow. Throughout, my philosophic reflections are pervaded by religious feelings. Of Orthodox grandparents, I was born a Jew; but I was raised without formal religious affiliation. Yet I constantly quested after religious roots, yearning both to recover those of my ancestors, from which I felt somehow cut off, and to discover new roots for myself. Thus, today, I am continually drawn toward religious concerns. Subtly or overtly, this fact conditions my treatment of every theme in this work.

My own sense of religion is deeply personal. As a Jew, I feel pride and reverence for the faith of my fathers, stretching back to Abraham; for the monotheism first crystallized by my revered ancestors; and for the great and abiding humane values which they shaped for themselves and linked to their God, the God of the ancient Hebrews of Scripture. To these people of a dim but noble past I am linked by blood and by spirit. Yet I feel an equally profound affinity and love for Christianity. For, insofar as Judaism celebrates origins, so that my past never ceases to dwell within me—and for this I consecrate the Jew in myself—I, with equal strength of conviction, look forward toward a future which both faiths manifest, each in its own manner, pointing the way toward destiny. In their respective paths of opening up into the future, Judaism and Christianity incorporate a vision of God (prefigured in its deepest contours by the earliest Hebrews), which, by their particular routes, is consummated and made a true, a living, reality. Indeed, for me, the most profound moment in all history, the one moment conditioning all thought, especially that of any *concrete* philosophy of the person, which is what this study purports to be, is the great time in which Christ appeared: the way in which he was celebrated, in the progressive stages of his revelation, in the manner set forth by the Gospels. For, *at the very least*, whatever one's faith, Jesus must be regarded as the last of the Biblical Hebrew prophets and the first of the Christian saints. Beyond that, surely mystery haunts the transition between Hebrew prophecy and Christian consecration.

Moreover, the contemplation of the astounding miracle of the faith of the early Christians has always inspired and haunted me. For their acceptance of God incarnate at this unique historical moment is witness to the same spirit, and emulates the endless genealogy, of the martyrdom of the Jews, when *they* proclaimed, and with stubborn dignity refused to relinquish against overwhelming odds, their faith and their love. For a profound inner bond, continuity, and affinity prevail between the Judaic and the Christian visions, despite the schism between these faiths in regard to the issue of the divinity of Christ. Indeed, the mystery of Christianity replicates on many profound levels a great succession of mysteries, portentous secrets which imprinted themselves upon the Jews, and thus prepared the way for at least one culmination of those mysteries. Hence, I feel myself drawn ever closer to that strange and compelling moment, as, somehow, a paradigm of the veridical Present, a present which is truly constituted by the insinuation, and all-pervading presence, of the enduring into the transient: this ever-deepening, ever-enriching present which, germinating within the Eternal, ever expands toward a new and larger coincidence with the Eternal. Here, I find the fullest exemplification of Plato's immortal dictum that time is but the moving image of eternity.

And so I see the passage toward the past (for Christians, the route of Judaism, and for Jews *one* ground of Judaism) and the passage toward the future (for Christians, the route of Christianity, and for Jews, the other ground of Judaism) as complementary and equally valid and vital ways, each a hope, in its fashion, of enriching, deepening, and suffusing the sacramental powers of an ever-expanding present; and I see this Present, both literally and symbolically, as the momentous juncture of these great and coeval faiths, so much akin. For, as Thomas Mann wrote,

> the deeper we sound, the further down into the lower world of the past we probe and press, the more do we find that the earliest foundations of humanity, its history and its culture, reveal themselves as unfathomable.[4]

Yet, within this abyss, at the very point of their uttermost concealment, great mysteries illuminate themselves and, indeed, therein reveal that God

> sent out of the substance of His divinity spirit to man, in this world, that it might rouse from its slumber the soul in the frame of man.[5]

For the final mystery lies at the beginning and at the end; and the beginning and the end are one; and, as one, they, each converging toward the other, together converge upon the Truth, the inner depths of the here and the now. Surely, the proper task of philosophy is to probe the symbolisms of the here and the now, to understand their patterns, to interpret their meaning and their import, to penetrate the mysteries of the personhood of man.

And so it came about that I write as both Christian and Jew—the two faiths are for me complementary and, indeed, at bottom, are they not, in the profoundest sense, one and the same? Indeed, I seek to illuminate those mysteries, the hidden ground of Truth which, ultimately, cannot be comprehended apart from an acknowledgment that to grasp the personhood of man, which is, after all, my subject matter, is both to apprehend, and to relate, it to the *person* of God. For me, I stress, such an acknowledgment most explicitly presents itself by the routes of Judaism and Christianity. For the acceptance of this perhaps unorthodox view of these faiths, a view which is implicit throughout my argument, I owe a special tribute to my dearest friend, subsequently to be commemorated in this Preface, John W. R. Thompson; to my childhood associations, equally treasured, with Christians and with Jews, equally pious; to a few great rabbis I have known, notably Benjamin Kahn, Leonard Beerman, and Menachem Schneerson; and hardly the least, to my dear Jesuit friends and spiritual intimates, too numerous to mention, at Fordham University, and the spiritual community in which they have encouraged me to work and to evolve my thoughts. As well, and perhaps most important, I cannot refrain from stressing the enormity of my debt to the memory, by which I am perpetually haunted, of my maternal grandfather, Laibe, of whom I am privileged, in humility, to be the namesake; a man whom, in the flesh, I never knew, but with whom, in the spirit, I am ever in communion, a pious Jew beloved and revered by all who knew him.

Whither this double, and yet to me profoundly unitary, commitment will lead me, I cannot yet foresee: this faith of my fathers and this faith of those among the earliest Christians, who after all were also my kin, pious men who brought to fruition the love, concern, and respect for humankind first articulated by the ancient Jews. For I feel as though my searchings have only begun. Yet, as a commitment, it is inseparable from my work. It is woven into the topics of this book, and will pervade every book which will succeed it. To summarize the intellectual impact upon me of these personal experiences, experiences also profoundly affected by my philosophic studies, and such studies are, at bottom, *Greek*, is no easy task. Yet I essay a quite brief statement.

From the teachings of the Hebrews, I learn of the wholeness of the person, of his obscure yet momentous depths, and the hidden labyrinth of the mysteries of spirit which reside within his very physicality; I learn of those aspects of things which, however fixed and seemingly immutable, are nonetheless transitory and evanescent, hence grounded by the Word—the dynamics of speech, in its inmost processes and its endless flux and ferment, its rootedness within God as an efflux of His spirit and His intent: like the shifting sands of the desert, and its great mounds of renewing fertility; I learn of the power of speech, in all its resonances —those concealed and those manifest—to unite men in tenderness and in love, each to the other and, as a Nation of men, all within God; and I learn of the purposiveness which suffuses the cosmos, both in its rhythms and in its redemptive historicity, and of the eternity of its Creator.

From the teachings of the Greeks, who in matters of philosophic probity remain unsurpassed as the teachers of us all, I learn of lucidity, like the light of Greece itself which brings forth the drama and subtlety of contrast between rock and sea and stark tree against the sky: a preciseness with which the different functions, dimensions, and aspects of the person, and, indeed, of all creatures, may be distinguished; I learn that, in their very demarcations, these ingredients of reality are interwoven as unitary complexes; I learn of the numberless ways in which reality manifests itself and may be re-created by the hand of man for his delight and his edification; and I learn of the high moral purpose, the humanly liberating consequences of an intellectual search into the subtle dialectics of Being and Becoming, and of how, contrary to the Hebrews, the Word, powerful and elastic though it be, is essentially subordinate to the Thing—even the drama incorporates the word not as elusive and obscure but as etched with the very clarity of things.

From the teachings of the Christians, who in a certain sense have united Hebrew thought with Greek thought, I learn of the luminosity of the person, and of how he extends himself toward others to shape a universal community of brotherhood; I learn of how the myriad expressions of man, first contrived by Hebrew and Greek—his art, his poetry, his music, his intellect—bear witness to the spirit of man, and both transmute that spirit and, in the most diversified shapes, transmit it from one person to another; I learn that these works multiply immeasurably, immeasurably enriched, in an immense efflorescence like the infinitely variegated regions of the most diverse climes and contours throughout which this faith has spread, and how the Divinity, inscribing itself through the agency of man, becomes visible through them; and I learn how the community of persons is universalized as love incarnate by these embodiments of the human spirit, so that the innermost depths of the Hebrews and the outermost vision of the Greeks, together the repository of the most profound spiritual resources of humankind, may with ever-increasing clarity be etched upon the consciousness of mankind.

From all these, Hebrew, Greek, and Christian, I learn of wonder, of integrity, and of reverence. In the account of the person I here set forth, I draw equally upon the gifts, both unique and shared, of these marvelous cultures. And if I do not mention the other great civilizations in the epochs of man, it is rather from ignorance than from lack of respect. For I am a man of the West. My roots are sunk deep into its ways: its history, its landscapes, its customs, its art, its religion, its intellectual life. In this sense, my search cannot pretend to completeness. Yet I am open to the future. For, instinctively aware of the momentous impact of cosmologies quite different from those of the West upon the great peoples who partake of the cultures, proud and enduring, of the East, I would rejoice were values focal to those cultures explicitly synthesized with modes of conceptualization peculiar to my own peoples—values which by my personal limits must only immanently condition the thoughts of this work. Yet since, ideally, my categories ought to approximate the requisite generality of any search which may legitimately claim to be philosophic—that is, a quest for *universal* wisdom

—I shall always be receptive to their amplification and emendation in such ways as those more learned than I might propose. For, ultimately, a viable philosophy of the person requires a veridical syncretism: the orchestration of all authentic modes of affirming human being, modes which incorporate the values which lie deep within the consciousness of *all* the peoples of the earth.

Always, however, in the end, I must express my deepest gratitude to my many friends with whom over the years I have had countless conversations which have imprinted themselves deeply into my thoughts and my feelings. There are so many, and they must be unnamed, with whom my encounters, brief but intense or sustained and enduring, have, each in its own way, shaped my thought and helped me to come closer to what I increasingly feel as my inmost convictions. To these many, and to the special few, I can only echo Emily Dickinson:

> Meeting by Accident, We hovered by design
> As often as a Century, An error so divine
> Is ratified by Destiny, But Destiny is old
> And economical of Bliss, As Midas is of gold.[6]

But since for me the intimacies and communings with actual people are more valid and sustaining than even the most potent of intellectual impacts, I must stress certain particularly personal debts: my gratitude to my mother and my grandfather Nathan; the most special loving obligations to those who, in their ways, from the beginnings of my life never ceased to affirm their faith in my value as a person, and in the intrinsic value of all persons—namely, my grandmother Esther, my aunts, Anna Smelo and Fanny Krasney, and, without even a momentary interruption, my uncle and aunt, Frank and Nettie Smellow; my gratitude to my former wife, Blanche, who, especially during the earlier years of my maturity, never ceased to replenish my hope, and who, over many years, endured the prolonged birth pangs of this book with constant and, for me, essential reassurances of faith in its eventual completion; and my thankfulness for the innumerable friendships and special carings by which I am so fortunate to have been blessed—the memories of all that can never die.

Among my friends, though few may be named, those who have quite directly affected the writing of this book, and the research for the larger work of which it forms a kind of prologue, merit certain quite particular acknowledgments; and I earnestly trust that should anyone, by chance, be omitted from specific mention, it is not from lack of deep and abiding gratitude but, rather, that the list probably ought to be extended indefinitely, so numerous are those who in one way or another affected the writing of my book.

To David Meranze, who with that singular devotion of a rare and true teacher, long ago set me on my way toward a philosophic career; to Justus Buchler, whose philosophic depth and uncompromising honesty had a strong and most personal effect upon me, and whose courage and originality inspired me to turn away from a more secure but less bold and rewarding style of philosophizing to seek my own intellectual destiny in a life devoted to the pursuit of metaphysical inquiry; to Edmund Hillpern, whose spiritual integrity, warm friendship, and, above all, compassionate reaching out toward me in times of trial have never failed me; to William J. Richardson, S.J., whose abiding friendship, probity, trust, and encouragement made it possible for me to resume a philosophic career, after having for a time moved along other paths of knowledge, and in the context of a university in which I found great spiritual inspiration; and to Quentin Lauer, S.J., who has always stood by me with quiet support as a rock of integrity and friendship, after having specifically invited me to teach and dwell in intellectual tranquillity at that university: to all these men I owe deep gratitude. In addition, to the generations of students whom I have had the honor of teaching over many years, for their loyalty, their enthusiasm, and their perceptiveness, I give my heartfelt thanks. Finally, to six very special people in my life who have profoundly affirmed me in most special ways, helping me to free from a kind of bondage in which they had been held the germinal ideas which now culminate in these books, I also express gratitude: Harry Bone, Erich Fromm, Anna Gourevitch, Pierre Rubé, Ernest Schachtel, and Heinz Westman.

In particular, I acknowledge a special debt to my dear friends Lillian and Leo Kovar, for whose generosity in providing me with a context for writing, a tender presence, and a beautiful locale, without which this book could not have been finished, I am grateful beyond words. For the friendship of James Lee, who also provided me unreservedly and with generous care a home of exceptional tranquillity far from the turmoil of my customary home, and was the first to read the manuscript, and from whose sensitivity to style as well as to philosophy I have benefited, I am grateful. To my friends of so many years, always constant and true, and endlessly encouraging, Patricia and Louis Carini, who have never ceased to sustain me throughout the writing of this book and the research which preceded it for a larger project, and indeed have lovingly read and deeply resonated to everything I have ever written, and who, beyond even this, have provided me with priceless interludes in their home, I express everlasting gratitude. I gratefully acknowledge too my debt to Gerald A. McCool, S.J., who, with generous patience and profound understanding, read the manuscript, and to Elizabeth M. Kraus, who not only reviewed the manuscript and gave me constant cheerful succor, enormous spiritual support, and ceaseless encouragement, never failing to affirm her belief that this work was worthy of my continued labor, but also, by her profound philosophic intuition and deep personal caring, endlessly inspired me. All these people, including those previously mentioned in this Preface, symbolize for me such qualities as constitute each an embodiment of Albert Camus' aphorism regarding the only true kinds of nobility, taken in their most inclusive senses: *la noblesse de la pensée, la noblesse du travail*.[7] "For my part," he proclaimed,

> I have never admitted any aristocracies but those of work and intelligence, and now I know that together they form a single nobility; that they can find truth and . . . efficacy in union; that separated they can be vanquished one after the other by the forces of tyranny and barbarism; but that together . . . they will become the law of the world.[8]

As a community, all those whom I here acknowledge exemplify such a law. For, in the end, *il n'y a qu'une noblesse: celle de l'esprit*.[9]

In addition, among my acknowledgments, hardly the least are to a certain reader selected by Fordham University Press—a distinguished professor of philosophy whose anonymity must be preserved—who both read the manuscript and offered invaluable suggestions for its improvement, including certain proposals which I have incorporated within the Prologue; to Clyde Walton, for a conscientious proofreading of the manuscript and excellent comments on the text; to John McNaughton, who gave generously of his time in discussing this book with me; to the editors of *International Philosophical Quarterly* and the *Annals of Psychotherapy* for allowing me to use material previously published in their journals; to the members of the staff of Fordham University Press, especially Mary Beatrice Schulte, for her remarkable editorial skill and perceptive understanding of my thought—to these and to so many more I express my heartfelt thanks. Further, to Fordham University and to all my friends and colleagues, who, with their support by a most timely Faculty Fellowship, enabled me to have the leisure in which to complete this book, I am deeply indebted.

Finally, and most of all, across the mists of time I send my everlasting gratitude to John W. R. Thompson. Rare poet, wise philosopher, luminous teacher, exemplary physician, and beloved friend, he inspired me at our every meeting; without his affirmation, this book could not have been written. By the wonderful clarity of his life, he has given me a glimpse that to be truly alive is to be utterly simple and without dissimulation. To his imperishable memory as the most marvelous man I have ever known, an exemplar to me of what a person *is* and *ought* to be, this volume would be dedicated (as will indeed my third book, for that will be most fitting to commemorate his ceaseless affirmation of the dignity of man), were it not for the singular fact that, above all else, as the ever responsive source of my energies to continue my labors against what at times have seemed insuperable obstacles, my work is the spiritual symbol of a father's immeasurable gratitude: for the deep and abiding love I have for my children, and the inutterable inspiration which the wonder and the beauty of their existence hold for me, so that from it I draw so much of the sustenance which gives me the hope by which I live.

Fordham University   LEONARD CHARLES FELDSTEIN

NOTES

1. Shakespeare, Sonnet 87.
2. Benedict Spinoza, "Essay on the Improvement of the Understanding," in *Works of Spinoza*, trans. R. H. M. Elwes (New York: Dover, 1955), p. 7.
3. Benedict Spinoza, "Ethics," ibid., p. 271.
4. Thomas Mann, *Joseph and His Brothers* (New York: Knopf, 1942), p. 3.
5. Ibid., p. 25.
6. Emily Dickinson, No. 1548, in *The Complete Poems of Emily Dickinson*, ed. Thomas H. Johnson (Boston: Little, Brown, 1957), p. 645.
7. Paraphrased from remarks by Albert Camus in a speech delivered in Saint-Etienne on May 20, 1953, and conveyed to me by Pierre Rubé.
8. Ibid., trans. Dr. Rubé.
9. Ibid.

HOMO
QUAERENS

PROLOGUE

IN THIS BOOK, I set forth the general tenets of a method for systematic philosophic inquiry into the person. I intend my examination of method to be prefatory to a more extended investigation, one in which I unfold, in stages I herein enumerate, the substantive groundwork for a general human ontology, together with such ramifications of that ontology as will locate man in the larger cosmos, and this from within a double perspective: the perspective of pride and the perspective of humility. Under the first perspective, I shall treat the person, in a number of books, in terms of the several traits which constitute him a being unique among the creatures of the earth. In those volumes, I shall use the method herein proposed to study the variegated facets of man; and I shall conduct my study from an essentially developmental point of view. Further, I seek to evaluate the roles of these facets as they pertain to the essential being of man. Throughout, the person is regarded as center and prime focus of the orchestrated rhythms of the cosmos. In a sense, he is conceptualized in his *ego*centricity, or more broadly, in the communo-centricity of the interpersonal relations within which matrix he arises, plays out the drama of his life, and brings his destiny to consummation. However, under the second perspective, I shift my concern from man's essential egocentricity to a *deo*centric orientation toward his value with respect to the cosmos as a whole.

Both these perspectives interweave throughout the work; indeed, I regard them as inseparable. Nevertheless, in the earlier books, the first perspective will dominate my reflections. On the other hand, as I proceed through these volumes, the second perspective will increasingly give rise to the principal motif of my concern. Accordingly, in the final book, I gather together the theological and metaphysical assumptions which progressively emerge, though in fragmentary and often desultory form, throughout my inquiry. At that point, I shall generalize the method proposed in the present volume to allow these diverse themes to converge upon a cosmology. Crystallizing hitherto disparate topics, which nevertheless are pertinent to my argument in setting forth a theory of the person, I draw these topics to systematic unity and coherence as both the ultimate ground upon which the earlier and more constricted themes rest and the justifying principles by reference to which those themes may be supported and, wherever possible, validated.

Hence, this volume on method is intended to introduce the forthcoming volumes. In it, in addition to framing a theory of a philosophic method for studying the person, I sketch many of the substantive issues which will more cogently, and in greater detail, constitute the topics of the other books. These I enumerate seriatim, in the hope that the titles alone, with but a short accompanying explanation, will suffice to indicate, however tentatively and cursorily, the general drift of my approach. Accordingly, following this volume, the sequence unfolds: *The Dance of Being: Man's Labyrinthine Rhythms*—here, I treat the relevance of the thingly aspect of man and his organismic aspect for his strictly *personal* being, always within the guiding context of the latter; *Choros: The Orchestrating Self*—here, I treat the dialectic between consciousness and the Unconscious in a matrix wherein the person is construed as achieving integration both through his private searchings and through his encounters with other persons, and in each instance by dialogue, explicit or immanent, in which the symbolisms of his presence are woven with the symbolisms of the compresence of each with each; *Metamorphosis: The Odyssey of the Self*—here, I treat the orchestrated rhythms and symbols of comportment by which the person reveals the sequence of crises and resolutions of crises, the transformations and the transfigurations, through which he proceeds along his life's journey; *Apotheosis: The Divinizing Self*—here, I treat the person as the locus wherein the great cosmic reverberations articulate themselves and, by man's committed and directed searching activities, come to fruition within the orbit of his potential cognizance; *Cosmos: The Crucible of Man*—here, I bring my work to its penultimate conclusion in a theory woven of ontologic, cosmologic, and theologic components, in effect reversing the orientation of the preceding volume by deriving man from the cosmos, that womb of his being wherein all that is true and good and beautiful is borne to confluence in a doctrine I designate transcendental trinitarianism; but a trinitarianism which is dynamic, progressive, and endlessly revelatory of novel facets; *The Person: A Cosmic Perspective*—here, having adduced from a systematic theory of the person a general cosmology, I explicitly deduce the principal categories of a human ontology, each category condensing yet going beyond the themes proposed in the earlier volumes, by using cosmology as a paradigm, hence, by now construing the person as a veridical microcosm.

Though my treatment of method is contained within but one book of a number of volumes, all of which deal with themes which repeat themselves with varying ornamentation, and accordingly may only be *fully* understood within the context of the complete unfolding of these themes, it is also intended to stand on its own as an autonomous study. It is so meant to be read. Nevertheless, Method reveals its inmost dynamism only through its actual application to subject matter. For it is by a concrete working through of the tenets of that method, within the context of the specific resistances those tenets meet upon each new attempt systematically, coherently, and comprehensively to coordinate a welter of details, that Method perfects itself. With a kind of presumptuous chaos, particular matters of fact confront methodic inquiry with their import. Thereby, as it proceeds through diverse subject matters, Method progressively emends itself,[1] correcting and sharpening its own tools, never blithely but only arduously and always with circumspection and a groping tentativeness. In particular, these considerations are crucial for a method of philosophizing about the person. Indeed, this very self-emendation lies at the core of Method itself; it is Method's most typical and recurrent characteristic. For the method most felicitously adapted to inquiry into *human* being, so it is my persistent claim, is quite distinctive; it differs markedly from methods relevant to study of any other kind of entity.

According to my proposal, and prefiguring succinctly the argument which will follow this prologue, one deals in most inquiries with objects in their generality. Concern with a particular object is limited to its status as an instance of a class of objects. True, no merely random objects are ever chosen. Rather, a small group is selected—by intuition, with anticipation, on principle; the objects chosen are exemplars, entities deemed paradigms for that class. In this sense, individual and particular features of an object are always relevant to investigation. Yet, in his experimentation, the methodic student attends only those aspects of the exemplars which are strictly generalizable; and this approach is usually designated by such terms as "objective," "detached," or "disinterested." Granted: in such inquiries one "listens" to the manifold qualities the object exhibits, and one listens intently; surely, one attends in an in-depth fashion, even with empathic orientation toward the object and the situation within which it functions. An epistemologic obligation weighs heavily upon the inquirer: ignore no facet which, by generalization, might be converted to a variable which is relevant, from the standpoint of an ultimately systematic theory of the class to which the object manifesting that facet belongs, to precise specification as functionally connected to other analogously adduced variables. Indeed, the more one listens, and therefore searchingly addresses the object with appropriate questions, the more that object will (in effect) respond, and respond in ways heuristic for the framing of a theory of the behavior of classes of like objects under duplicable and recurrent circumstances. The injunction prevails: seek those properties of an object which are invariant within an inclusive class of relevant situational transformations. In these respects, inquiries into all entities, including persons, do not essentially differ.

Yet I maintain throughout this book that methodic inquiry into the person is unique and distinctive. For, alone among "objects" of inquiry, the person manifests his being through symbols, which are the same kinds of symbols as those by which the investigator himself conducts his inquiry: symbols of speech and symbols of comportment. The consistency, continuity, and substantive equivalence between the items composing respondings establish the crucial difference between inquiry into *person* entities and inquiry into *non*-person entities. Further, and indeed as a consequence of this critical maxim, the person subject to inquiry is himself a subject, a self-determining user of symbols. As such, his uniqueness, the radical absoluteness of his individuality, manifested through the self-engendered symbolism of his presence, becomes of impressive concern to the inquirer.

To repeat: it is not that uniqueness does not pertain to other entities; nor is it simply that there is a kind of quantitative difference between the uniqueness of persons and the uniqueness of non-persons—a difference the increments of which sum into a qualitative difference. Nor is the element of randomness in selecting exemplars for study wholly lacking in the study of persons. Quite the contrary. For persons as well as non-persons are instances of a class; hence, one may, and, as an inquirer into the person, one *must*, be concerned with universal and recurrent traits of persons in order that a viable philosophic theory of the person may be framed. Rather, *only* the person is unique in the sense that he is, by nature, problematic. Alone among entities submitted to methodic investigation, the person is self-creative; he is a veridical specimen of the concrete universal. For, while surely resembling other persons in the same sense as any entity may share traits with other entities of the same class, the person alone changes, and, by his nature, never ceases to change, the contents of his ever-expanding and his ever-deepening subjectivity. And his very self-changings are part of his reaction to the inquirer; the more the latter searches his nature, the more elusive that nature becomes, the more evanescent, the more ethereal. For to inquire into the essentiality of the person is to dwell with that person *in* his subjectivity. It is to allow oneself to be drawn further and further into its labyrinthine depths; it is to allow the analogous efflorescings of one's own subjectivity to blend, mesh, and join intimately with the efflorescings of the very person into whom the investigator inquires.

Accordingly, three interrelated sets of circumstances and qualities confer distinctiveness upon inquiry into the person: *symbolic dialogue*, rather than monologic interrogation; *concrete universality* dominated by a dynamically construed uniqueness, rather than synthesis of an inert particular with a precisely formulable general; *an object which is also subject*, endlessly efflorescing in transactional connectedness to an inquirer analogously composed. From these factors, a special injunction of Method follows: inquiry into the person consists of a peculiar oscillation and combination of ("objective") *de*tachment and empathic *at*tachment. In consequence, I have chosen as subtitle for this volume *Method Become Ontology*. For the very method by which the person is studied, *in toto* and *in concreto*, is essentially sympathetic searching: searching in which no encounter is unreciprocal; for all human encounter is mutual. Indeed, as I later argue, all human beings are constituted by their encounters. What Method preeminently reveals is that the "substance" of the person, his ontology, itself consists in searching, and in searching committedly and sustainedly—in a word: methodically. Hence, the more profoundly Method is applied to human investigation, the more its divergent strands flow together, and the more these strands are progressively transmuted into strands of ontology. Applied with consummate methodicity, method is transmuted into ontology. In the very context of an unfolding inquiry into the person, the *substance* of the methodic inquirer, qua methodicality, becomes one and the same as the *substance* into which he inquires.

Moreover, this book might have been subtitled "Freedom's Ambiguities," for I propose two guiding and pervasive tenets. First, the person qua person is conceived as radically free; the texture of his being is open, the creations of his spirit are unpredictable. Secondly, emerging within his very openness are constellations of deterministically interwoven schemata. For certain purposes in (more restricted) inquiry, these constellations as such prevail; yet deeper penetration of their own constituents reveals, at the very center whence emanates determinism itself, a core of ineluctable, irrefutable freedom. Throughout this book, and in those which follow, I assume the burden of explicating, with increasing systematicness, the dialectics of this ambiguity. For the moment, I rest content with the triadic formula: applied to the person, Method *is* Ontology; (Human) Ontology *is* Freedom; Freedom *is* Ambiguous.

However, the title of this book, *Homo Quaerens: The Seeker and the Sought*, has been chosen for a special reason, a reason already partly indicated. For Method reveals that the object sought, man himself, is no object at all, but rather a subject who seeks. In consequence, *Homo Quaerens*, or "questing man," is intended in a double sense: the quest for *who* man is, his *quiddity*—*what* he is qua objective phenomenon is subsumed within this who-ness; and the belief that *who* he is is, at bottom, an *activity* of questing. By this formulation, I stress my conviction that any questing after man is pervaded by an attitude of *reverence*; and that man sui generis, in his inner core as quester, is himself profoundly reverent—no matter what merely contingent self-denials or degradations have obscured this primordial fact of his existence.

In the twentieth century, this theme of reverence has been demeaned by a pervasive cult of cynicism, a cynicism even institutionalized in countless spheres of human activity; its practice has been fragmented by social decadence and holocaustic horror; its moral force has been perverted by an allegedly "scientific" and certainly technological view of man's intrinsic being, a view based on a shallow, and fallow, reductionism, indeed the crassest kind of materialism. Increasingly, the person has been regarded as but a bundle of roles, needs, and functions. In numberless ways, his powers of *giving* have been shunned, mocked, and ridiculed: giving selflessly out of inexhaustible depths of energy, energy spiritual and energy vital; giving in total dedication and without reserve. In consequence, although our century has witnessed the flourishing of almost every systematically human and spiritually human activity, at the very same moment it has been assaulted by a false scientism, a denigrating technologism, all converted to dogma and implying a deformed notion of *who* man truly is.

I am especially sensitive to the degradations which have swept over the traditionally most reverent of the intellectual strivings of man: namely, philosophy itself. In these decades, I have observed people addressing other people's serious and searching questions regarding the inmost being of man, questions of haunting concern to all mankind; and I have seen those authentic seekers mocked and polemicized by ad hominem wit, even such as is masked by a grotesquely courtly demeanor in the very act of ruthlessly destroying committed inquiry. I have experienced philosophers—so called, in our time—philosophers of eminence, or, more accurately, of fame and power, publicly prefer to draw attention to their own facility in empty verbal acrobatics than seriously, and reverently, to respond to issues addressed to them honestly and without guile. I have read journals claiming respectability and, indeed, declaring themselves the vanguard of the *new* "analytic," "behavioral," "rational" modes of search; but they employ ancient and honorable words perverted from their original import—granted, at times, with consummate skill—to mock, to tear down, to pulverize, to suck the vitality from the *wonder* with which philosophy began its ancient and noble task; wonder which, nonetheless, will never be crushed, even by those insipid though shrewd minds which seek, on every front, not merely to diminish wonder but to convert it to sequences of trivial propositions, bickering over vacuous and mere abstract usage—these minds which are the silent allies of all forms of man's alienation from man.

This is an age of strange idols. Whosoever fails to worship at their feet—any protagonist of a rich, poetical, speculative, and, above all, devoted pursuit, however frail and inadequate the results—is, in fact, declared a heretic. And the sophistical mockers of wisdom confront him, not as a respectable intellectual adversary, but as an enemy. So often, in addressing their enemies, they bow and nod and simper with seeming gentleness and even a pretended humility; yet, too often, these gestures are hypocritical concealments of *their* quest for power *over* men—that understated watchword of this age—rather than power to potentiate new powers *of* men; and certainly, power to manipulate decadent ideas rather than power to shape new ideas. Doubtless, this book, and perhaps even more those which will follow, will create for me, at best, a host of enemies, and, at worst, multitudes who will not deign to read it—on grounds that it is not philosophy at all, but "poetry," full, perhaps, of dazzling metaphors, a veritable psychedelic experience: poetry indeed, that latest term of philosophic denunciation by which, of course, is meant *bad* philosophy and *worse* poetry, a designation used so glibly to dismiss serious quest to understand man as *reverence*, man's seeking to understand man as *reverence*, man's philosophizing about man as *reverence*.

Yet I have also beheld those rare and gallant souls who, under circumstances requiring courage, nobility of spirit, and high probity, have affirmed, in timelessly memorable defense, eloquent and profound, the veridical dignity of man. It is these "happy few," either those who acted on their commitments or those who quietly assented to those who have so acted, whom I address in these pages. For I seek to do battle with no particular man or woman, or, for that matter, with no particular style of philosophizing, since I shall not again refer to either the iconoclast or the sophist who would destroy philosophy. On the contrary, I wish only to affirm *all* men and *all* women, that is, human being as such; I seek to point the way toward a Scripture-based renewal of trust in man's capabilities and his powers, of hope for their fruition, and of love for his ceaseless quest— for even though it must so often fail, at least it can fail honorably; I seek the meaning of the great Greek triad of truth, goodness, and beauty, as they constitute a vital perspective under which man may be understood; I seek the Christian synthesis, as the fusion of the Greek ideal with the Scriptural and Hebraic ideal, to comprehend all the phases of man's consciousness: his power for justice, integrity, and wisdom; and I seek to understand the diverse modes, and the dialectical unfoldings, of the moments of his wisdom.

In my inquiry, I am seeking to respond to a century of human alienation, in which even as he affirms his powers in art, science, religion, and philosophy, and all the variegated forms of his creative expression, man has so diminished his specific potentialities for systematically joining the fruits of his labor that he has fragmented his destined role in the universe, his role as locus wherein *its* diverse facets reveal themselves coherently and comprehensively. In effect, I strive to reconcile a relativist perspective upon the person with an absolutist perspective. For while I seek the *invariants* of human activity qua human, I recognize that, once they have been discovered, and the horizons within which they function revealed, these invariants declare themselves to be but variations upon new and deeper-lying themes; and I acknowledge that no method can provide in advance of its specific utilization the criteria for its own effective functioning. In consequence, only the shell of the person, his behavioral manifestations, and never his underlying reality, may be conceptualized by methods the norms of which are explicitly set forth prior to their concrete application. Hence, one must begin ever anew, and always from new and more inclusive starting points; one must, as it were, rework the argument, from a point now illuminated by prior search, in the quest to understand the person as quester: *Homo quaerens.*

Accordingly, this constant self-reinterpretation advances through philosophic dialectic. Since each particular item revealed by correct application of Method changes, the connections between any set of specific items are relative to the overall context in which they appear. One mode of patterning succeeds another, each more inclusive, coherent, and adequate to the facts as they emerge. Hence, something positive is asserted by every item, and this positive element is preserved despite all contextual variations, though the overall import of that positive content is ceaselessly changing. In effect, perspectives are engendered of increasing generality, precision, and systematicness of articulation. Throughout contrast and opposition, something remains inviolate and imperishable; yet schemes of greater vibrance and human impact are interwoven ever anew. Thus, my method does not exhibit a linear pattern of ideas, each deducible from those presented earlier. On the contrary, its structure is spiral in character. At first starkly general, I proceed through the circle of my themes with successively novel incarnations, transfiguring them, as it were, via deeper interpretations revealed in the spiral. For I am presenting a philosophic scheme in which I blend and interweave the empirical results of modern investigation, hoping to retain whatever durable may be extracted from art in general, the diverse cognitive disciplines and, indeed, the moral acts of mankind. Nevertheless, though I endeavor to make my theory applicable to the person as a concrete bio-psychical organism, I strive toward a theory with the requisite generality—hence, self-referentiality—of a metapersonal ontology. In brief, I regard my reflections as constituting a transcendental personalism, rooted in two great traditions: philosophic realism fused with philosophic idealism.

In effect, I propose two types of investigation: philosophical psycho-logy and philosophical physio-logy. In the first inquiry, I study the person from the point of view of his *psyche*—his mind, and his soul. In the second, I study the person from the point of view of his *physis*—his natural and bodily processes, within their circumambient milieu, behavioristically understood in its broadest and least pejorative sense. Yet the more one probes the first perspective, the more one discovers as pervading his very subjectivity—his thoughts, his feelings, his appetites, his perceptions, his very interests—a grounding, archetypal objectivity: an interior and subjectivized objectivity. Analogously, the more one probes his naturality, the more will be revealed, as any biologist or physicist can state, bizarre and other-worldly configurations such as only mind can conceive: an intersubjective component, an ideational contrivance which suffuses the object itself and discloses itself as unfolding in labyrinthine layers and stages. Thus every subject conceals an inner object strangely different from an immediately presented objective datum, and every object conceals, on sustained inquiry, an interior thought likewise peculiarly different from the introspective data of immediate subjectivity.

How, in an account of the person, to join these correlated perspectives! How to join them without losing the validity and the power of either! Could it be that a *nested* series of objects surrounding subjects, like mutually enclosing Chinese boxes, tends toward a kind of infinite regress? If so, the endless revolutions of the spiral in which, as it were, a clockwise circle would proceed from object to subject, effecting a never-ending sequence of reductions, would lead toward a dialectically nested philosophical idealism; and, in counterclockwise rotation, a similar spiral from subject to object would lead toward a dynamically nested philosophical realism. Two circles which each time round exhibit new fleshings upon a skeletal frame! Yet, relative to the clockwise–counterclockwise asymmetry, both circles are equivalent. But is such a solution really different from a psycho-physical parallelism, and all its attendant difficulties?

Spinoza sought an answer to this quest for a deep, inner relationship between these series by reducing both series to a third: *substance*. Yet does this notion not imply an overly objectivist or naturalist bent? For the very term "substance" suggests solidity and changelessness. Kant sought an answer in the *noumenon*. And yet he was forced to hover between a strictly logical and a transiently onto-logic contrual of this invisible and esoteric realm which presumably is intended to ground both thinking activity and physical activity. Hegel sought an answer in *Geist*: "absolute spirit." Yet this idea, suggesting an ethereal flux and ferment, surely implies an overly idealistic and mentalistic bent. In our age, Dewey sought a solution in still another concept. In his reflections, subject and object are but crude and abstract though convenient foci *within* "experience": *experience* which is subtle, resilient, stretchable, of multiple depths and recesses, open-textured, composed of ingredients partly self-actional, partly interactional and yet, as a totality, transactional since it may be divided into numberless kinds of configuration. Still, even "experience" is nebulous. Beyond that, restricted to the interpersonal sphere alone, it does not allow of a definition of the self *as* self, in its interiority, and as internally (and metaphysically) linked to the cosmos. On the other hand, Whitehead sought a solution in *prehension*, or generic feeling, an idea of sufficient generality to apply to all entities; and he treated this notion in terms of contrasting intensities of depth and interpenetration, a thoroughly concrete relational matrix exhibiting many levels, a labyrinth of interiorities. More general than Dewey's "experience," yet containing the same multitude of nuance, Whitehead's category nonetheless lacks a sufficiently strong sense of personal identity and continuity. For the strands which bind the "occasions of experience" to the unity of personhood are too composite, too elusive, insufficiently unified.

In effect, I seek a synthesis of Hegel's *Geist*, Kant's *noumenon*, and Spinoza's *substance*, a synthesis which will preserve the endless subtleties of the Deweyan and the Whiteheadian proposals, and yet allow for the mysteries of a solid bond both of personal identity and of persons with persons: something akin to Heidegger's *Dasein*—a Being-in-the-World, a locus wherein being articulates itself, but a concept more concrete, more rooted to the human situation, more cosmologic in import, more humane, more moral. I designate my position *transcendental rhythmicality*. In it, I seek (in my own way) to preserve the element of the transcendental as well as the empirical; and I strive to combine requisite metaphysical generality with subtlety of nuance, clarity of formulation, coherence in coordination of detail, and adequation to the variegated realm of fact.

Throughout, whenever I qualify a term, such as "rhythmicality," by *transcendental*, I mean to stress that the term thus qualified pertains to a realm of activity which comprises many layers, ineluctably wrapped in mystery, and only to be adumbrated by human vision, a composite realm which, at the same time, is united and indivisible; further, I stress that this realm is the unconditioned ground for what is customarily and even consummately experienced, though it exhibits continuities with experience; finally, *transcendent* will be distinguished from *transcendental* in that the former term will pertain to a realm of activity which, in principle, may, under appropriate circumstances, be absorbed into an ever-expanding experience. A close approximation to my "transcendental" is Kant's noumenon of the third *Critique*; alternatively, it is Spinoza's determination by negation—i.e., the n-attributes which do not positively determine a given mode; yet all modes are *of* the same substance.

Yet I cannot avoid postulating a certain paradoxicality as residing at the very core of the being of man, and, indeed, under the cosmologic perspective, an *ambiguity of freedom* concealed within all entities, persons and non-persons alike. Albeit unconsciously, by the dynamics engendered through this paradoxicality the person constantly engages himself, and this in a variety of ways: his ideality (or *is*-ness) vis-à-vis his actuality (or *ought*-ness); his functionality vis-à-vis his substantiality; the relativity of his nature vis-à-vis its absoluteness; his historicity and radical uniqueness vis-à-vis his ahistoricity and his utter universality; his empiricality vis-à-vis his transcendentality. Five sets of paradoxes, all equivalent, though each with a slightly distinctive emphasis! What do these paradoxes portend for a metaphysical theory of the person, especially with respect to the method for questing after that theory?

Correlative and analogous, these five dichotomies express different perspectives upon the essential paradoxicality of man, the dialectically imbued ambiguity of freedom, which resides at his very center, shapes his engendering dynamism, and constitutes the *vis vitae* whereby reverence comes about—reverence, that quintessential trait of man: man the inquirer and man the inquired into. Throughout, I deal with man both as he is and as he ought to be. Yet the descriptive and the normative, the actual and the ideal, are not set over against one another as though in radical and total opposition. On the contrary, they are profoundly interwoven, each—for its fullest formulation—conditioning, presupposing, and, indeed, requiring, the other. At the core of man, there resides a paradox, and hence a mystery. For he ceaselessly, though not necessarily consciously, engages himself in what he is, his living and vibrant reality, and in what he is by the contingencies of his life, with what he might become by the values and the strivings for transcendence which dwell within him. The consummation of man's powers consists in the vitality of this dialectic, this self encountering self, and in the grounding of its self-encounters within a community of mutually engaging and dedicated seekers. Herein is achieved the concrete embodiment, the fullest exemplification, of these powers as his distinctive and unique, though always universal, nature; for each particular existence is but a variation and a repetition upon a theme, yet a variation profoundly and endlessly subtle in its distinctive nuances. The *ought*, what man would be were he de facto to embody the ideals shaped and evaluated by the collective wisdom of humankind and adapted to the peculiar needs and proclivities of each person, arises through the interplay of dissident and divergent beliefs, each a partial truth, yet, together, in their composite plurality, an approximation to the whole truth. Amidst their clashes and their cacophony, penultimate though never final harmonies and attunements emerge: Truth, in the democratic republic of inquiry, is thus asymptotically approached. For, by "democratic," I mean: let all inquirers freely declare themselves, and, at the outset, be presumed to entertain opinions so regarded that the weight accorded each is deemed equal to the weight accorded all; and by *res publica*, I mean: let all competing opinions enter the public scene, so that consequent upon their interactions and confluences the consquences of these declarations may continue to dwell within the public domain, but now evaluated, purified, and transformed, and, hence, available for renewed search.

And yet, this Truth-not-yet-become dwells as a still and ethereal presence, a transcendental *noumenon* within the heart and the soul of man, subtly illuminating and guiding his inmost aspirations and yearnings. For reality exists on many levels. It occupies, as it were, the interface of these levels; it hovers about their interstices; and all levels interfuse and interpenetrate. The *to be*, the *not yet is*, and the *ought to be* are parts of a process of which the *already been*, the *once was*, and the *now is*, in its full contemporaneity and presence, are phases. As the Artist imprints *his* presence, silent though vibrant, within his work, effaced yet pervasive, so the *Ideal* (that shaper of actuality) never ceases to pervade the actuality; it is transcendentally present within it. My task is to explicate the status of this ideality of the present, from the methodologic point of view in this volume, from the ontologic point of view in the intermediate books, from the cosmologic point of view in the final ones.

In effect, I am declaring: possibilities, powers, potentialities, actualities, anticipations, premonitions, memories—those perishings of past to present and those growings from present to future—are all intertwined, woven into myriad patterns and modes. In a later book, I shall discuss the *luminosity* of the person: how the "unconscious" shines forth, making itself visible in multifarious ways. It illumines the fabric of his comportment; it integrates the diverse rhythms of comportment; it manifests itself through the symbols formed by constellations of these rhythms. All the variegated facets of a person—those ideal and those actual —come to confluence within this "unconscious," and flow forth from it to constitute the overarching rhythms of his transcendentality.

Within this dynamic context of self engaging self, the unique qualities of a person, qualities conditioned or even created by his particular historical status and determining his masks, his roles, and his functions—in a word: his *persona*— act conjointly with his inmost substance: those ahistorical, deep-lying aspects of man which are out of time and out of space. For I am committed to the supposition that Platonic ideals are not external to man as mere subsistent norms to be striven toward but never reached; on the contrary, they are, as *eternity* is, constitutive of man as the uttermost ground of his being. They interweave with his regrets, his fears, his hopes, his dreams. Surely, what we are as means to the end of what we might become exhibits qualities analogous to the qualities of that end. Were such continuities and trajectories not so intimately to bind means with ends, the radical divorce between means and ends would, on the one hand, degrade man to dust, and in effect, consign him to hell, and, on the other, constitute his aspirations the exclusive prerogatives of angels who are the exclusive inhabitants of paradise. John Calvin's view of man is diametrically opposed to the view which I am setting forth in these pages. Hence, each under its own perspective, person qua substance and person qua function, illuminates the paradoxicality of flux and stability, the quest for roots and the peace of rootedness, the restless migrations of man and his endless return to a secure and tranquil dwelling place.

Granted: I am here stressing an ideal image of man. And twentieth-century man *is*, after all, alienated and fragmented. But philosophy is not primarily concerned with setting forth the conceits of an age; nor does it explicate man's pathologic condition—though it is competent to search for plausible reasons for his "fall from grace." For, first and foremost, philosophy deals with man, not as he crouches in the dark recesses of the cave, but as he nobly steps forth from the cave, and envisages ever new possibilities for his own concrete growth. In consequence, philosophy cannot be bound to the particular vicissitudes of a particular epoch; nor may it confine itself to delineating the character of that epoch. In its mode of speech and in its style of presentation, philosophy is undoubtedly affected by the biases of its age; it is burdened by so many of its presuppositions. Yet philosophy qua philosophy cannot be the spokesman for *that* age so much as the prophet for *all* ages. Whatever the social scene at any given time, man's *ultimate* values are functions more of his potentials for growth than of where he actually stands at this special moment of history. An empirical approach to his nature wedded to a transcendental approach takes cognizance of such of his frailties as derive from his inevitable participation within his age, a participation *through which*, however, he arrives at a vision of what dwells absolutely and timelessly within his inmost being.

My own concept of philosophy, and, in particular, of a philosophic inquiry into human being, has nowhere been more eloquently stated than in these lines:

> History is not an unbroken stream of existence in truth, but is interrupted by periods, or is shot through with levels, of deformed existence. This period, or stratum, of deformation . . . can impose itself so massively on a man that he conforms to it and consequently deforms himself by making deformed existence the model of true existence. And the philosopher who has made deformed existence his own . . . can deform the historical field of experiences and symbols by imposing on it his model of deformation. The deformed sectors of the field acquire the status of true reality, while the sectors of true existence are eclipsed by the imagery of deformation. . . . We are all sufficiently familiar with the age and its usurpation of authority, for we all have had our encounters with men who, sternly rejecting their humanity, insist on being modern men and, in so-called discussion, try to bury us under the rhetoric of deformed existence. This kind of "age," it is true, cannot be avoided by the philosopher in our time; it is the social field into which he is born, and it presses in on him from all sides. But he is not supposed to succumb to its impact. The philosopher's way is the way up toward the light, not the way down into the cave. . . . the search for truth makes sense only under the assumption that the truth brought up from the depth of his psyche by man, though it is not the ultimate truth of reality, is representative of the truth in the divine depth of the Cosmos. Behind every equivalent symbol in the historical field stands the man who has engendered it in the course of his search as representative of a truth that is more than equivalent. The search that renders no more than equivalent truth rests ultimately on the faith that, by engaging in it, man participates representatively in the divine drama of truth becoming luminous.[2]

In numberless ways, man seeks this luminosity. He never ceases in his quest after the *good life*: the true, the good, the beautiful; he endlessly strives toward the *pious life*: trust, hope, and love. Nor does he desist from seeking the synthesis of these lives in the *spiritual life* which unfolds, through phases of justice and integrity, toward wisdom. Finally, at the end of the way, he realizes that wisdom itself is but a lesser peak whence he gazes upon endless stretches of mountain tops the contours and challenges of which he cannot even yet discern.

NOTES

1. This concept of method as self-certifying in the context of its employment derives directly from Spinoza, "Essay on the Improvement of the Understanding," pp. 12–41.

2. Eric Voegelin, "Equivalences of Experience and Symbolization in History," *Eternità e storia: I valori permanenti nel divenire storico*, ed. Istituto Accademico di Roma (Florence: Vallecchi, 1970), pp. 215–34.

I

Rhythm Incarnate:
The Problematic, Man

1

METHOD AS ONTOLOGY

PREAMBLE

In this chapter, I sketch the kind of object into whose traits I inquire, and the general contours of the method by which I inquire. Approaching my object by a metaphysical route, I pursue several interrelated objectives. First, I expose the presuppositions underlying the several disciplines which, under one or another perspective, treat the variegated aspects of the object. Next, I unify these presuppositions, in the light of a more inclusive perspective which takes cognizance of the most significant ingredients of its component perspectives, to create an integrated cognitive manifold which adequately represents the object as integral and indiscerptible. Finally, I probe the inner content of the postulates underlying this synthesis in order to disclose how initially naturalist and personalist points of view, each complementing the other, are progressively displaced, the more profoundly the object is examined, by a transcendentalism in which the dominant element is the luminosity of the object even while it is enshrouded in mystery. For, the person, the understanding of whom *in toto* and *in concreto* is my veridical objective, is construed as a labyrinthine ferment of novel efflorescings, cavernous recesses, sharply contoured mosaics—in a word: a matrix of subtly orchestrated rhythms and symbols. Indeed, my transcendental method conceptualizes the person, not as an object per se, but as a *pro-ject*: a self giving itself by its own volition in myriad ways, all interwoven as a finely modulated texture and penetrable by numberless routes of exploration; a self in quest of drawing forth from the inmost regions of its being those strands of existence by which it might relate to the larger cosmos.

My intention is to delineate the contrapuntal interplay of rhythm and symbol which *is* the person; it is to show how, by methodic inquiry, they may be drawn forth from his hidden essence. Further, I seek to exhibit this method as pre-eminently a method of empathic searching, a searching which by its intrinsic nature is substantively linked to the very substance it strives to disclose. For, I argue, methodic inquiry into the person is characterized by rhythmic communings with him, communings which reveal the richness of the interior being of the seeker as (internally) continuous with the interior being of the one who is sought. In a reciprocity of givings, each to the other—searcher and "object" of search—and both witnessed in the quest by others who likewise search, the intrinsic composition of all becomes manifest and luminous. In principle, an egalitarian community of inquirers, each complementing the other, implicitly or explicitly, formally or non-formally, and whatever the specific role differentiations assigned by that community, collectively strives toward Truth, the truth of the being of *human* being. By an inner necessity, all persons engage in analogous searching activities. By these activities, the metamorphoses of each, along the stages of his life's journey, are so facilitated that, at the end of the way, a veritable transfiguration of all may, in principle, be achieved. Accordingly, when applied to the person, method and ontology are inextricably bound together. Ultimately, they converge upon the same enterprise.

A · THE PRIMORDIAL ENCOUNTER OF MAN

(a) Toward a True Image of Man

Many images of man have been framed by poets, scientists, artists, and philosophers over the centuries. With varying explicitness, scope, and coherence, each purports to give an account of *who* man is—man in his essential character, man in that which sets him apart from other things and other creatures. Among these we find seemingly diverse and even disparate, and yet at bottom often overlapping and always quite related, portraits of him: uniquely, he is the one who reasons, who symbolizes, who is self-aware, who purposively uses tools; uniquely, he is the one "within" whose intricate biological makeup psyche arises to animate and suffuse his being—perhaps as a "natural" expression of physico-chemical processes when they have reached a certain degree of organization, perhaps as miraculously conferred upon those processes as an entelechy in accordance with some inexplicable principle of vitalism; uniquely, he is the one who seizes upon the world and reconstitutes it, imprinting his own image onto its texture, or, again, he is the one who alone is capable of experiencing, as he acts, a vast range of feelings with fluctuating intensities and myriad nuances—joy, ecstasy, despair, equanimity; uniquely, he is the one who in trembling dignity declares himself a privileged being before God, persuaded of a special personal (and transpersonal) rapport with Him.

Such characterizations could be multiplied indefinitely. Indeed, a sufficiently informed inquirer might extract from every poem, every novel, every symphony, from every product which man may create, some pithy statement of the traits immanent within those products which, *in essence,* qualify their creator. Were this to be done, many fragmented but quite valid characterizations of man would be available for philosophic scrutiny. In each instance, over the limitless field of such accounts, one finds recurring, whether implied or stated, the expression, *the one who, constituted in such a manner and by factors of such and such a kind, performs, acts, or orients himself toward a something or a some "who" in this or that way.* The differences among these diversified and often aphoristic summings up lie in the varied terms by which one specifies the parameters "in such and such a manner," "of such and such a kind," "in this or that way," and how such words as "who," "constituted," or "acts" are to be construed.

But rarely have attempts been made, systematically and comprehensively, to develop a theory sufficiently generalized to be adequate to the insights provided by the sciences which deal with man, the intuitions one finds among the artists, the esoteric hints suggested by the more occult disciplines, ways of life, or even cults, the moral and ontological predilections of dedicated men, the spiritual callings and theological reflections of those committed to a particular religion. Sufficiently examined, such a program might provide the *fons et origo* for penetrating to the core of this multitude of portrayals, for integrating their essential contents as mutually complementary and presupposing, and, further, as reconstituting all their portrayals as but aspects or perspectives into a more inclusive, adequate, and valid treatment.

This is the task I set for myself: namely, to indicate more effective and more potent values for the suggested variables than those hitherto proposed. In my study I freely draw upon seemingly disparate realms of inquiry and belief, but my intent is to give neither a summary nor a classification of definitions of man. On the contrary, it is to extract such insights as will allow reformulation as elements integral to a generalized theory of man, a metaphysical account of the person. My goal is to present themes relevant to working out a philosophic theory of the person which takes cognizance of a sufficiently wide variety of points of view.

I aim at a measure of comprehensiveness with as little sacrifice of precision as is consistent with statements of a high order of philosophic generalization.

In this work I set forth an approach by which an answer may be approximated for the question: "What, essentially, and from a philosophic point of view, is a *person?*" In effect, I search the meaning of this question, and, to render it, the ideas of "essence" and "person" in their mutual bearings will be explored. Fully explicated and systematically set forth, the emerging themes would constitute an actual answer. Yet the latter task is so arduous that numerous volumes would hardly suffice. By way of the lesser inquiry, I here but sketch these themes with admittedly insufficient elaboration. Their development will be contextual. No key idea can be analyzed without reference to all key ideas; hence, I proceed by approximation toward greater cogency of statement.

The work is intended as a systematic, generalized, and speculative inquiry into the essential traits of the person. My approach is twofold: (1) interdisciplinary, for I draw upon materials belonging to the natural sciences, treating different aspects of the person, upon relevant theological and philosophic doctrines, and upon various non-systematically articulated sources; and (2) synthetic, as constituting an effort both to probe the fundamentals of these disciplines (whether formally executed or non-formally constituted searches) in order to draw from them what they might offer of relevance to understanding the essential person and thereby to propose a scheme of ideas into which these insights might be translated, and within which they can be so incorporated as to exhibit their more significant ramifications.

My quest belongs, as a special and limited task, to the province of metaphysics. By "metaphysics" I mean an account of the foundations of all encountered phenomena, their *conditio sine qua non,* and of the sense in which each phenomenon is a manifestation of being—however its disclosure as an explicit doctrine is interpreted. Though in the long run the more generalized philosophic formulations concerned with "being in general" are relevant to the more particular formulations concerned with the "being" of persons, I here confine myself to the latter.

(b) Man as *Datio*: The Person

When I speak of "a high order of philosophic generalization," I do not mean excessive abstractness. For by a metaphysics of the person I intend the person *in concreto,* the person as datum construed in an active sense—a *datio.* To construe the person as mere datum is in effect to truncate what is most essentially his nature: it is to prescind from his status as actor and agent; it is to deform and to pulverize that nature into a mere conglomeration of static elements and to deprive it of its consummately active and accordingly privileged status in the make-up of reality. In fine, it is to diminish the nobility of his destiny. Granted: by his finitude man cannot escape the ultimately tragic status of his human predicament, a creature frail and anguished. But there is a profound sense in which all men are co-participants in what is eternal. Durationally constituted, they concelebrate eternity. As concelebrants, they sanctify eternity. Thus hallowed, eternity is the matrix wherein they dwell, the fount and sustainer of their being. How to specify *eternity?* How to justify its designation as a *matrix?* For the moment I am compelled to resort to metaphor, even to a combination of seemingly incongruous metaphors. Later, this characterization will be abandoned in favor of one more precise and articulated with a greater measure of philosophic clarity. For, in a later book, I shall argue that the essentially philosophic concept of time and the essentially theologic concept of eternity are concretely interwoven. Complementary to and conditioning one another, they are also mutually reinforcing. Philosophic reflection and theologic reflection, so I shall claim, cannot be conducted along entirely autonomous routes; each requires and presupposes the other.

Thus I declare: this matrix—namely, *eternity*—is a labyrinth of infinite recesses and infinite spiralings, of hues infinitesimally graded, of tonalities and resonances and nuances of kinds imaginable and of kinds which exceed all imaginings. Herein reigns the drama of *silence*; yet it is a stillness not vacuous but endlessly rich in its ever-changing "substance." Moreover, it is a labyrinth unified amidst its infinitely diversified contents; a labyrinth pervaded by a unity which, though immanent within its every part, is transcendent with respect to man's capacity to relate to it, and to relate specifically and uniquely. In personal dialogue, as the perception of this unity haunts him, and the latter (perceptum) so to speak ceaselessly hovers about him, a unity now "moving" deeply into his own interior and private depths, now "receding" as a distant yet endlessly compelling star far beyond what he can properly claim his own, it reveals itself to him as he, reciprocally, reveals himself to it. Do I dare yet introduce the term "God"? For herein, or rather, *here in whom*, man roots himself; herefrom his life derives meaning, affirmation, value, solidity—and this despite his temporal fragilities. Herein is the source of man's nobility, his power ceaselessly to seek and in his seekings to transfigure both himself and that into which, or into whom, he seeks.

Above all, I wish to avoid any species whatsoever of Whitehead's "fallacy of misplaced concreteness." What man *is* is never mere body, or mere mind, or some contingently linked composite of the two. What he is (in his essential makeup) is not a set of (two) parallel (and when conjoined, incongruous) series of deterministically patterned *res extensa* and *res cogitans*—though up to a certain limit and under a certain perspective he is, indeed, thus constituted. On the contrary, he is an activity of both *bodying forth* and *ideating forth*—but a single and integral activity, a "potency-in-act" which only *as* actualized may be designated now body, now mind.

Yet, ontologically speaking, the actuality can never be divorced from its "originating"—and, indeed, compresent—potentiality. Nor is he to be understood as a paradoxical but inexplicably and miraculously compounded blend of determined elements and free elements. To abandon this fallacy, I must imply the reduction of man's status neither to that of sheer determinism (in either a Laplacian or a logical sense) nor to that of sheer voluntarism (according to a Schopenhauerian or a Bergsonian model). For at the outset I understand the person not merely as a given, a passive object. Quite the reverse. I construe him, in the first instance, as a *giving*, a self giving himself in freedom and in spontaneity, but a self required by his inmost nature thus to struggle, and thus unremittingly, to give himself.

This conflict is primordial. When the dialectical character of its dynamism is clarified, the conflict is revealed as the engendering source of both his "free" *and* his "determined" aspects. As an agent the self both acts on *his* behalf—and this out of the inner necessity of engaging his own conflictual makeup—and *freely* constitutes himself the medium or instrumentality through which other like agencies act. True, the given*ness* aspect of him cannot be denied, nor consideration of its import be circumvented. Yet in my account this is but an aspect—in effect, the negative moment, the shadow, if you will, of what a positive appraisal discloses as one who, by my definition, constructs his own existence and never desists from this activity no matter how quiescent his movements or his thoughts.

For the person is truly a *power*, a power of affirming or denying, a power to opt to orient himself now in this manner, now in that manner. He is an activity whose elements are specific and concrete acts. More precisely: he is a succession of potencies-in-act, a succession the members of which are internally and not merely contingently related and one wherein each member is not divisible into an antecedent potency and a consequent act—as though "potency" were an entity among other entities, like actualities.[1] On the contrary, in his makeup potency and act are so inextricably linked that neither can be construed without the other. He is a process of self-actualization, and he actualizes himself in and through his every *seemingly* discrete and individualized act. Moreover, each act casts up particular and completed products. But these products are only a deposition. Whatever the appearance of a deep intimacy of connectedness, they are products essentially detached from or, at least, but tenuously linked with the activity itself. Yet always amidst this disengaging, like rivulets becoming isolated through geological upheavals while their mother stream does not cease to flow, so the stream of action remains integral and indiscerptible.

By this construal, I mean person as an opening up and a disclosure of powers to him who searches into his nature—person not as already completed, a past and perished datum, but in his immediacy and in his aliveness. I intend the Spinozist distinction between the person qua *"natura naturata"*—the engendered product—and the person qua *"natura naturans"*—the engendering activity. More precisely, to follow Spinoza's usage, he is a particular "mode," a quite privileged region of nature—not nature in a narrow and merely empirical or even a naturalistic sense, but nature as "substance," as the totality of cosmic processes.[2] Some of these processes are luminous and some are perpetually concealed from human vision; other processes are enmeshed with one another, not, at bottom, contingently but "by necessity," i.e., as a coherently ordered and ultimately unified manifold—a manifold within which, though he cannot specify its ultimate character, the person roots himself and from which he draws his sustenance. He is that region, that concrete locus, wherein reality, i.e., *substance* (within which he himself is embedded as co-participant) is pre-eminently revealed to him, revealed in its many laminae, in the infinite subtleties of its texture, in the multiple rhythms of its polyphony, in the endlessly intricate cycles of its unfolding.

In the first instance, he is in effect a *res extensa*, an object to be studied behavioristically, a patterning of existents—e.g., identifiable gestures, facial expressions, vocal inflections—existents which may be classified and organized in various ways and explained by various hypotheses according to the purpose of the quest. In the second instance, a person is regarded as *res cogitans*, but a *cogitans* which is to be interpreted more broadly than merely mentation—a total and active *experiencing*. Here I reinterpret the Cartesian *cogitans* to mean, not the person qua mere subject, in the ceaseless flow of disembodied thought, fantasy, and feeling, but as subject incarnate. Thus conceived, he engenders himself and in this activity casts up as both manifestation and residue of his every act some specific "object." But object now is construed, not as existent sui generis, like a datum of natural science, but as a *symbol* which when properly deciphered discloses the character, the phases, the dynamics, of that self-engendering activity. Too, like Spinoza in his *macro*cosmic metaphysics, I shall argue the claim in this micro-cosmic metaphysics of the person that in the last analysis what he is as either is what he is as the other. Both are at bottom one and the same: person qua assem-blage of existents rationally ordered, person qua assemblage of symbols intuitively penetrated. The symbolical analysis of the person and his existential analysis are the two methods, each having parity with the other, the complementary and mutually presupposing means by which insight into man's *essential* nature is to be attained. Indeed, either method pursued sufficiently far leads precisely to con-clusions regarding that essence to which, pursued sufficiently far, the other leads.

In these preliminary remarks I have used a number of terms, none defined with precision, for each is assigned its fullest meaning only in the context of the unfolding of my thesis, each in part in its customary sense yet each in a quite special way. The key terms thus far introduced, in addition to the abstract char-acterization of the person as "the one who . . . ," are "image of man," "datum as given and *datio* as giving," my adaptation of Spinoza's words "mode," "substance," "*natura naturata*," "*natura naturans*," and "privileged region," "assemblage of existents," "assemblage of symbols," "rationally ordered," "intuitively penetrated," "a complementarity and parity of methods." These terms involve one another. None can be fully clarified without reference to all.

The cumulative evolving of my argument will reveal with increasing precision how these terms are to be understood. They may be roughly classified as involving two sets of problems: (1) methodological, i.e., how and with what justification (i.e., in accordance with what norms and specifying and vindicating in what way these norms themselves are to be grounded) the rules and principles of pro-cedure, the tactics and the methods emerging in my inquiry, might first be established as plausible, and then validated; (2) ontological, i.e, how the specific themes, dimensions, and categories for specifying the essential traits of the per-son are to be delineated and woven systematically into a unified "image" of man. Though I treat these topics sequentially, and under each heading specify more explicitly the meanings of the indicated terms, in its fullest sense neither topic can be considered as autonomous, separate, or independent. Each requires and presupposes the other. But justification of *this* claim must be deferred until, in my next chapter, I begin to treat the topic of method in systematic fashion.

(c) Man *in concreto*: The Person

According to my central thesis, the person—in his humaneness, his intentionality, his organicity, his integrality—unfolds his potentialities before us; he reveals who he truly is. As we observe him and in observing him join ourselves to him, he shapes experiences already past to a unified *Gestalt* which flows imperceptibly into something yet to come. In his essential dynamism, he constitutes a datum (actively construed as *datio*) in which are compressed, in a continuous whole, past, present, and a trajectory toward the future. From the caverns of his memory, full of numberless things, even such as one cannot but dimly or remotely feel, he draws forth, consciously or unconsciously, such contents as enable him to shape and solidify, in each instance of his existence, his very self. In its rhythms of discord and harmony, orchestrating myriad patterns of events remembered and events perished into the hidden recesses, the inmost labyrinth of his memory, he constructs his own identity. As these memories stream together, he becomes a coherent union of impressions and movements, and he can begin to discern the connection between the beginning and the end of his life. He then perceives a pattern and a style which is utterly his own. Transiently revealed in this pervasive quality, in its sheer uniqueness and vitality, this living man journeys forth from birth to death in living association with, and perpetually witnessed by, a humanity which is likewise ceaselessly venturing into *its* unknown realms. And yet, despite this ineluctable vanishing, man stands in solitude eternally there, rooted in a "something" which does not cease to be, the living exemplification and embodiment of universal man.

Only by a philosophically conditioned and informed confrontation of a *single* person—this is the force of my thesis—in which I, the knower, stand in cognitive harmony with all mankind while I receive all that is peculiar to this particular man, may I understand him in a mode appropriate to his nature, his powers, and his destiny. For in this confrontation and in the fusion of the datum (again, more correctly, *datio*) which that encounter yields with all relevant historical, scientific, theological, and artistic perspectives upon him may be disclosed the *concrete essence* of the individual—a moral creature who may opt to shape his life in accordance with his own specific and non-duplicative endowments—as illustrative of the *general essence* of man. To comprehend how the traits of this or that man are special ways of orchestrating themes universally present in humankind is the root task for a philosophy of the person.

By "person" I accordingly mean here, by way of adumbrating my conclusions, not a legal entity nor an abstraction nor a fiction of any kind but any specific, living individual man *as* man: a locus of movement, intention, and agency, the source of all activities of experiencing, knowing, shaping, or exhibiting. Moreover, the boundaries of a particular person, the influences which mold him and the works which issue from him, or even indeed the very concept of person as locus, source, entity, or bounded agent cannot be assumed as delineated without philosophic specification. Nor are the matters of what constitutes his being alive, his individuality, or even his specificity, or (again) whether these traits themselves are integral to his defining "essence," self-evident or, indeed, philosophically settled.

Nevertheless, I do not assume an inquiry without presuppositions. Quite the contrary, I adhere to definite substantive commitments; there are no substantively presuppositionless questions. In my account, these commitments center on the theme, as the root idea governing my inquiry, of "rhythm," in particular, of *concatenated* rhythm. The concepts proposed here are intended to lay the groundwork for clarifying this focal idea. Closely related, as I later indicate, are the notions of integrity and identity. What, I now ask—in a philosophic setting— are those general characteristics of the entity which may variously manifest itself as biological man, psychological man, economic or social man? How does it come about that man reveals himself in the myriad forms and ways in which diverse special investigations have construed him? Wherein consist the characteristics, namely, in terms of which may be defined the integrity of this entity, its identity, and, at bottom, its *rhythms* as a unique individual?

Accordingly, I develop the thesis that in essence a person is a meshwork of integrated yet ramifying processes which rhythmically unfold; he is a locus of activities interwoven as cycles, epicycles, and systems of cycles which, in replicating itself, from instant to instant of his duration, and in transmitting a living image of that matrix to a new locus, amplifies and reconstitutes those rhythms. Powers but latent within any phase of his existence, or even concealed throughout his existence, are potentiated as altogether new modulations of former rhythmic patterns. Utterly novel cyclic modalities are from time to time fashioned. For, on the one hand, a person is self-replicating; hence, he is a "theme" which preserves its resilience and its vitality though upon it are inscribed the most diverse variations. On the other hand, as self-mutating, a person projects himself beyond what he had been, or what the type of which he is an instance had been, to an instance of a radically new type. Naturally, such a transformation may occur only within certain limits. But at this preliminary stage of my inquiry I cannot prejudge the character of these limits. Moreover, I say "*utterly* novel" and "*radically* new type," for I stress how each new factor emerges from a progression of syntheses and confluences. Though at each stage a determinate context within which this factor functions must be presupposed, nonetheless the entire progression is grounded in a primordial principle of absolutely free creative activity. Suffice it now to say: a style of existence which seems imperishably rooted in the biological and social conditions of a person's life may, in either personal or cosmic crises, evolve toward a style which had quite unpredictably been germinating within that existence. Only in retrospect when what is new but germinal has evolved to living actuality can a hitherto unpredicted style be specified. What follows elaborates this compressed formulation. My aim, as I have already stated, is to coordinate and systematically to unify the points of view of the several disciplines which deal with man, and to extract a new set of ideas which may more effectively illuminate his essential and focal nature.

B · SYSTEMATIC APPROACH TO THE STUDY OF THE PERSON

(*a*) Toward a Unitary Frame of Reference

In my overall inquiry into the metaphysics of the person, I intend two emphases. First, by a *metaphysics* of the person—hence, a quest for a theory of man which is foundational to diverse approaches to explaining his nature—I presuppose (and partly assume the obligation to explicate) a general metaphysics. Indeed, I argue that in the end one cannot separate a special metaphysics of the person from general metaphysics, and, moreover, that each is immanent within the other. A dialectic is operative in which each search requires the other; the illumination of one makes possible new insights into the second. In this sense, neither has priority over the other. In effect, a theory of man and a theory of the cosmos—

in general, a theory of being—may evolve only in reciprocal and interdependent inquiry in which stress on the former alternates with stress on the latter.

Secondly, by a metaphysics of the *person*, I mean to emphasize that man's nature is ultimately conceptualizable without reference to a cognitively denotable "quality." It is my belief that at the core of man there resides a mystery which may be alluded to but never stated. At bottom, his being is ineluctably elusive with respect to any imaginable method of inquiry one may use. Yet in another sense his being is open to penetration by reason; and new schemes for comprehending it, and surely schemes which within their spheres are valid, are perpetually disclosed to his searching acts. A paradoxicality inheres in every attempt to frame a rational account of his nature. But much can be formulated about that paradox.

In addition, when I in effect designate this book a prolegomenon to a treatise on a generalized theory of man, I intend two further emphases. First, though my aim is at *systematic* formulation, and though I hold before me as methodological ideals such (Whiteheadian) criteria as coherence, adequacy (with respect) to available facts, and scope in the sense of completeness in regard to those facts, the subject matter with which I deal is so vast, so diversified, and (since man himself is perpetually changing) so intrinsically incapable of demarcation that not even an attitude of intellectual arrogance—to say nothing of the modesty which alone befits a quest for wisdom about man—could presume even to approximate a cumulative and, by necessity, endlessly growing *treatise* on the innumerable topics pertaining to his nature and required for its clarification. Yet if the tentative scheme of ideas I set forth is to be of any value, then at least in principle it must be possible to derive from its chief hypotheses such information as might point toward a plausible (though I cannot claim true) conceptual image of man, an image of maximum generalization and one which is consistent and (reasonably) comprehensive.

When, in keeping with the aims implied by my title and its subtitles, I speak of the person as a *meshwork* (of processes), a *locus* (of activities), a *matrix* (of rhythms), and when I refer to his *latent powers*, his radically self-projective and yet eternally invariant (and self-identical) character, and when I reiterate in varying ways and with differing degrees of explicitness, as the ceaseless refrain of this work, his essential being as *rhythmic*, I am implying a fairly definite set of philosophic convictions. In particular, I shall assume the obligation to analyze this rhythmic being in a way which resolves (by reference to a dialectical process) the apparent paradox between its fluctuant and its changeless nature. A preliminary statement of these convictions, and of how they may be specifically appropriated for a philosophy of the person, is now indicated.

By "meshwork" I imply that the person is a *natural* phenomenon, one among the many "complexes" of nature, an interplay of processes and ways of behaving which may be studied and, in some sense, deeply revealed, in the very foundation of its being, by empirical or behavioristic science. But this disclosure may occur, I hasten to add, only when the ideas framed by science are not distortedly construed. For I distinguish the *stating* of a scientific explanation about this or that aspect of man from the *interpretation* of that statement. Science, certainly any particular science, is not competent (so I here claim) to delimit, save by negation, the region within which its ideas may be validly applied. What I am suggesting is that the truth about a phenomenon with which a science deals is established, not by affirmation, but either by indicating the conditions under which its ideas may be falsified or by unambiguously stating which of its suppositions are, in fact, supposals and, hence, subscribed to on grounds (whatever *their* justification) of *convention.* By "convention," I mean what is deemed a conceptual device by the community of competent inquirers in the field—a convenient instrument for co-ordinating the data, and hypotheses about those data, elicited from the phenomena by accepted procedures of scrutiny. Moreover, a convention expresses the decision of that community to treat as a *postulate* what, in another context of inquiry must—if its latent and potentially explicable contents were to be drawn forth—be regarded as a *problem.* A scientist (if he is to construct a network of ideas expressing the functional relationships constituting the phenomena of his interest) deliberately desists from probing what he must simply assume as not further analyzable. But it is precisely those latent contents which contain richer (albeit suppressed) insight into the phenomenon the explanation of which requires an enlargement of the scientific context itself, reaching into domains hitherto considered not in the province of that scientist. Such conceptual extension, and the making available of what heretofore was merely the immanent content of the indicated discipline, entail the interplay of a variety of contexts. Indeed, to achieve this extension, one must frame a philosophic theory (in the case of the present study) of the person involving *all* disciplines concerned with him. Unless there occur this dedicated engaging of the root ideas of each science by those of every science, insofar as all pertain to the person, the theory framed by a particular science is but an abstraction which is true within a narrow sphere and likewise useful and illuminating, but always on the verge of constituting itself a caricatural representation of the person.

For example, a person is, in part, a process of energy transfers and transformations; and what that energy *is* is, in part, stated by physics, in part by chemistry, in part by biology, in part by psychology (I am assuming that a precise account of "psychic" energy may, in principle, be given). When, accordingly, I spoke earlier of person as a "locus" of movement, intention, and agency as well as a "meshwork" of processes and a "matrix" of rhythms, I meant to indicate my conviction that there are endless layers of meaning which may be assigned to such notions as "energy," that no particular specification exhausts what is potentially suggested by that notion, that the person *himself* is problematic, and problematic in all the dimensions of his being, in his every manifestation and activity, and in his multifarious ways of engaging the world. I do not mean locus in the sense of an abstract or empty location wherein unfold natural (i.e., spatio-temporal-material) processes. On the contrary, by "locus" I mean a concrete source and dynamism; and by "concrete" I mean (quite literally) a flowing together of myriad factors, some already discernible, some to be discovered, some perhaps never to be detected. Deriving from both the "surrounding" cosmos within which the person is embedded and the intrapersonal forces the interplay of which is also part of a more inclusive cosmos, these factors develop, in their reciprocal dependencies as a compact organization, into a peculiarly intricate yet absolutely unified organism, into a peculiar intensity of self-awareness. The person is pre-eminently the locus wherein the cosmos—granted: under the perspective of his own finitude yet perpetually haunted by infinite reaches beyond him—reveals, in reflecting it-self into itself, its own essential makeup as a matrix of fathomless and endlessly ramified yet co-dependent relations. I here assume a cosmological principle of re-flexivity, a principle so operative that every region of the cosmos mirrors the entirety (within the limits of its own specific character) and is, indeed, *consti-tuted* by that self-mirroring.[3]

Moreover, by "locus" I mean the person as a generative agency, hence, a *rela-tively* durable configuration of autonomous processes, who stands forth sharply etched in his *in*dependence of the cosmos, an agency who reveals himself both predictably (thus in ways formulable by science) and quite surprisingly, indeed miraculously. For the marvel of the person is that he brings novelty into the world from the recesses of his own existence. Fully contemplated, that existence inspires awe which never diminishes. He is not merely a phenomenon which may be un-derstood, hence brought under the rubric of natural laws. For the person is a creative and a self-creating agent, and as such he is a mobile, endlessly fluctuant "matrix," a pattern of rhythms nuanced with infinite subtlety. In his intricate coadaptation to other persons, and in their reciprocal influences, each constitutive of the other, while mysteriously standing forth in his own identity, autonomy, and integrity, the person is a repository of seemingly inexhaustible powers which he himself potentiates, and potentiates anew. As a member of a community of persons, of ultimately the entire community in all its historical unfoldings, and in its opening up into the as yet concealed future (yet, in our glimpses of eternity, a future perpetually revealed), he attains a destiny which ever lies before him while in its very futurity it enters as an active element into the immediacy of his present. At the same time, each person is analogously rooted in a nature seem-ingly impersonal, yet a nature which is a treasury of mysterious unfoldings—its own swirling rhythms to which alike he, in his very essence, is inextricably linked.

A person's characteristic mode of being thus linked is such that he is, among all creatures, pre-eminently the one who searches—a *rhythmical* searching, as I shall always stress. And his searching is a *double* searching: first, he *intro*spects the infinitely subtle intraorganismic world, symbolizing it in myriad ways; sec-ondly, he *extro*spects the great spectacle of nature, analogously symbolizing that realm. Through these two routes of symbolization he traverses the indefinite stretches of the inner world and what lies without. Yet always in this searching, whether self-directed or world directed, he is by his essence *witnessed* by another —first, by one or two (perhaps the primordial parental presence), then by a community, and finally by a personal center beyond all those he can, through any natural means, specify and conceptualize. Both witnessing and searching involve processes within him and about him, yet processes so interwoven that no sharp demarcation can be supposed to separate the one from the other. And each, the witnessing and the searching, is, as constitutive of his being, a rhythmic interplay.

(*b*) Toward Transcendental Naturalism

Accordingly, the person is (though not exclusively thus to be conceived) a dy-namic and laminated structure, a living structure which is in fact a set of functions, but a set which itself is a function, an activity in which may be distinguished three "primary layers" of rhythm: rhythms of space, time, and matter; rhythms of metabolism and replication; rhythms of reflection and encounter. In every instance where I treat these layers, I begin my account from within a *naturalistic* frame of reference. What is revealed by a variety of scientific disciplines is indeed pertinent to my account: the disclosures of the physicist and the chemist about the fundamental character of such phenomena as energy, entropy, elementary particle interaction, simple intermolecular reactions; those by the biologist about protein and nucleic acid formation, macromolecular interplay, production of mutants, natural selection, gene structure and formation, embryo differentiation and growth, electrochemistry of nerve impulse transmission; those by the psychologist and the sociologist about learning activity, "unconscious" processes, the structure of awareness, the role of community in personality development and interplay. In sum, what empirical investigation guided by the canons and procedures of scientific method reveals as the focal ingredients of any particular science are here presumed to be relevant, when properly construed, to a generalized theory of the person.

When I say "properly construed" I mean, first, as understood in the manner intended by physicist, chemist, biologist, psychologist, sociologist, but, more significantly, as interpreted in the light of the fact that every scientific formulation provides a more inclusive context within which some other scientific formulation may in its deeper relevance to understanding the person be *re*interpreted. Through its encounter with any particular formulation, every formulation is amplified with respect to its power to penetrate more deeply and effectively into the *essential* person. For example, the biological aspect of the person provides one context wherein the relevance of his physico-chemical aspect may be established. Further, ideas focal to the latter must be reinterpreted in the light of the former in order for their character as truly germane to understanding the person to be established.

Analogous considerations hold for social and psychological inquiry with respect to both the biological and the physico-chemical spheres. Yet contextual reinterpretation operates in the reverse direction as well. For the seminal ideas—for instance, of physics and chemistry—properly construed are profoundly relevant to an understanding of the biological, social, and psychological aspect. What I am proposing is that philosophic inquiry into certain leading ideas in *all* the behavioristic sciences provides a schema for understanding the person qua person, especially with respect to that understanding for achieving mutual fructification across the discipline barriers. Analysis of *physical* time, for instance, leads to a concept which involves and, indeed, requires as complementary to it the concepts to which one is led by analysis of macromolecular reactions and unconscious processes. In short, the inner meanings of physical, chemical, biological, social, and psychological ideas are reciprocally illuminating; and a context of inquiry in which *their* relationships are made explicit alone provides that dialectical method (of cross-fertilizing basic ideas) by which be evolved the notions, internally coherent and systematically formulable, for conceptualizing the person in his integral unity, his autochthonous and most concrete *personal* rhythms.

Disclosure of the interplay of ideas engendered by the dialectical approach to the contributions made by the various scientific frames of reference I designate *transcendental* naturalism. For, although it begins *within* the naturalistic field, the probing of such contributions (e.g., "space" in the light of, and in juxtaposition with, the idea of "consciousness") requires that one pass beyond the restrictions of each particular science into a new sphere of inquiry. Herein one reflects upon the connection between notions so constituted that, although each refers to a special discipline, the totality, as a complex of interrelated factors, pertains to all (natural) disciplines. Such reflection requires not simply the assemblage of whole sets of such ingredients so that by insight into them a more comprehensive picture of the person is revealed, but also, what is far beyond mere assembling, the systematic integration of the ingredients which individually integrate systems of data on the several scientific "levels." Thereby alone is the actual character of the person disclosed.

Accordingly, throughout, I develop a philosophic position which construes the person as a *trans*natural locus of activities. Although every activity can be analyzed as a phenomenon, all phenomena (i.e., appearances or "behavings") are "centered" in an initially unspecified "point" which subsequent analysis shows arises from an altogether new realm, a realm which may be specified only in terms of ideas of which the "natural" is to be understood as but a negative moment. For example, the scheme of ideas wherein such notions as "energy" are defined is quite different from that scheme whence derive such notions as *heat* energy or *light* energy. The latter refer directly to encounterable phenomena. As we say, they are "operationally definable" by reference to specific human experience and activity. But they are also to be construed as particular values of the unspecified parameter, energy qua energy; and such notions as *energy* may themselves be conceptually and systematically analyzed though not necessarily in the context of, say, theoretical physics as we know it today. The ideas which herein emerge—namely, those functioning as *axioms* in the special sciences—are the central thematic of a transcendental naturalism.

In sum, the problem I emphasize at the outset (but only as preliminary to my major concern) is, namely, to understand the person as body, an organization of "material" energies, studied abstractly (i.e., *in abstracto* with respect to the full concrete being which is the person) by the various natural sciences. What, I ask, is the *natural foundation* of the person, the naturalistic basis of a personology —the person as rooted in nature, as participant in nature, as one with nature, as the culmination and the fruition of a natural cosmogenesis? I construe the entire (natural) universe as a vast, unfolding, and endlessly ramifying process— a process which is a plurality, for it is made up of countless events, classifiable under the rubric of the empirical sciences, yet a process which is unitary since its components are integrally enmeshed and interwoven as a system of reciprocal dependencies and coadaptations, of equilibria formed and equilibria shattered, of events which now endure seemingly timelessly and then flash in and out of existence with minimal instantaneity. Only by such a construal may the full drama, the authentic history of this process, be understood, i.e., as consummated in the shaping of a single, unique, individual person. And yet I assume (qua naturalist) no *a priori* assignations of a purpose, a telos, to this process either as immanently at work or as (transcendentally) directing it from without. Nonetheless, every layer of complexity of the phenomena cast up in this surging cosmogeny becomes (by whatever kind of destiny) an integral constituent of that most intricate of all phenomena, the person, upon whom it appears to converge.

Further, I assume that, embedded as he is *within* nature, and looking out upon it, so to speak, from its interior, the person witnesses a spectacle which insofar as he is detached from it appears to him a plurality, but insofar as he is empathically related to it constitutes itself for him a *unified* presence. Precisely what it means for a person to relate to a *totality* of which he is nevertheless a part is not easy to specify. In a future book, I shall explore some aspects of the architecture of the cosmos in its connection to the architecture of the person, which indeed it includes as one of its essential components. Sufficiently explored, a cosmology would be seen to require a personology. But the converse holds as well. Hence, a subtle dialectic needs to be worked out which will do justice to the exceedingly intricate architectonics of person-in-relation-to-cosmos. As referring to both person and cosmos, "substance" is progressively revealed by a kind of spiraling method: the uncoiling of the mysteries of one is the occasion for the uncoiling of the mysteries of the other.

(c) Toward Transcendental Personalism

By my argument, one task of this work (emphasized especially in the earlier portions) is to conceptualize hierarchically the several conventionally distinguished levels of energy organization—roughly, the physical, the chemical, the biological (and what is revealed by such intermediate disciplines as physical chemistry or biochemistry), and, though by analogy (for "energy" is differently employed in the latter), the (behaviorist) psychological and sociological sciences. A single problem is treated in its many ramifications and reveals itself as of intricate and labyrinthine character. A single focus is specified in which is integrated an often disparate variety of data drawn from both the conventional disciplines and the "in-between" disciplines. How I propose to relate and to correlate the focal ideas, the germinal and the seminal notions, of these diversified realms of human inquiry I can only indicate in the sequel. But at the outset I must never cease to stress that these coordinating ideas which conceptualize the person under the diverse perspectives of biochemical processes, psychobiological processes, sociopsychological processes, at each level and in every instance though formulable with precision, systematicness, and coherence, conceal a mystery. What from a naturalistic point of view is a sharply definable, logically ordered set of (operationally definable) concepts, economically and consistently organized, reveals on deeper probing—when one strives to grasp horizons beyond those traditionally (and naturalistically) demarcated—a realm strange and paradoxical, a realm beyond the test of "instruments" of observation currently available or conceivable.

Insight into the facts about man assembled on each layer of a "naturalistic pyramid" discloses notions which are deepened by what is revealed through exploration of every succeeding level. Thus biology leads to the evolving of a less restricted chemical theory of man. Sufficiently explored, not only does biological theory reorganize ideas focal to the more restricted (chemical) theory, providing the broader setting within which alone the latter may be understood, it in fact alters the basic and most elemental integrative ideas of chemistry. For I affirm the principle that *contextuality is reciprocal*: a more "elementary" analysis provides the context for a more "advanced" analysis; however, once formulated, the latter changes the former. And in the latter process, a set of non-naturalistic notions, i.e., transcendental ideas, is shaped. These, in turn, enable one to leap beyond what has already been transfigured from a "mere" naturalism into a transcendental naturalism, but, more strongly, to a radically *personalist* theory of the person. For one *transcends* the empirical to grasp the inner import (i.e., insight into claims about the indicated phenomena which are implicitly being made) of each notion framed in the context of scientific method. A series of such steps (i.e., of efforts to penetrate further this continually expanding context of import) successively converges upon a view of the person under the perspective of what I shall designate *transcendental personalism*.

By this I mean the laying bare of a transcendentally naturalist theory of the person, i.e., an unfolding of ideas central to the several sciences insofar as they are regarded as pertaining to man. Thence follow a speculative leap beyond these ideas and a preliminary reordering of the resultant interpretations; this constitutes an enterprise which itself is but a preamble to a more deeply reconstituted inquiry. As analysis proceeds, the notions emerging as the central theme of a transcendental naturalism are seen through their own deeper elaboration to evolve, by a necessary process of reasoning, into new themes which reinterpret the "substance" of the person as radically different from anything which can readily be extrapolated from a behaviorist or empirical approach. The structure and norms of the mode of reason needed to illuminate depths of the person (i.e., in *transcendental* personalism) concealed but yet immanently present within naturalism, even in its transcendental reconstitution, may only be disclosed in stages. For no canon of inquiry can be framed apart from its exemplifications in practice; it is within practice that the canons themselves become explicated and indeed constituted in their inner meanings. For their immanent contents are revealed *as* they are applied and not prior to their application. Only through the working out of a problem and by inspection of the involved activities as they are revealed *in concreto* may the governing standards and principles be discerned, indeed, even themselves be shaped in their essential character.

Concern with the person qua body—not mere body, but body alive, thinking, mobile, *rhythmic*—that is, transcendental naturalism, is itself accordingly sublated into a transcendental personalism. Herein alone may the true, inner unity of psyche and soma be conceptualized, a unity not of parallel and correlative, or even of deeply coordinated and conjoined, activities, but of a single activity upon which the spheres of mind and body are but perspectives, each illuminating the person in its own terms, each a heuristic way of viewing the person. But neither is sufficient to indicate the paths along which inquiry must proceed to reveal the true character of the other. Yet the ideas relevant to framing a unitary theory of the person are so thoroughly different from those ideas customarily used (by the sciences) that a preparation is needed in which insight into the extraordinarily relevant data constelled by the (behavioral) sciences must be secured, then reinterpreted, as propaedeutic to the second task.

But this propaedeusis is no mere pedagogical device. For in itself it anticipates

and even prefigures the altogether novel themes unfolded in the second inquiry.
Hence the three (naturalistic) layers of rhythm I have mentioned—namely,
space, time, and matter; metabolism and replication; reflection and encounter—
must each be fully investigated so that the notions relevant to the overall enterprise may be revealed not abstractly but in their full concrete particularity. Each
layer provides a context wherein the next may be more significantly explicated.
Once understood, each succeeding layer requires modification of its antecedent.
A lesser dialectic between these naturalistically construed rhythms prefigures a
larger dialectic between (transcendental) naturalism itself and the later evolved
personalism. Yet each sui generis points the way toward the very themes which
when fully elaborated will constitute the person as a transcendental integrity, a
substantive unity amidst the manifold functions, activities, and dimensions of his
being. What in retrospect may only be regarded (but not pejoratively) as the
coarser rhythms (i.e., those more evident and more amenable to lucid conceptualization) of transcendental as well as of empirical naturalism become but like a
skeleton, albeit mobile, but relatively fixed and rigid, the flesh of which is composed of the subtler, less easily delineable rhythms of trust, loyalty, prayer, art,
dance, music—in a word: the spirituality of the person; and the latter both presupposes and yet, in a strange way which may only at the end of my inquiry be
revealed, is presupposed by his "naturalism." In the end, person qua natural and
person qua spiritual are one. Indeed, spirituality and "naturality" are themselves
(I shall ultimately seek to prove) but one and the same. Otherwise expressed: it
is *natural* to the person to be *spiritual*. Were he less than spiritual his naturality
would be demeaned; were he in any way *un*natural his spirituality would be
diminished or deformed.

Yet prior to the building up of this thesis a comment is in order concerning
my use throughout this book of the seemingly archaic term "transcendental." The
image of man to which I have just alluded is, in my usage, a transcendental image,
an image composed (as I have stated) of both "naturalist" and "personalist"
factors. Moreover, it is one in which the former, treated as though constituting
for the *scientist* of man a self-sufficient set of themes, are, when systematically
coordinated, for the *philosopher* of man but one factor, albeit a most significant
one, within the broader frame of reference I call personalist. Justification for
both using this terminology and juxtaposing these terms in the way I have is
provided in the detailed working through of my thesis.

At the moment, it suffices to remark that naturalism is the study of man "from
the outside," i.e., in his exteriority. It is the summation and the explanation in
terms of ideas which are either conventions linked definitionally to specific operations or actions (experimentally) performed upon him. Transcendental naturalism is the view that every "exterior" behaving conceals, as latent but laden
with dynamisms, an "interior"; and it speculates about ways of conceptualizing
this interiority and bringing it into systematic relatedness with other "interiors."
For *transcendental* naturalism is a predelineation of the idea of interiority (i.e.,
of animating psyche) as, in an as yet inexplicated sense, the *power to give rise
to* behavioral manifestation. I say "manifestation" in order to stress the idea of a
making evident of what from the point of view of transcendentality is an as yet
concealed dynamism.

On the other hand, personalism involves the idea of person as a *unity* of behavings, each of which is an "appearance" of the unity, a self-diversifying unity but one whose mysterious character is not specified. *Transcendental* personalism is the doctrine that what from the point of view of naturalism are data are *in fact* "givens." They are given by a *giver*, the person himself; and the person qua donor of that wherein he shows himself is also the one who, by and through that showing, also reveals a "substance," a complex of rhythms which *cannot* be exhaustively stated by naturalistic explanations of behavior.

On the contrary, though mystery will always reign, fuller and ever new disclosures are always possible. Against Kant's view (and significantly influenced by the Hegelian critique of Kant's noumenon[4]), I here affirm the doctrine that no limits to knowledge about the person as source of his actions can be formulated which themselves cannot be altered, and this by cumulative inquiry which uses a method which includes yet transcends scientific method. Disclosure of the tenets of this method (of transcendental personalism) can be fully made only by first traversing the terrain afforded by a strictly naturalistic account of the person. In my account, to avoid what in its fullest details would be an extraordinarily lengthy enterprise, I interweave both approaches.

C · TOWARD A PHENOMENOLOGY OF THE PERSON

Having indicated the broad contours of my thesis—namely, that the person is a rhythmical being who searches, communing interiorly and dialectically with a personal witness to his searching—I stress the following points.

(*a*) Dimensions of Searching

(i) Interior searching and exterior searching are but different phases and foci within a single phenomenal world, a world which stretches out "before," "around," and "within" the person. Their demarcation, and the apparent dichotomy they constitute, are always such by reference to a convention and never an absolute criterion. "Before," "around," and "within" are but different perspectives upon *what* is felt by that "center of feeling"[5] which *is* the essential person. Hence, figure and ground are interchangeable. Should two sensations be compresent, such as hunger pangs and a specific perceptum such as that of a flower, and should the first be sufficiently acute, the second is relegated to the periphery of awareness; but when the inverse occurs, the former is experienced as a vague kinesthesia. In general both *my* body, in its usual sense, and the "body" of that which lies outside me are equally, however attenuated, my experience of either, my authentic experiential manifold. Together, and as a continuum, they constitute the world under the perspective of the physical. Whether I experience myself in detached relatedness or in empathic relatedness I am empowered to inquire (with equal validity)—whether sustainedly, tentatively, randomly, or systematically—into the *unitary* texture of the corporeal.

(ii) In consequence, my searching is conducted not in radical detachment from objects strictly external to me, whether such objects be the source of such sensations as an inescapable heart-thumping or, alternatively, a compelling landscape; on the contrary, as intimately interwoven with those objects, imprinting my subjectivity upon them, thereby durably altering their character, they conversely in a kind of reciprocation impinge upon my subjectivity. Analogously, I am durably transformed by the impact of the object world upon me. For as I look about me, or introspect my own "private" feelings, I find myself already within the world—a world which surrounds me, pervades me, haunts me, suffuses me—a world which is paradoxically distinct from me yet one with me.

According to this view, by my "mind" I mean the interplay of two systems of "resonances": impulses which both circulate and are sent forth in a patterned and coordinated way within me, traversing "antennae" morphologically defined as a ramifying network spreading throughout my body—a network which constitutes my nervous system; and complementary impulses which traverse subtle, fluctuant, and mobile "structures"—in effect, those *proto*morphic channels, which invisibly yet ineluctably extend themselves into the "outer" world. When these systems cofunction, those signals are transmitted which convey to me "information" about both that single and unitary phenomenal world—the corporeal—and even, by a kind of *positive* negation (like Whitehead's "negative prehensions"[6]), a strange, awesome and numinous "realm" perhaps forever inaccessible to me. Reciprocally, "information" about *me* reverberates throughout those realms.

(iii) By a peculiar sort of empathy, I am capable, in my searching, of feeling my way into the very feelings as and in the manner in which they themselves emanate and radiate from other centers of feeling. Thereby, I come to touch the very heart of the subjectivity which pervades the cosmos. Moreover, each felt center of feeling which feels, and which I emphatically feel through sympathetic resonance, is as privileged as any other center of feeling. Radical democracy, not anarchic, but integrated and organized, reigns throughout the cosmos of "centers of feeling," and this however feeble their capacities to feel.

In effect, no privileged frame of reference may be specified, save this: the "origin" of every "coordinate-axis system" is one and the same as the cosmos itself. What I am stressing is the supposition that any claim on behalf of such a privileged frame of reference is a claim of *egocentricity* quite analogous for a metaphysics of the person to the geocentric Ptolemaic universe in its relevance for physics. Ultimately, centeredness is transferred for every *res extensa* and *res cogitans* (i.e., durational things) to a "something" which is *no* thing—an object which is not *ob*ject but only subject in the sense of grounding the panoply of centers of feeling—in effect, a *deocentricity*. Through the multitude of specific transformations which define the world of contingency, a pattern of reverberatings remains invariant, though in subtle and mysterious ways this invariant itself might ceaselessly though imperceptibly be changing.

Applied to persons, this doctrine states that empirical selves, i.e., persons locatable as incarnate selves in the spatio-temporal-material world, transcend themselves in their mere external relatedness. In this process, a web of deeper, archetypal, *transcendental* selves weaves itself as a pattern at times arcane, at times luminous. Such selves are the true invariants amidst the multitudinous transformations of the façades the empirical selves present to the world—namely (in the case of the former), those selves into which each empirical self is empowered, indeed (by a certain ultimate morality) enjoined to risk, to leap, to delve, and to probe. Far from being solitary and isolated, these transfigured selves, in their very inwardness, are internally related to one another and constitute a vast reticulation which spreads over the cosmos; throughout this network resonances of deeper communication echo and re-echo. To these resonances persons-in-relation increasingly attune themselves; by this attuning they draw that sustenance and vigor by which they are perpetually renewed.

(b) Modes of Searching

(i) Every searching act expresses itself as feeling in the process of articulation. Hitherto unrevealed feelings, indeed, recesses of feeling deeply concealed from the seeker himself, transmute themselves and endlessly ramify. Here, I am presuming that feeling is a fundamental category, such that all differentiated mental activity derives from feeling as one or another of the *specified* modes. Intuitively perceived as a polyphony but nonetheless an undifferentiated synchronization of rhythm, the cosmos is experienced as an orchestration of many themes in all their variations and their infinitely nuanced tonalities. Yet in its very symphonic character there is preserved a sense of the vast mosaic, of the cavernous interiority, of the infinite recesses of the cosmos. A sense of mystery as well as a sense of order pervades. Mystery is revealed to him who engages the world with all his powers—those known to him and those unknown and unimagined. A mighty schema reveals itself in patterns of subordination and superordination, constellations of centers of feeling; and all centers, particularly those so subtly and delicately constituted that we designate them persons, enter into dialogue with the one all-unifying and overarching Center.

Every dialogue unfolds through a dialectical process. Part and whole engage one another. In reciprocity each is reconstituted and reconfigured. Though essentially private, dialogue in its very inwardness is dialogue witnessed; and such witness is always personal. This witnessing is of the nature of a sacrament. By it the rhythms of dialogue are hallowed and sanctified. Within the context of dialogue of each with All, a communing of each with each unfolds. Knowledge, morality, beauty arise through diverse ways of oscillating between the unifying of a diversity and the diversifying of a unity; each is a distinct modality of orchestrating personal with cosmic rhythms. Integration amid unification perpetually recurs. By "integration" I mean the intimate intermeshing of diverse phenomena. By "unification" I mean that same intermeshing under the perspective of its status as an integral totality. Ceaseless activity spirals ever outward and inward to embrace more inclusive and deeper modulations of those cosmic rhythms. The apprehension of this concatenation of rhythms constitutes wisdom. Yet there is always an ineluctably tragic diminution of intensity and scope. For, too, wisdom arises when man becomes vividly aware of his finitude in confronting an infinite cosmos—encountering it humbly yet in dignity, at times in anguish but often in tranquillity.

As mere *relatum*, autonomous, and turned in upon himself and the inexorably limited world he occupies, man is forever doomed to solitude. But this closure may be perforated, if only transiently, for man is empowered to opt to open himself, in a mode appropriate to his gifts and his nature, to cosmic rhythms which are at once turbulent and tranquil, ecstatic and quiescent. Herein he attains for the brief span of his existence a freedom, a spontaneity, a power of giving which is increasingly potentiated by his every affirmation of an indefeasible link to a supreme and beneficent Donor, a Donor whose ultimate gift to man indeed consists in that very power of giving.

(ii) The searchings upon which man is, by nature, impelled to embark are traditionally of three kinds: the cognitive or theoretical, the practical or moral, the aesthetic transformative or exhibitive. Though I cannot claim, nor need I for my argument, that these classes include all modes of searching, they surely are not mutually exclusive. Moreover, they interpenetrate and enmesh; each presupposes in its own activity some immanent activity of the others.

By the first kind, the cognitive or theoretical, the texture of reality is conceptually penetrated. Ideas adequate to its structure, its contours, its mode of patterning, are framed. Only when qualified, if but implicitly, by coherence, unity, and completeness do they acquire consummate status.

In the second kind, the practical, the person comports himself toward the phenomena which the first kind conceptualizes. Initially only attitudes, proclivities, tendencies, or impulses are expressed. But this mere assemblage, at worst inchoate and anarchic—a cacophony of conflicting values—is synthesized into a unitary yet richly nuanced orientation which may only be designated a *calling*. Yet the devotion with which this calling is pursued requires an attuning of the person to every new resonance of his experience as each is cumulatively woven into his calling.

In the third kind, the aesthetic, objects are actively taken hold of. Given their specific potencies and the limits inherent in these, they are manipulated to a new texture to which one can relate. Each textural transformation can be shared with the entire human community, shared in joy, delight, horror, equanimity, shared with the entire range of human emotion, but only so long as the contemplation of every texture is active and reciprocated by others. Acquiring powers and influences of its own as an autonomous source of inspiration to mankind, these ever-renewed textures ceaselessly enrich the human community and (together with shared cognitive and moral values) ineluctably solidify that community.[7]

In sum, in every instance of what is asserted, comported toward, or exhibited, there are both factors of assimilating and factors of reshaping, factors which comment upon phenomena and factors which reveal something of the character of the one who comments. These factors constitute symbols which, properly deciphered, enable each person to experience more profoundly his own *vis vitae* and, by extension, that of the community of which he is a part. A mosaic of symbols is created; and this mosaic is limned against an ever more finely reticulated cosmos. But these symbols are not merely to be construed as inert and static. Quite the contrary. Save within narrow limits, the image of "mosaic" is inadequate to do justice to the dynamic character of authentic symbols. A more effective metaphor would be "an orchestration of rhythmically fluctuant and most delicately nuanced tonalities—meaningful silence (or fragile densities) woven with meaningful 'sound' (the more compact densities)." Indeed, the cosmos itself comes to be perceived as composed of agencies within which, through which, and owing to which its every region may function as a veritable (and vibrantly alive) symbol, a symbol the resonances of which spread far beyond itself to activate the reverberations of multitudinous contexts of like symbols.

(c) The Integrity of Searching

(i) In these indicated kinds of searching, man as searcher is doubly construed. On the one hand, he penetrates an interior manifold given him as an assemblage of disparate internal (i.e., intraorganismic) objects. On the other, he inquires into an external manifold given as contingently related persons and things. Both manifolds are but foci within a single phenomenal field.

His primordial quest, which is to unify both manifolds, each in its own intrinsic unity, delineates the contours of his being. In this quest, he, *first*, so probes each manifold that a double unity emerges as ground and condition whence emanates the double plurality; and this double unity is further revealed to him as itself encounterable though perhaps in the last analysis unspecifiable. For mystery always remains.

Secondly, he so brings to culmination this probing that the unity of the interior manifold and that of the exterior manifold increasingly reveal themselves to him as coinciding. In effect, they become one and the same unity. The *ultimate* unity of unities (of which the two separate penultimate unities are but adumbrations) is itself to be identified as the "center" of the cosmos; and this center man is capable of both contacting and being contacted by. In this latter quest, many laminae of the cosmos are disclosed. As it appears, each lamina presents itself to him as an active and activating presence: a presence which dwells both within him and about him; a presence which is a *presenting* to him, as a kind of gift, by an unknown and perhaps unknowable cosmic "essence." Yet this is a presence which nonetheless becomes in its inmost recesses constitutive of the person's own existence, an existence which ever "thickens" and thereby becomes richer, more inclusive, and of greater depth.

(ii) Finally, the quest itself is a *witnessed* quest, witnessed both externally and internally. On the one hand, the entire community both "listens" and responds to every instance of searching. It provides, negates, or changes the norms and standards for comportment; it formulates and specifies conditions for the application of rules of validation and procedure. On the other hand, the community dwells *within* each searcher as a living and vital presence, a haunting presence in varying gradations of intensity, scope, and articulateness of its proscriptions and recommendations. Now certain members of the (internalized) community acquire significance, as conscience incarnate, in approbation or reproval; then, in endless alternation, those personal imprints recede in importance, and others dominate.

Imprints may be deformed or authentic, fragmented or unified. Not only a single imprint but a multitude may emerge into effective internal operativeness; and this multitude itself may be a deposition now integrated and coordinated, later disintegrated and inchoate—and in both cases with varying modalities and modulations.

Many of these considerations apply, of course, to the community construed as external witness. In either instance, this witness may be malignant or benign.

Sometimes it terrifies; at other times it reassures. It may be tender, concerned, condemning; always it is a haunting presence. As internalized, the witness may be experienced as split asunder into sound, odor, taste, sight; and each of the latter may itself be dismembered or integrated, or projected outward as hallucinatory, or each may perish within him to evolve in conjunction with other such factors as his inmost and *ownmost* "voice"—his willing, his thinking, his appetitional, his believing *I*.

All factors become in varying ways and degrees synthesized with that *I*, an *I* now invigorated and renewed. Alternatively, when these internal presences perish incompletely into his being, his *I* becomes deprived of its potency, and his existence is accordingly enfeebled or deformed. In general, any such presence may be composed either of depersonalized and internalized "personal" imprints, or, since each person dwells among an assemblage of things as well as other persons, of personalized and internalized "non-personal" imprints. Many combinations are possible. However constituted, a vast and endlessly mutating interior network of intricate relationships emerges, a web which once effectively absorbed may either liberate and transform him so as to potentiate and potentiate anew his already given powers, or so constrict and crush him as to negate those powers.

(iii) In conclusion, I now proceed systematically to set forth a conceptual scheme which comments at length upon the preceding anticipatory survey of the essential nature of the person. Construing him as a *witnessed activity of searching into the rhythms of the self-in-relation to the cosmos*, I am but abbreviatedly stating what will contextually unfold as the meaning of the equivalence between two different perspectives on the person: transcendental naturalism and *non*-transcendental personalism.

Transcendental naturalism affirms that body as *human* body is body to be understood reflexively. For no body which is to be designated the body of a person can, ipso facto, be regarded as a mere aggregate of inert parts. Quite the contrary. Insofar as it is organized as human body, it must (so my argument will run) be apprehended as reflecting into itself an image of itself in relationship to its own "parts" and to the "parts" of the world to which it is (externally) linked.

Personalism holds that all feeling, cognition, willing, appetite, desire, and the like is ideation (or, better, idea*ting*) incarnate. For ideas reveal, express, manifest, or, in general, symbolize themselves through the agency of what a mere naturalism asserts to be mere body.

The axiom of equivalence reigns. It is among my principal claims that its rule is powerful. Carried sufficiently far, I contend, the probing of either perspective discloses a single person-*substance*, a substance which is integral, indefeasible, not static but potency-in-act, and indiscerptible.

The essential unity of these positions—namely, transcendental naturalism and personalism—is grasped under the rubric of *transcendental personalism.* This doctrine, which it is my purpose to work out, elaborates the themes pertinent for conceptualizing this "substance." The immediate implications of transcendental personalism will be seen to define (in my abbreviated formulation) the invariant factors (here designated "transcendental") amidst the multitude of (empirical) transformations, whether the latter be in the realm of body states or in the realm of mind states.

But I stress: this invariant is here construed not as an axiom to be entertained abstractly and merely formally. On the contrary, it is my very problematic. For what is initially stated as ground and presupposition for affirming the indicated equivalence must itself be continually reinterpreted so that its inexhaustible contents may be increasingly drawn forth and articulated.

In the final analysis, the doctrine of transcendental personalism emerges in the context of inquiring into the implications of both a transcendental naturalism and a personalism; and this doctrine is concerned pre-eminently with elucidating the *integrity* of the person. By "integrity" I mean (in a preliminary way) the person as integer, a unified transaction among the many parts of his being. In illuminating this notion, I construe him as a multitude of concatenated rhythms orchestrated with contrasting intensities, luminosities, densities, and fragilities; I treat him as constituted, not by inflexible structures, but by functions which transiently crystallize into durable patterns of elements; and I conceive these functions as correlated activities, activities which form designs woven and rewoven as motile and kaleidoscopic textures. My use of such terms as "rhythmic," "function," "kaleidoscopic" clearly underscores my desire to avoid a rigidly structuralist interpretation of integrity.

In the succeeding chapters, I present from the standpoint of method, and under varying perspectives and in its myriad modalities, this elusive constant: the persistent and essential core of the person. This core of integrity is thus to be understood: every facet is dynamically attuned to every other facet; every facet is dynamically attuned to the assemblage within which are bound together all facets. My reference to a "constant" suggests that I hardly imply that "something" invariant does *not* persist. An organization of processes, integrity is certainly *some* kind of invariant, precisely *that* kind which transcendental personalism delineates. But I must never refrain from emphasizing that this invariant is incomparably more subtle, more refined, and more arcane than any persistent factor which may conceivably be subsumed under either a naturalist or a personalist rubric. It is my intention, in a number of books, to state this thesis and to elaborate its implications; the purpose of the present volume is to set forth the key tenets for methodic inquiry of the kind which will allow for substantive development of the thesis in subsequent books.

NOTES

1. Here, and elsewhere as I shall indicate, I am indebted to a remarkable work on Spinoza, H. F. Hallett's *Creation, Emanation, and Salvation* (The Hague: Nijhoff, 1962).

2. See "Ethics," Part I.

3. Later, I elaborate the implications of "self-mirroring." At this point, I am not committing myself to either a Leibnitzian or an anti-Leibnitzian construal of morals.

4. I here assume that Kant's noumenon is progressively transformed as he passes

through the three *Critiques*, from possessing strictly logical status to possessing a status which, in my judgment, tends to be ontological in Hegel's sense.

5. F. H. Bradley, *Appearance and Reality* (Oxford: Clarendon, 1946). See indexed section on "feelings."

6. Alfred North Whitehead, *Process and Reality* (New York: Macmillan, 1967), p. 42.

7. See Justus Buchler, *Toward a General Theory of Human Judgment* (New York: Columbia University Press, 1951), pp. 48–49, on the distinction between assertive, active, and exhibitive judgments.

II

Strands of Inquiry:
The Emergent Person

2

THE FIRST PHASE OF
METHOD: INTERROGATING

PREAMBLE

In this chapter, I write of reasoned interrogating, the first phase of methodic inquiry into the person. Throughout inquiry, the "object" to be systematically questioned is construed as both a *who*, autonomous and self-determining, and a *what*, a manifold of deterministically interwoven relations. All questions addressed to this "who-what" complex, in effect a *datio*-cum-datum, converge upon such responses as will allow a generalized, coherent, and systematic theory of the person to be framed, a theory which nonetheless is adequate to the range, subtlety, and myriad nuances its "object" manifests. From the standpoint of its deeper ontologic import, the essential being of this "object," in actuality a *subject–object*, is inseparable from being in general. Hence, the philosophic personology I herein begin to set forth cannot be dissociated from an implicit philosophic cosmology, the penumbral suppositions which confer meaning, value, and import upon the person. To achieve my end, the questions methodically to be addressed the person must derive from many disciplines, formal and non-formal, and arise within an attitude of empathic concern for the person addressed. In consequence, every question is asked from within a larger frame of reference, an orientation which requires, at the very moment specific and circumscribed questions are being asked, a total listening to the person. Indeed, as an *a priori* condition of the inquiry, a decision has already been made by the investigator to join the responses of his subject–object with an integrated and comprehensive interpretation of those responses, an interpretation linked to an implicit general metaphysics.

In applying my method, a *previewing* of the person is first needed, a cursory glancing at this or that aspect of his being—in effect, an *anatomizing* of his personhood. Hence, at this stage, the relevant questions are concerned with understanding the person as a mere assemblage of parts, disjoined from one another, and interwoven, not by an intrinsic bond between them, but by a conventional and postulated bond. But the more one questions, the more a natural taxonomy emerges. For each question provokes a new set of questions; soon it is as though a natural movement takes over, as an autonomous force immanent within the questions already asked directs the flow, confluence, and differentiation of the questions *to be* asked. For as the "object" is revealed in its inner depths, a deep relationship between questions and "object" manifests itself, a kind of inner link. More and more, this link prescribes the trajectory the questions will take. Accordingly, though initially the methodic inquirer possesses the "object," directing the several routes of inquiry by his own freely chosen questions, as the process continues, the inquirer himself becomes, so to speak, possessed by the "object." A dialectical interplay among the questions supervenes. Guided at first implicitly by this interplay, then with increasing determination, the person searched into allows fuller disclosure of his variegated facets; perception of the inherent unity and coherence of the person becomes increasingly vivid and persuasive.

Hence, not only are the relevant questions guided by the taxonomic attitude, an attitude which seeks to classify the diverse parts of the person (at first, by convention, and, later, by his natural constitution construed as "object"), but continual repetition of those questions is required, repetition of a kind which leads the inquirer to an altogether new sphere of searching—a sphere which lies beyond ordinary taxonomy. Questions are asked, and asked anew. Upon each asking, subtle nuances are inscribed within each question subsequently to be asked. In effect, the "object" is held up under many perspectives; each seemingly identical question is implicitly conditioned by the particular perspective within which it is asked. In this process, a dual injunction of Method emerges: seek the invariant set of traits which characterize the "object," traits which remain constant through a multitude of circumstantial alterations; once this invariant has been formulated, direct future questions toward the invariant itself. Accordingly, what had been presumed an axiom is now regarded as a problem. Various persons deemed exemplars of a class are questioned; a single person is questioned many times. In this double context of inquiry, the invariant is opened up to reveal its hitherto undisclosed content; these contents themselves are questioned. Hence, the person is ever more deeply probed. Progressively, he reveals himself to be a dialectical interplay between structures which he himself determines, yet structures which in themselves are deterministically ordered—structures cast in the wake of the ceaseless ferment of freedom which *is* the person. By this approach, the person discloses himself, by the kind of questions he himself now draws forth from the inquirer, to be one who implicitly directs questions to the inquirer. Now the "object" of investigation is revealed as himself a methodic searcher. Thus far, the structure of inquiry is shown to consist in the compresence of two searchers, each questing (in dialogue) after the universal characteristics they share, yet each haunted by the utter uniqueness of the other.

A · THE FIRST MOMENT: PREDELINEATION

(a) Preliminary Survey of My General Approach

Mere shadows of a person's intrinsic qualities, the mental and the physical are often explained by notions which fragment a truly indefectible experience of his "being." This deficiency holds for explanations belonging to both science and common sense; since each appropriates key notions from the other, they may chase tails while all that lies beyond the vicious circle thereby created is denied. To achieve greater precision and more useful rule-of-thumb techniques, the multilayered yet cohesive fabric of reality is insufficiently respected. The make of the universe is ever changing; only as a skeleton devoid of flesh does it lend itself to what from the standpoint of authentic experience is facile schematization. One "sees" distortedly and cursorily through habits of vision cast in the mold either of everyday precepts or of scientific principles which refine precept. Though the latter are like maps which guide one through unknown regions of experience, clarifying that to which common sense has merely alluded, they are but sketches, representations—and quite inflexible ones at that. Unwittingly, the investigator regards his actual perceptions from a point of view rooted in conventions which resist change, owing to their success in coordinating apparently disparate experiences into schemata for predicting natural occurrences.

By the restrictive character of the very method of science, the utility of which rests upon its capacity cognitively to isolate events into their "natural" classes by deliberately ignoring those features which cannot be specified according to some pre-existing conceptual scheme, this frame excludes from the scientist's ken countless penumbral meanings, rich and subtle perceptions. At times, these are so strange or, indeed, so veiled in obscurity that they invite radical dismissal as not warranting "rational" consideration. I do not deny that the structures of science may reveal novelties of experience or disclose its hidden recesses. The power to illuminate inhering in these structures is surely great. But from the standpoint of general ontology, they are isolated impressions extracted from a more full-bodied experience than that upon which science usually rests. Themselves based on analogies to experience, these impressions are woven to a phantasmagoria which is less alive, though always suggestive in its status as a great metaphor, than the experience which is its source.

Moreover, I stress as a desideratum of metaphysical inquiry the formulation more of what poets discern than of what scientists may acknowledge. For I hold with Wordsworth that poetry is the "breath and finer spirit of all knowledge."[1] And I would apply his dictum to art in general; I shall even defend Keats's idea that there are "ethereal presences,"[2] celebrated in the media of art, which as disclosures in some way of the *inseitas* of reality should fall within the province of the philosopher. It is his duty, I propose, to detect and explain them, these experiences of a reality glowing with endless layers of singular meaning, a web of undertones woven of the sensuous yet pointing toward a haunting presence, an uncanny "beyond" which by art becomes luminous. In whatever symbolic medium, this portrayal of our most responsive and delicately ordered feelings is a profoundly reliable source of intuitions for framing a general theory of the person, provided its teachings be systematically investigated within the appropriate empirical setting and controlled without losing scope or depth by the precision of data.

Though I develop a conceptual scheme which takes account of the cognitive adventure, the artistic posture will accordingly be of special concern. When authentic it is freer from ritual and stereotypy. It epitomizes a fresher, more spontaneous receptivity to experience. By the nature of his work the artist is more open than the scientist to its many-prismed character; he attends to facets of experience too readily dismissed by the latter. A zeal to avoid obscurantism or mysticism assumes greater importance than the scientist's natural proclivity not so much to dispel wonder, for this is indeed his proper task, but rather to exhibit wonder, to perpetuate it, and always to seek new topics for *inciting* it. Surely, his most basic theories themselves are instances of such topics. What is uncanny, sublime, or eerie, what provokes a sense of awe and mystery, what stirs a feeling for the numinous not reducible to any strictly cognitive system (and expressed only by the allusive components of religious and metaphysical doctrine), what reveals itself in myriad shifting tonalities which may not be rendered by the fixity of customary or of scientific language—these experiences are as important for philosophic notice as the stable, approximately recurrent, and readily conceptualizable phenomena to the clarification of which the scientist devotes himself. Indeed, the very language of philosophy is but an instrument, tentative and corrigible, for probing, uncovering, and denoting, for capturing in vivid metaphor, and exhibiting in the manner of the artist, more than for asserting and thereby merely schematizing the elusive aspects of experience.

To be sure, the language of science is also alterable, for it must respond to experience as its newly disclosed facets ever press for recognition; analogies are woven into that language; and experience is rendered as exemplifications of certain mathematical patterns rather than as simply conforming to the naïve assertions of common sense. Still the essence of science is to negate the numinous and but to sketch the clear; content where necessary to be allusive, philosophy at least strives to be comprehensive. Granted: my formulations are indebted to, and indeed founded upon, disciplines which in the manner of science treat the special topics pertaining to the nature of man. Moreover, my presentation itself is essentially in the assertive mood. Nevertheless, I propose a *generalized* theory which, while comprehending these disciplines, acknowledges the centrality of artistic activity for depicting more responsibly than science a genuinely clarified experience of persons. For that special precision which evokes multiple associations and the countless overtones of significance inhering in experience is both more refined and more accurate than precision based upon an abstraction of qualities from the fabric of reality which falsely simplifies experience.

I do not claim the uniqueness of the notions constituting my theory. They comprise but a *possible* basis for illuminating special theories, a matrix within which these theories may fructify one another. Many alternatives might have been conceived. And innumerable ones which will succeed the theory here offered will be truer to an ever-growing experience of man. But whatever basis is chosen, it, like art, should be inclusive and plausible with respect to the experience of its formulator, however constrictive in the cumulative human adventure that experience will prove to have been. This basis is subject to two conditions, coherence and adequacy. By "coherent" I mean that each of its elements will require the remainder for its full expression and that no pair of implications from any combination of these elements will be inconsistent. By "adequate" I mean that a significant range of ideas comprising the special theories may be interpreted by it—in effect, that all experience to which these theories allude will be taken into account. These criteria for an effective philosophic interpretation will later be further specified.

In sum, I propose a systematic, generalized, and coherent theory of the person. The data to which I appeal in formulating the elements of this theory derive from my own experience. Whatever in that experience constitutes a sound appraisal of reality will yield valid judgments, though the criteria for validity must themselves be stated. And what arises from my distortions will proportionately render my account defective. Accordingly, though my experience includes a deep commitment to the major philosophic and literary portrayals of the person, I offer in the last analysis a personal interpretation. The risk of failing genuinely to communicate is not small. To reduce this risk, I shall set forth the principles of hermeneutics I adopt, recognizing that they themselves require interpretation. I conceive a work of philosophy as I do a work of art: though it may be evaluated only within a cumulative tradition of actual specimens, it stands or falls in the measure that it has been drawn forth into symbolic utterance from the authentic experience of its creator. Naturally, I am obligated to defend the particular sense of authenticity I employ. I stress the personal character of this work because I do not wish it to be judged by reference to any presumed claim for *scientific* validity. Any use of my theory for the special sciences concerned with persons must be inferred by the reader. For nowhere do I trace, save impressionistically, connections between my philosophical conclusions and the premises of extant theories of science. However, since my duty is to communicate as well as to express, I shall wherever I can define my designations concretely and specifically so that, in principle, they might be applicable to more restricted but explicitly formulated disciplines treating the person. Indeed, the success of this inquiry is dependent upon the cogency with which I define the root notions of my theory. But I do argue that every philosophic definition is contextual. Thus it is only in the detailed working out of this theory that the full meanings of its terms may be illuminated and thereby rendered adaptable to contexts outside the immediate scope of the theory.

(b) Relationship Between Method and Ontology

In my inquiry into the person, I propose a distinctive method. To conceptualize his uniqueness, his individuality, and his unity—and this is my aim—one must attend not merely to the generic traits of an "object," as with most entities, but to its correlative subjectivity as well. By this fact, the associated methodologic tenets acquire special features. For, pre-eminently reflexive in his own makeup, the person is capable even as he himself is investigated of methodically searching; indeed, of searching into the very one, perhaps at the same moment, who is reflecting upon him. As a consequence, that makeup is problematic. It cannot be characterized independently of inquiry into the very activity of searching. Further, inquiry into a person requires *in principle* that (at least) two persons conjugately inquire into one another; beyond these two, the entire community is implicated. Accordingly, in investigating persons the veridical objective of method *is* that very method interwoven with its own object—namely, the one who searches, and searches by that method. As pertaining to the person, ontology and methodology are inextricably bound together. Some comments on this issue will introduce the themes of the present subsection.

It is my intent to speak methodically of the person: not only to disclose his nature with respect to the manifestations of his behavior, nor indeed to their underlying causes, but, while incorporating both these concerns, to look beyond them to the person in his essence. For I aim to clarify that peculiar fusion of a *who* and a *what* which distinguishes him from other entities and constitutes him a person. Surely, to speak of the person *essentially* requires that the logos of his being, his ontology, be formulated, that his nature (and his spirit) in its inmost features be illuminated and laid bare. What these "inmost" features are in their general contours, though not in their specific details, and how they may be identified is precisely my problem. In this book, my focus is upon the "how"; in the next, upon the "what."[3] But as I shall not cease to stress, as a pervasive refrain of this investigation, these foci cannot be divorced. They are complementary; indeed, they interpenetrate one another.

The problem of the ontology of the person cannot ultimately be separated from the problem of ontology in general.[4] Clearly, there are many kinds of metaphysical factors essential to a general ontology, factors discernible and formulable though not necessarily individual, ultimate, and indivisible; among these factors I include such classes as relations, possibilities, qualities, things, persons. There is no *a priori* reason for imputing ontologic priority to any particular class. Nor is the being of one factor necessarily dependent on the being of another. Yet a general ontology requires the systematic interconnection of these—i.e., of those fundamental sets of factors I shall call "categories." And any particular ontology implies that general ontology, if only as a background of implicit presuppositions. In my study of the person I refer to that background. More specifically: every particular ontology (e.g., of the person) presupposes a general scheme which weaves together as a coherent system all particular ontologies (e.g., of things, relations, possibilities, etc.). It is the bearing of the general problem of ontology, as presupposing such a scheme, upon the particular problem of the ontology of the person, one element in that scheme, and reciprocally the bearing of the latter upon the former—with a view toward indicating themes relevant to my original question ("What essentially, and from a philosophic point of view, is a person?")—which I here investigate.

In my account, I do not explore the issue of whether, and how, ontology is bound up with the activity of disclosing its own essential categories—an activity, indeed, of particular individuals. Perhaps this activity itself is a category of ontologic parity with the remaining categories. But I do argue, as a special case, that the task of characterizing the meaning of a searching into the being of a person and the task of setting forth the structure of notions in terms of which that being may be characterized are but components of a single enterprise. Again, though searching into any ontologic category is a human activity, I cannot presume that the laying bare of the inner nature of that search requires prior knowledge of *human* being. The issue of the connection between being in general and human being in particular cannot here be decided: the latter might be a species of the former; alternatively, the former may presuppose the latter. In general, the "naturalists" opt for the first view, the "existentialists" for the second. On the other hand, I do claim that all searchings, whether into the being of persons or into the being of any ontologic factors, are mutually implicated. In the final analysis, they are species of a single, integral inquiry. Moreover, I assume that "person," like "relation" or "thing," is a *basic* metaphysical category. And an essential trait of this category is that the structure of the search into one of its specimens, perhaps unlike the other categories, cannot be separated from the structure of the complexes revealed in that search: the searching is bound up with the very being of the person—in fact, one of my conclusions will be that the person *is*, at bottom, just such a searching, a searching to unconceal his being and *pari passu* the being of another who stands to him as complement. For the essence of a person is dialogic; it is a communing with his fellows. In the frame of dialogue, the "being" of a community of selves is disclosed, and this in a context in which nature, composed of things toward which each member of that community orients himself, is *itself* revealed. It is too wide a claim to assert that metaphysical man occupies a special and central role in the metaphysical scheme. In any event, I do not for the present deal with this claim. What I am asserting is that the *notion* of metaphysical man involves the idea of the intimate connection of the structure of inquiry into his nature with the structure of that nature.

In addition, a second kind of search is needed for characterizing the person, a search conventionally called psychology. But the term "psychology" is too narrow to designate the matter I now stress. For, in its usual meaning, psychology is concerned with the logos of the psyche—the spirit or the soul, i.e., psychic phenomena in general. Yet the strictly empirical study of the person *as* person is, in essence, a *person*ology. For this, logos should be considered meaningful, systematic discourse about all kinds of traits and qualities of the person, physical as well as psychic; more deeply, it treats the inner connection between these classes of phenomena.

The datum with which an empirical study of the person ought to deal is neither psyche nor soma. Certainly, inquiry into each of these aspects is valid, and the endeavor to show their interconnection is essential for understanding the person himself. Nevertheless, I am proposing an independent discipline concerned with the person himself, the person as agent and concrete datum—the integral of diversified traits, some lying in the psychic sphere and some in the physical sphere. Further, the basic ideas belonging to both are, in all the subtleties of their interdependence, correlative and complementary. What I am suggesting, in effect, is the need to clarify Heidegger's distinction[5] between ontologic inquiry into *Dasein* (the ontologically essential person, "metaphysical man") and *ontic* inquiry into "empirical man"—i.e., inquiry into the qualities which the person presents to the scientific in contradistinction to the philosophic interest. How to distinguish these modes of inquiry is at the moment not my concern. Suffice it to indicate that by "scientific" I mean inquiry into a particular aspect or constellation of traits of man, whereas by "philosophic" I mean disclosure of the character of the entity who, as source and agent, manifests itself as these aspects and traits, in their multiplicity, their diversity, and their interrelations.

Empirical man is treated by various sciences. Thus anatomy, physiology, psychoanalysis, sociology are concerned with different aspects of his nature. By facile interpretation of these themes, each tends to hypostatize a particular aspect of his existence as primary or as, in effect, expressing his "essence." From this point of view, these special disciplines create abstract images of man which may purport to represent man himself, man *in concreto*. Moreover, though ideas germane to a particular discipline may validly be explained in terms of ideas germane to another (e.g., psychology vis-à-vis physiology), the reduction thereby effected is methodologic and not, as is sometimes implied, ontologic. In any event, the quest for the "essential" person requires that the ideas pertinent to all these disciplines be systematically correlated to form a unified theory of the person *as* person. What is designated "philosophic anthropology" is either an anticipatory survey of such a theory, a tentative sketch or map the details of which are elaborated by the special sciences, or (alternatively) a plan concerning the general nature of man inferred from their findings. The notions forming the basis of this theory, notions discerned by collating the leading ideas of the disciplines concerned with man, ought to converge, the more explicitly they are formulated, upon the notions central to an ontology of the person. And, as I have suggested, this empirical inquiry is subsidiary, from the standpoint of the capacity of the concepts emerging within it to disclose the "essential" person, to ontologic inquiry, though certain of these concepts will subsequently be outlined. The meaning of the question "What, essentially, is a person?" is itself essentially elucidated in terms of the latter mode of inquiry.

It has been my persistent claim that the datum of my inquiry, the person, is a composite of factors which can never be exhaustively characterized. Many technical languages have been designed to conceptualize the various dimensions of his being; each language is valid in its own sphere. Responding to a person in his particularity, and not merely as an instance of a class, every language collects data concerning him by using certain techniques and methods of observation, and coordinates these data under the perspective of a particular conceptual scheme. To some extent, these languages (e.g., physiology, psychology) are intertranslatable. By reference to the relevant norms and conventions of usage, one may be partly "reduced" to another, allowing its key notions to be defined in terms of the key notions of the other. Taken together, these languages constitute an ever-expanding, systematic attempt to articulate the "structure" of the person. Yet that structure is not given but emergent. For only in the context of particular approaches and procedures is the datum to be discovered, and discovered anew.

Since each language systematically, and with varying precision, renders some aspect of that datum, all languages have parity. And though no language may claim to encompass all aspects, each nonetheless fructifies the others. In my search, I propose still an additional language. But my formulations are neither systematic nor precise. On the contrary, aiming at generality, I try to discern the object of ultimate concern to all approaches. Therefore, I sacrifice explicitness of formulation for scope. Wishing to encompass as many facets of the datum as possible, I can only *allude* to their focal and unifying principle. For the datum "itself" perpetually eludes all attempts conceptually to acknowledge it.

Indeed, deeper analysis of the central ideas I evolve—namely, *integrity*, *identity*, and *rhythm* (among others)—leads directly to the heart of general metaphysics. Only in the latter context may themes relevant to a particular metaphysics of the person adequately be delineated. Moreover, since I can express only aspects of action, i.e., specific acts, and not, in the final analysis, the source of action, I may only propose the latter as a *postulate* for understanding the multiplicity of parts, whether spatially as integrity or temporally as identity and rhythms. If this postulate is not demonstrably necessary, it is, at least, fruitful; moreover, implied by the use of this postulate is an "entity" which may itself (potentially) be experienced. Surely, the ultimate unity of the person may not be directly conceptualized. Only its manifold expressions are formulable. Every attempt to hold it in an idea fails, and just another expression appears. For unity is elusive. One can simply live it as a kind of "pragmatic" *a priori* of action. Yet, I believe, the source of unity is immanent within a plurality of actions. Binding them together and constituting their foundation, it is concrete and particular and not merely categorial, historical, and abstract. Thus I cannot affirm that source of unity but only allude to it; its *ipseity* cannot be captured. Ultimately bathed in mystery, it is grasped by a symbol; I point toward it; its ineffability may be summed up in a poem.

Further, the matrix for suggesting and validating the postulate of unity, general metaphysics itself affords, in its various systems, different perspectives on the ontology of the person. For one can extract from each system, or theory of being, some significant dimension of *human* being. Accordingly, we must search in different ontologies as well as different sciences to formulate notions pertaining to the person. I am proposing a complementarity of ontologies, of sciences, and of science and ontology, with respect to the task of framing a philosophic theory of the person.

Although, I have argued, the special sciences tend to hypostatize one or another aspect of the person as *the* central tendency, correctly interpreted they do not hypostatize distortedly. On the contrary, science provides matrices of ideas which are correlated and generalized in the context of metaphysical inquiry. Moreover, its several leading ideas tend to converge (in effect, asymptotically), through systematic coordination of their diversified contents, upon the very datum which metaphysics seeks more allusively to capture—a datum which, as emergent, is always problematic. My method combines rational detachment with, I trust, informed empathy; oscillation between the two is at the heart of metaphysical procedure. My intent is more to exhibit than to express. It is to suggest an image of man, not man in his manifold expressions and historical unfoldings, but man as he presents himself in his individuality; and this image purports to be essentially monistic and, moreover, one which views man not only as a natural complex but also as suffused with mystery. I call for dialogue between all the disciplines concerned with man, recognizing that no image can be more than tentative.

(c) The Triphasic Method

To what norms of inquiry ought this dialogue to conform? Clearly, a criteriology should be framed which is competent to deal synthetically, and not merely eclectically, with the kinds of information provided by experimental science. No less must it subsume the principles, usually but tacitly operative, governing the sifting of the relevant data from the irrelevant in such direct encounters with persons as both the therapeutic and the manipulative, modes of encounter which by no means always coincide. Surely, it must be cognizant of the unformulable depths of man disclosed in religious experience, creative activity of any kind, the empathy of love and friendship. It follows that the method incorporating such diverse standards, rules, and procedures for gathering and evaluating evidence must itself be exceedingly intricate. As a heuristic device for bringing into a coherent manifold, a unified methodology, the numberless pertinent strands of approach, identification, technique, and specification, I here suggest a comprehensive activity of searching which proceeds in stages—stages arbitrarily demarcated yet precisely formulated. In part, each stage recapitulates its predecessors; in part, each prefigures its successors. Hence, the method I recommend is cyclically or spirally phasic. Through ceaseless emendation of one phase by another, an "image" of man progressively emerges from fragmentation, distortion, and obscurity to clarity, coherence, and unity.

In my account, I propose three phases, phases at first glance autonomous, but, when their deeper import is discerned, interdependent and reciprocally co-determining. Sequentially related, one phase unfolding and passing into the next, these phases at the same time comprise a triphasic organic whole. In turn, the latter is so constituted that each phase implicates the remainder, transfiguring and reconstituting it. For, cumulatively evolving by the impact of each on each, the separate phases are but elements of a single configuration which as a totality itself evolves and is systematically transformed. In the present subsection, I merely distinguish (to a first approximation) these phases; and I speak of a few salient features. Subsequently, I set forth in greater detail their key characteristics; and I exhibit them as but aspects of a single process. Now briefly treating the phases, I designate them, quite simply, *interrogating*, *listening*, and *interpreting*, in each instance, with respect to the person whose essence is to be articulated within some conceptual scheme.

In the first phase, there is a questioning of (empirical) questions already posed, or proposed to be posed; and there is a questioning of the responses framed. In each instance, questions and responses are either systematic and articulate or they are vague and haunting; in both instances, they concern matters, remote or proximate, pertaining to the nature of man. In the second phase, there is a listening, intense, directed, and purposeful—in a word: *intentional*—a listening conditioned by an attitude of absolute receptivity to questions and answers, and an impartial, uncritical, and (as a limiting ideal) radically *total* assimilation of what is heard, abandoning nothing and, without conscious judgment, retaining all. In the third phase, there is an interpretation of everything heard and absorbed, an interpretation which is comprehensive and systematic but corrigible and revocable in the light of what might be revealed by new searching. Through rigorous application of this method, I aim at a schema generalized and precise, yet one consistent with man's mysterious depths. Though I derive this schema from varied disciplines, I intend it, within its very pluralistic character, to be unified and self-consistent. Thereby, I propose to illuminate the person, his ontology, his origins, his metamorphoses, his symbolisms, and his destiny; and I seek to indicate the cosmological and theological consequences of this doctrine for a general phenomenology of man.

The three phases I have specified—namely, interrogating, listening, and interpreting—I first examine seriatim. Next, and primarily, I expose their mutual relations and both their procedural and their ontological presuppositions, and I propose them as constituting the *organon* of inquiry of this metaphysical investigation. As an organon, the (triphasic) method itself is a posing of questions, but a posing on a deeper (and as I designate it, transcendental) level of inquiry than the posings constitutive of any of the subordinate phases. It is a questioning of an incomparably more integrated yet richly diversified and subtly nuanced man than of the man disclosed by questions put to him as exemplar of this or that "image" constructed by the specialized disciplines subsumed under the first phase and interpreted by the last.

Moreover, whereas previously I merely referred, as the force of my thesis, to "a philosophically conditioned and informed confrontation of a single person, in which I, the knower, stand in cognitive harmony with all mankind whilst I receive all that is peculiar to this particular man," and I suggested that my goal is to disclose "the concrete essence of the individual . . . as illustrative of the general essence of man,"[6] I now indicate systematically the *method* (composed of the indicated phases) by which this metaphysical comprehensive may be attained. An "object" (the person) will be constructed, as well as discovered, by use of this method. More intricate, more labyrinthine, more mysterious, and yet more profoundly unified and integral than the *apparently* actual person dealt with in either our immediate perceptions or our scientific investigations, this "object" is held (in my argument) to be truly the *real* person. Merely approximated by sense and science, this "reality" is associated with an "actuality" capable of maximally concrete and substantial acts—acts which are elements in a more perfect action than the privative and pulverulent action imputed to the merely "empirical" person of sense and science. The method itself must be revealed as guaranteeing this achievement; and the generic traits of the "object" thus constructed (i.e., by rigorous application of this method) will themselves be delineated sketchily in this volume and with increasing detail in subsequent books.

A root supposition of this claim, a supposition which itself can be justified only in the context of the innumerable investigatory activities set in motion by the method, runs thus: our initial and primordial knowledge of particular cases (here, of persons), whether it rests on the immediate testimony of sense or on the more sophisticated and mediated dicta of science, is defective, impoverished, and merely potential. To frame a viable and generalized yet authentically individualized metaphysical image of man requires numerous stratagems of knowing. In every instance, an immensely complicated but, at bottom, conjoined and unified set of steps is involved. More exactly: whole systems of sets of steps must be brought into systematic relatedness; manifold and diversified ways of being related to other things (i.e., persons) or to a knowing subject (i.e., the investigator) are implied. Usually, most of these steps and ways must be fully explicated. Only subsequent to search of these intricate dimensions and phases may a person be *truly* (i.e., integrally) encountered, encountered over the entire spectrum of his significant traits.

Moreover, *that* search (i.e., the *system* of searchings) must itself be systematically and comprehensively rational. For it is a search which (pre-eminently) draws synthetically and integratively upon a multitude of ways of conceptualizing man. It alone allows a consummate encounter of the person. For it sums up and coordinates, and indeed involves a heuristic leap beyond, already established (and conventionally sanctioned) searchings. By these considerations I mean the following: the search which alone will reveal man *in concreto* is constituted by a true synthesis and not a merely eclectic assemblage of disparate items of knowledge. The sensory, the perceptual, the empathic or intuitive, and the rational–conceptual modes must be so joined that each discerned aspect, dimension, or part of his (apparent) being may now be apprehended as a fully valid symbol of his transcendent being, i.e., of his being as a fully concrete person.

But this synthesis is not arbitrary. It is not simply the joining together of abstract portraits of man. On the contrary, it is truly a discovery, a discovery in which as each "abstraction" is constituted the way opens for an enrichment of the portrait. One by one, the veils which conceal his concrete and authentic nature from the investigator are stripped away; and this disclosure (as by an artist) is literally an opening up of new horizons, the reversing of "closure." All the investigative resources accessible to the inquiring community—its gifts, its techniques, its innovative possibilities—must be mobilized. By heuristic fusion of all *abstract* images, man *in concreto* is brought to presence. For each abstraction is a drawing forth from the object (the person) of some significant set of features, features composed of qualities actually resident within the object. In combining these varied "drawings forth" (literally, *abs-trahere*) in the appropriate manner, a true *concretion* flows forth—a flowing *together* into an immeasurably enriched and more subtle content of what had separately, and, as such, impoverishedly, been drawn.

To clarify this implied distinction between a fragmented, deformed, and wholly inadequate immediate appraisal of man's nature and an integrated, precise, and adequate appraisal which truly conforms to his being, I treat sequentially the topics Method and, in the subsequent books, Ontology. Only by joint in-

quiry into method and ontology may that consummate being itself be conceptualized in its systematic totality, a totality construed as relational both internally
and externally. By *internally* relational, I mean relational with respect to the constituent elements of the pattern which that totality forms; by *externally* relational, I mean relational with respect to the bonds which it sustains to similarly
constituted totalities. Only by framing and using the techniques for constructing
this relational totality may that dialectical interplay between abstractness and
concreteness (viz., drawing forth and flowing together) be depicted wherein the
person is revealed in his full vibrancy: the rhythms of his own circumscribed
being; the multifarious attunings which, breaking through his customary boundaries, link him to the cosmos—a cosmos which at once dwells within him, about
him, and beyond him.

B · THE SECOND MOMENT: TAXONOMY

(*a*) Primary Interrogation

In this moment—namely, taxonomy—I distinguish (primary) interrogation from
(primordial) interrogation of interrogation. By "primary," I refer to several kinds
of realms of inquiry. On the one hand, I mean investigation based upon experimentation. Here, the person is construed strictly as an object to the observer. The
realms of inquiry are already established; or, alternatively, they may be anticipated
as likely to be established. Every conventionally designated discipline, each concerned with man, every realm uses its characteristic techniques, ways of isolating
relevant aspects to be conceptualized, and theoretical foundations. However, either
these disciplines deal with him focally, *as* man, or they treat topics deemed (by
some acceptable criterion) in some indirect way pertinent for understanding him.
In the first instance, I include such sciences as psychology, physiology, anatomy; in
the second, I include the relevant chapters, for example, of physical chemistry,
biophysics, biochemistry, and even, for that matter, certain branches of nuclear
physics and gravitational theory.

On the other hand, I mean (by primary interrogation) ways of dealing with
man which involve experiment only in a peripheral or at least a less sharply
delineated sense, ways which, on the contrary, stress association with man. In
this case, he is encountered in his "subjectivity." Here I emphasize self-searching
as exemplified by introspection, psychotherapy, relationships of friendship or
love—in short, by any unmediated contact with man. In no instance need an
organized discipline of learning be implicated, though in some instances such a
discipline de facto conditions the encounter.

In both cases, that involving an "objectivist" approach, or experiment *upon*,
and that involving a "subjectivist" approach, or association *with*, an "object–
subject" is constructed; and this construct derives its features from the particular
method an indicated approach employs. I use the locution "object–subject" since
no way of speaking about man entirely eliminates his status as both object and
subject. This statement needs qualification. For, when one treats "parts" of man,
his subjectivity need not be explicitly mentioned; it is relegated to an implicit
context of conditioning factors. Alternatively, when one relates empathically,

the "object" character is dismissed into irrelevancy: it is the suppressed ground upon which the "figure" of subjectivity plays, perhaps hauntingly, perhaps in vivid clarity. With varying emphases, every encounter of a person entails a foreground of object against a background of subject *and* a foreground of subject against a background of object. It follows that all human encounter is the matrix for the oscillation and dialectical interplay of these contrasting tendencies. This fact is of significance for both an ontology of the person and, throughout the present book, for a methodology of that ontology.

Whether sharply and systematically articulated or obscurely and tentatively etched, the methods incorporating primary interrogatings are as efficacious as they are manifold. No "natural complex" of factors can present itself either for "direct" experience or as an object, hypothesized or presented as sensible data, for experimental inquiry save in the context of some methodic activity. Granted: every such activity implies the pre-existence or contemporaneous presence of some complex. Nevertheless, the *durable* discrimination of the relations which pattern those elements requires deliberate and inventive reflection upon the relevant method, and its imaginative application in effecting further lasting distinctions.[7] Moreover, the method itself may be construed as a patterned complex; as such, it is always evolving toward intimate relatedness not only to other methods but, indeed, to the very complexes its employment discloses. From the first preliminary taking note (as by cursory glance) of the relevant complexes, every primary method is in its very use re-formed, as are, reciprocally and in correlation to this transformation, the complexes it presupposes—complexes whose real inner constitution it with increasing detail reveals and elaborates.

In its most inclusive sense, method—*any* method considered from the point of view of its own consummate development—is a disinterested engaging of its subject matter. But it is an engaging up to the point where, inexorably, a reversal occurs; and, so to speak, the now well-articulated subject matter itself engages the one employing that method, hence, the method itself. In this activity, its dicta, norms, procedures, and assumptions are, as it were, scrutinized by the newly emergent subject matter; and scrutinized to the point where the method, as originally conceived, is now in process of conversion from possessing "natural" status (since its employment is with respect to natural complexes) to possessing "transcendental" status. For, at this point, the hidden and not merely empirical contents of its object are increasingly disclosed.

However, to anticipate the character of this conversion (a veritable transmutation), I must leap ahead of my present account to a prevision of a doctrine crucial to my argument: namely, diverse methods diversely employed, and employed perforce to treat diverse subject matters, tend, in the long run, when they are exercised vigorously and appropriately, not only toward self-emendation, but, more dramatically, toward a state of confluence, one with respect to another—in effect, they tend to form a dynamically equilibrated system. I am enunciating what interrogation of interrogation will reveal as an ultimate cohesion of methods. This tightly-knit manifold constitutes a limiting ideal. Prescribed, in effect, by every particular method, this ideal is already prefigured, in varying gradations of clarity and scope, as inhering in each method. But the generic traits of method itself, in particular of methodic inquiry into the person qua person, first truly disclose themselves only when one passes to a treatment of what I have named *primordial* interrogation, an interrogation which seeks the ground and justification for all empirical questioning.

(b) Primordial Interrogation

When I speak of interrogation of interrogation as "primordial," I mean a deeper construal of interrogation than that previously set forth. For I refer to the immanent basis which grounds the validity of *primary* questioning. Only when this basis is exposed may a philosophy of method be evolved, and its implications and larger import discerned. In my work, that philosophy concerns those particular methods which yield such information about man as will facilitate "constructing" the person in his total concreteness. By "constructing," I mean a reconstituting of the person, transforming a cursory and fragmented glimpse into a coherent and integrated portrait. Under the rubric of primordial interrogation, which ultimately aims at such reconstituting. I consider a congeries of questions: those already asked, or those which might be asked, concerning the import of the first (or primary) class of questions, and their underlying assumptions material and formal—namely, questions pertaining to the criteria by which the primary questions are selected as also being significant questions; the classes of "objects" emerging when they are asked; the ways in which these emergent objects compel revision of the kinds of questions posed; and the steps by which a particular taxonomy is vindicated or emended.

As the Method of interrogating methods progressively makes itself evident, it becomes increasingly clear that the question–response complexes which form the primary subject matter to be inquired into must themselves, *in their general configuration*, have already been presupposed, though not yet explicitly acknowledged, as (in a general sense) discriminated and classified. This schema emerges into the full light of (methodic) consciousness in the context alone of the activities involved in the diverse methods; and this context itself is an increasingly unified superordinate activity, subsuming those methods in a collective, not merely a distributive, sense. The vicissitudes of this process of unification are manifold. They constitute the factor of adventure within the emerging overarching Method. For to transmute a corpus of methods from an often desultory assemblage of contingent approaches into a coherent organon, in which each (primary) method finds its necessary role and location, the searcher must venture forth into unknown domains, and yet he is guided toward them as though by a distant beacon. Modified and transformed by the impact of its own results upon its constitutive procedures, a method which thereby emerges acquires a new direction and a subtly changed purpose. A veritable taxonomy of constructed objects, together with the correlative procedures by which these objects are constituted, expresses the first and merely preliminary stage in this acquisition.

Roughly, this taxonomy embraces a primary division and its derivative subdivisions. The former consists of subjectivist approaches to the person; the latter, of objectivist approaches. This dichotomy approximately, but not precisely, coincides with the distinction, introduced earlier, between association and experimentation. However, neither polarity is absolute. For, in both instances, when viewed from a "higher" (transcendental) standpoint, the oppositional element is negated; the conflicting factors are transformed into sublated moments within a more inclusive concept. With respect to these dualisms the regnant principles are *complementarity* and, more radically, *transactionality*. By the latter I mean: what had been distinguished, at first, as opposing factors, and, next, as contrasting but mutually presupposing factors, now emerge as but foci within an intricate relational complex—a complex which, under varying perspectives, presents a shifting constellation of foci, relatively enduring crystallizations of significant elements. For example, the transactional complex, a person, may under one perspective present himself dramatically as a constellation of gestural activities, whereas under another perspective his verbalizations emerge into prominence as the dominating factors. But this progression can only be regarded as the *terminus ad quem* of a series of taxonomies of which, for the moment, I may only set forth the *terminus a quo*.

To proceed: the subjectivist approach is further divisible into introspection and extrospection; and the extrospective, in turn, into searching into a solitary person and searching into a person in his relationship to the community. Alternatively, the objectivist approach is also divisible, but in a more ramified way. On the one hand, it involves those disciplines concerned with either the overall behavior of man—whether from a psychological, physiological, or, for that matter, any behavioristically scientific viewpoint—or the behavior of *parts* of man, living or non-living, insofar as an understanding of those parts contributes to an understanding of man qua man. In the first instance, I further distinguish the behavior of integral man *in solitudine* from his behavior *in communitate*. The latter concerns the relations between man and his environment, alive or lifeless. In the second instance, I distinguish, first, the behavior of parts of man *in summation*—i.e., man as assembled, as *body*, or, more strictly, as body *functioning*; second, I distinguish the behavior of parts of man qua parts, but parts nonetheless relevant to the total configuration which is man. Finally, in the last case, I distinguish those parts which may properly be called living from those parts which may properly be called lifeless. Nowhere in this initial taxonomy do I confront the crucial problems of continuity or discontinuity, of hierarchy or parity, or of priorities with respect to the issue of the reduction of living to non-living and the alternate but less prevalent view of the non-living as essentially an extract and privation, a deformation of the "purer" being, of the living.

Already, in this predelineation of the texture of primary interrogatory approaches to the study of man—an activity which comes under the province of interrogation of interrogation—the skelton of an ontological commitment emerges—more exactly, of an ontic or empirical approximation to an ontological analysis. A complex web of intentions, an intricate network of "horizons" within which objects are discriminated, a seemingly disparate assemblage of "worlds" announce themselves as a vital presence to the philosopher who would seek the essential person. The very inchoate quality of intentions, horizons, and worlds constitutes them as a challenge and a spur for conceptual revision of the crude taxonomy, and its conversion to a new and more integrated schema. That all members of this skeleton, however crudely articulated, are indeed relevant to a philosophy of the person is a matter which may only be established by primordial interrogation, as, surely, are further refinements and reconstitutings of the skeleton. The essential prerogative of *this* mode of interrogation is precisely to exhibit the process of *re*articulation of the skeleton. In the province of primordial interrogation dwells all preparation, including this rearticulating, for the second phase: namely, speculative *listening*.

Before passing to the issue of criteriology, viz., determining the norms and standards of research in accordance with which schema revision is effected, I diagrammatize the tentative schema thus far proposed—proposed, in effect, tacitly or explicitly by disciplines and approaches already extant.

(*c*) Implications of the Taxonomic Scheme

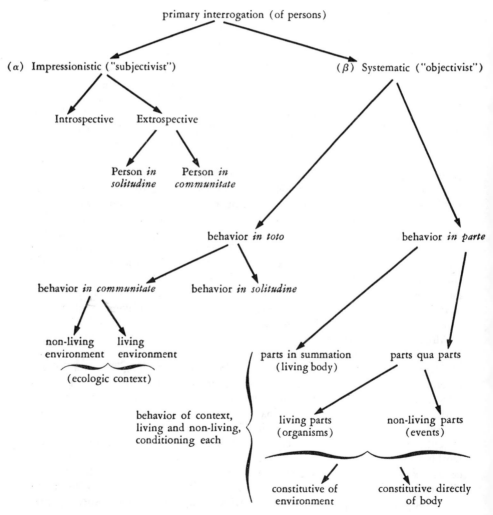

When I survey this simple diagram, I am led to several but significant conclusions —though, indeed, the "force" which leads me along this and not some radically different line of inquiry might, as the phases of my method unfold and disclose their as yet hidden content, itself be disclosed as based on a "convention," a convention, moreover, which is alterable and replaceable. Nonetheless, I pursue what for me is a natural direction of inspection.

Accordingly, the method of "impressionism" (α) is concerned for the most part, though surely not exclusively, with man in his uniqueness, his particular and individual character—his depths, his symbolisms, his self-identity—and this against a background of general information about man, of universal and recurrent traits without a knowledge of which the objective of impressionism cannot be consummately achieved. On the other hand, the method of "systematic objectivity" (β) is concerned with man, or parts of man, or the natural environment of man, in the *recurrence* of structures, functions, activities, and processes—in a word: of behavings as general and recurrent universal "forms"; and this against a background of the specific, thorough, and detailed examination of particular cases, of unique instances: a necessary ultimate condition for grounding the validity of empirical laws. On the whole, neither case, (α) or (β), precludes *in principle* a reversal of the indicated relations between the particular and the universal; in either instance, foreground and background are interchangeable. In quite the same way as the contrasting poles subjectivity–objectivity and abstraction–concretion may be negated by their subsumption under a more generalized perspective, here also, in the contrast between the indicated methods, (α) and (β), one must affirm a methodological principle of complementarity, oscillation, dialectical interplay, and transaction. As before, these ideas concern the dictum that through interchange of content both oppositional factors and conjugately related factors other than those originally discerned may be ascertained. But the full sweep and import of this principle may only be revealed as my methodologic inquiry proceeds.

An important exception to the principle of interchangeability of foreground and background must be noted, an exception which perhaps necessitates reinterpretation of the principle. For on the one hand, introspection involves only a *singular* complex, the self internally inspecting itself, a complex radically dissociated from a conditioning objective matrix. Even though this complex may be (internally) inspected from many angles and under varying perspectives, the multitude of self-inspectings tends in the long run to converge upon a single *inward-dwelling*—a dwelling, in effect, upon a "nothing," i.e., a no-thing (perhaps construed as a Kantian noumenon, perhaps as a Buddhist nirvana). To penetrate the very ground of subjectivity is to reveal the inmost rhythms of silence, perhaps a labyrinthine and subtly constituted pattern of rhythms but nonetheless an absolute and ineradicable stillness. The inmost core of the subjective is neither subject nor object. On the other hand, when from the point of view of extrospection a putative *ultimate* part is postulated, and as such also inspected, it, too, tends to acquire the character of a character-less entity—in effect, a mere point, an instantaneous flash of existence utterly devoid of subjectivity: for example, the quark of elementary particle physics. Here I assume that the horizon of objects which includes the quark is relevant to understanding the immeasurably more intricate yet indefeasibly unified "object–subject" (i.e., total) person. Moreover, does not the quark acquire meaning only within the complicated relational structure of physical theory? Further, must not the appropriate procedures of identification and recognition, circuitous as they are, be deemed by the physicists' convention an extension of our senses? Hence, as it is *in itself*, the quark is surely never encountered, on any interpretation of encounter, save as a universal. The particularity of the interior world passes over into a universal silence; the universality of the exterior world, so manifestly a relational complex, passes over into the particularity of an empty existent. For, in the deepest sense, at the uttermost extreme of the outer as well as that of the inner both subjectivity and objectivity absolutely vanish; the particular and the universal become indistinguishable.

Two limits, an upper: the absolutely unique encountered *no-thing* of consummate introspection! A lower: the absolutely universal (conceptual) no-thing (or minimal thing) revealed, consummately, by science! Yet at these limits neither particular nor universal has meaning. And yet, perhaps these limits—the first involving the plentitude of being, consummated personal being; and the second, the privation of being, the most elemental instance of existence (the consummate result of scientific inquiry)—themselves express perspectives upon a single *transcendent* being: a unified perspective within which absolute being is somehow revealed as embracing in an absolute (though paradoxical) unity the extremes of fullness and emptiness. In the very negation of each, particular and universal are conjoined as one.

I am proposing a cosmological principle of deep relevance to understanding the person. Both the path of the indefeasibly and most distant interior point (the self-seeking-itself)—the ultimate foundation of personal reality—and the path to the indefeasibly and most distant exterior point (the ultimate foundation of physical reality, in which the conventional notions of space, time, and matter collapse, and are replaced by altogether new ways of schematizing phenomena) terminate, when traversed sufficiently far, in a single locus: a noumenon which, properly construed, is indeed *numinous*—i.e., luminous with the strangely glowing light of absolute truth (perhaps, the "substance" of Spinoza). But I have already digressed too far from the main thread of my argument—yet it is a digression which must somehow be incorporated within the speculative theory I am setting forth.

C · THE THIRD MOMENT: REPETITION

(*a*) Variations

To return to the main line of my argument: further inspection of the diagram discloses an important relation between uniqueness and generality, a relation involving the methodological category of repetition. Deeply rooted in the "interrogative temper,"[8] indeed in the makeup of man himself, is the need for regularity, ritual, sustained meditation. No novelty or adventure or inventive deliberation is denied as an essential ingredient of method. Quite the contrary. What I am affirming is the dual character of method, as of all systematic query, as requiring synthesis of novelty and repeatability. Alone, neither element suffices. For both vanish, and method passes into mere routine or haphazard contrivance if either element is negated. Not only do the continuity and coherence of meaning and the very possibility of recognizing, identifying, and specifying complexes of existence (even the merely trivial) depend upon innovation, the unique insight, discovery of a new theme, distinctive and novel variation on a tried and secured theme; but a certain exactitude and fidelity in repetition are also required. Moreover, with each new application of method, new variations appear. In their cumulative character these variations may so insistently obtrude upon our experience as to compel revision of a given method, if not its frank revocation.

How do such variations arise? At what point do they modify the very method the repeated use of which gave birth to them? To deal with these issues, I reflect further upon the theme of repetition. Two modalities of repetition must be distinguished. There is repetition with respect to a single (perhaps singular) datum. There is repetition with respect to a set of similar or analogous data. I treat these modalities, and the ways in which their respective variations occur, seriatim.

In the first instance, a particular object is repeatedly held up for scrutiny, at first cursorily and then with increasing systematicness. Constituted in several possible ways, this object may be demarcated by immediate sense perception; alternatively, it may be specified by an instrument deemed a satisfactory extension of sense perception—e.g., the microscope: optical, in the case of "simple" visual extension; electronic, in the case of intricate visual extension. With respect to the latter, the criterion for "extension of sense perception" is established in various ways: a tacitly accepted habit or orientation, an explicit theoretical doctrine, a loosely worked out practical frame of reference. In either case, the object is inspected again and again, from many angles and vantage points. It is placed in varied contexts. Depending upon such factors as resistance, malleability, resilience, it itself may be subjected to internal changes of innumerable kinds. At first, whether internal to the object or in its milieu, random contextual variations become increasingly deliberate; and this by virtue of reliance on a specific method of selection. As that method for holding an object up for systematic inspection is variously deployed, elaborated, and modified, a distinct order, or set of orders, of variations is prescribed, and presented anew. In this process, the object itself is experienced as altered, and altered in systematic correspondence with these contextual shifts. Thus the initial distinction between object boundary, interior, and exterior may be changed, as indeed will be the qualities initially imputed to that object. Further, its relations to other objects analogously "held up for inspection" (in this dynamic construal) become fashioned to a web of often exceedingly intricate design; and new foci of "objectivity" emerge to displace hitherto discriminated foci—a *field* of activities is now conceptualized in its internal dynamics, a field whose *particulate* structure is constantly subject to change.

Governing this process is a rule of the following nature. Certain structures or functions are ascertained as invariant with respect to some set of contextual transformations, random or systematic. Once established, this invariant is deemed to possess a *substantive* character, a character symbolized by a pattern of symbols to which is accorded axiomatic status. Associated with each invariant is some set of variations of a specified kind and form. When through accumulation of new variations, variations hitherto undiscerned or unpredicted, this kind and this form are sufficiently altered, the image of *what* is invariant is itself correspondingly altered. What had been constant is now reinterpreted as variable. Interpreted as a new group of transformations, this (latter) variable is brought into systematic connection with other analogously produced variables—variables themselves constructed through demolition of what had likewise previously been entertained as constants. A new specification is now required. For, correlative with the now enlarged group of transformations, a new, more inclusive, and more fundamental invariant is posed. What had previously been deemed axiomatic is now held problematic. Deeper inspection of the inner content, newly revealed, of the problem discloses what may, in a more advanced stage of inquiry, be newly deemed axiomatic. And so, step by step, the process continues. Though here succinctly and abstractly stated, this process unfolds in such a way that the person emerges in his full concreteness from mystery to presence. How this emergence occurs I have yet to take up. Prior to this task, a few comments are needed regarding the second modality of repetition.

(*b*) The Invariant

In repetition with respect to a *class* of data, an assemblage of objects is chosen, an assemblage the components of which are deemed typical with respect to the properties intended to be classified, interrelated, and measured. On the basis of what measurement discloses, a new taxonomy is constructed; new properties are now revealed, as well as a correspondingly new pattern of relevant relations. To accomplish this task, a random sample is chosen from this assemblage, even a sample of one, chosen because reason indicates it an exemplar of the assemblage. In the light of this choice, the pertinent data are gathered, refined, coordinated, and revised. Discerned "within" these data are, as in the first modality of repetition, certain invariant factors with respect to transformations deemed, by theory or by convention, permissible. As before, these factors are construed as imperfect renderings of deeper and more significant factors. Accordingly, the searcher is enjoined to seek the invariants for an increasingly wide range of increasingly diversified, though not always precisely specified, transformations.

A significant problem for a philosophy of the person lies in the discernment of the inner connection between an invariant factor disclosed as bearing upon his makeup by *both* modalities of repetition. By illumination under many perspectives of a singular datum, a datum sui generis of commanding interest, the trajectory toward an "ultimate" invariant is disclosed. Through intense examination, in a multitude of contexts, of a group of like data, an analogous trajectory is disclosed. Pre-eminently for persons both modes of recurrent inspection are essential; they complement, complete, and elucidate one another—and this in a profound way. For each person is both of intrinsic interest, in and for himself alone—he is a veritable world unto himself—and of interest as an instance of the universal theme of person*hood*.

A vital concern of my quest for the essential person is the issue of the *coinciding* of the indicated trajectories. Is there an overarching invariant, so the essential question must be posed, upon which the inquiries involved in tracing these trajectories converge? Does a double invariant reside, indeed inhere, within each and every person—an invariant duplicated because it, in part, derives from the unique and particular essence of that person while, in part, it also derives from the universal essence of humankind? If so, in speaking of humankind may one affirm that *this* group constitutes an object no less a unitary existent than any of its instances? And if so, does not this *general* object, of indefinite and ever-growing—though, granted, at times contracting—membership yet (perhaps), despite the ceaseless change of its constituency, exhibit its own unalterable pattern of constants? Finally, if so, does not humankind command attention quite as compelling as, and revelatory of precisely what, in the final analysis, each of its members in his inmost implications reveals? I am here speaking of a double identity: one stemming from himself alone, and differentiating him from all others; the other deriving from his participation in the human community, and causing him to be profoundly like all others. The problem of the ultimate identification of these two identities is crucial for an ontology of the person. Its additional methodological import will be treated in the following chapter.

(c) The Recurrent and the Unique

In sum, any entity—and, in particular, a person—may be understood both as an instance of a recurrent phenomenon and as itself a novel and non-duplicative phenomenon. Though no encounter excludes either mode of understanding, in every encounter one mode predominates.

Thus a scientist, who typically uses the first mode, explains the behavior of an object by deducing a statement describing that behavior from two sets of premisses, one general—the desired explanation—and one particular. In the former, he formulates general laws which bind together factors, both experientially identifiable and theoretically stipulated, into a system of parameters expressing uniformities of behavior exemplified by innumerable similar objects. In the latter, he specifies the values of some of these factors for the particular object under scrutiny. By combining this specification with the explicit indication of the pattern of variables found in the initial premiss, he may derive (and this process of derivation is a process both of explanation and, when the conclusion to be drawn is not yet known, of prediction) the descriptive statements specifying the values of the remaining factors. His interest, however, is primarily (in his theoretical role) directed toward the contents of the major premiss, and in the possibilities for systematically relating these contents to those of major premisses relevant for deducing the behavior of other classes of objects. Concern for the contents of the minor premiss, in which are formulated the special conditions for the application of the major premiss to *this particular object*, is tangential to his ultimate aim: namely, to disclose the behavior of the object in question as an instance of successively more comprehensive classes of behavior.

Technically, I should add, some philosophers of science prefer to regard explanations as material-leading principles—inferential rules which permit derivation of instantial conclusions (the descriptive statements) from instantial premisses (the minor premisses in our formulation). This view has the advantage that it suggests that explanations are, like maps, modes of illuminating the realm of our experience, permitting us to move from one experiential point to another (these points being incorporated in the instantial premisses). Logically, however, the two formulations are, as C. S. Peirce has shown, equivalent.

Turning to the person as unique, one must distinguish an historical account from a non-historical account. The latter endeavors to apprehend him from the point of view of his full, living presence. Surely, science is significantly ancillary to achieving this end. But history aids in a peculiarly competent way. For, of all entities, a person most dramatically reveals *who* he is only when his particular unduplicatable history, the process of his *personal* evolving, is grasped and conceptualized. Typically, the historian elaborates the contents of what for the scientist is a mere minor premiss, instrumental for drawing forth conclusions relevant to the making of predictions, into a systematic characterization of the way an event is embedded and implicated within a network of events, a pattern of causal strands which binds those events together. Certainly, he is interested in explaining the behavior of the event by reference to a major premiss which includes general laws (e.g., of sociology, psychology, economics). Nonetheless, his first obligation qua historian is to render an accurate narrative (though he perforce selects and stresses certain elements to the exclusion of others in accordance with his own values and concerns) of the particular trends, forces, institutions, motives which brought about its existence and of how this complexus impinges upon the event to determine its specific activities and issue.

The enterprises of history (in this sense) and of science are, accordingly, complementary. Within what from a strictly logical point of view is an identical *pattern* of explanation, two different foci of inquiry may be chosen: by stressing the particular factors conditioning specific situations, expressed in the minor premiss of an inference, history unfolds; by stressing the general contents applicable to a class of situations, expressed in the major premiss, science unfolds. And, surely, for an understanding of a person, both foci are needed. I should like, nevertheless, to stress, for this will be important for my subsequent discussion, certain additional limitations inherent in science with respect to its power to elucidate the behavior of a person.

The scientist extracts certain elements, selected in accordance with the frame of reference defining the scope, presuppositions, and interests of his science; and he weaves these elements into a conceptual fabric which bears, at certain crucial points, resemblance to the object but which cannot fully comprehend the special qualities of its existence—much as an abstract painting dramatically focuses on lines, planes, and colors of an experience, yet intensifies and distorts these into a novel pattern. Though every science of man discloses something important about each particular man, it formulates but a single perspective upon him; it cannot grasp him in the integrality, the depth, the integrity of his existence. Nor does the multiplicity of perspectives afforded by the diversity of sciences succeed in unconcealing a jot more. Science surely facilitates understanding, but it is not the characteristic means by which the unique person whom we encounter is revealed to us in his individuality and in the special drama of his life.

The sciences of man, I am suggesting, cannot even collectively disclose the person, only his stereotype. They in effect construct a caricature of him, deliberately exaggerating certain features in order to illuminate relationships relevant to the making of predictions, not so much about this or that individual as about this or that aggregate of individuals. Numerous caricatures may, of course, be made of any particular person. The scientist is interested only in those which are, so to speak, isomorphic with caricatures drawn of all men. By conceptually slicing man's existence this way or that, science arrives at biological man, psychological man, economic man, social man, etc.

Accordingly, by the nature of its methodology, science reifies man. Focusing upon him as a passive, un–self-determining object, it studies only the *residue* of his existence. And, by that methodology, it must abhor any conception of him as immeasurably mysterious, as intrinsically capable—as I believe he is—of drawing forth from the wellsprings of his potentialities an unpredictable, inexhaustible multitude of interests, skills, motives. Science, I claim, necessarily reveals man as not fully alive.

To meet a person scientifically means, therefore, to meet him as an instance of a class: to focus on some aspect of his existence, to analyze that aspect into its constituent elements and relations, and to compare it with its analogues in other people. To encounter a person in his particular existence, on the other hand, means to focus at once on all aspects of that existence—on that from which the several scientific perspectives have been extracted.

When, however, I argue that the sciences of man distort, reify, frame caricatures, and disclose stereotypes, I do not denigrate science's unique contribution to a philosophy of the person—whether science deals with general classes of repeatable phenomena or with particular phenomena repeatedly. I only stress the dangers of construing that philosophy as exclusively, and merely, the summation of the results of using the procedures of science, implying that such an account of the person is reducible to some particular image constructed by science. Indeed, I am here rephrasing one instance of Whitehead's "fallacy of misplaced concreteness."[9] Equally, I argue, an exclusively historical approach suffers from an analogous flaw. For, like science, history deals with facts already completed, with circumstances and causes which belong to a *closed* past. And as I never ceased to stress in my first chapter my concern is always with the *actual* person, the person in the fullness of his presence: his immediacy and his concreteness, the person as a *who* and not merely as the *what* revealed by either science or history. Nonetheless, science and history alike have essential roles in this enterprise. The who-ness of man cannot be fully conceptualized, or even encountered, without an appropriate incorporation of his what-ness.

NOTES

1. William Wordsworth, "Preface to the Second Edition of the Lyrical Ballads," in *The Poetical Works of William Wordsworth*, ed. E. de Selincourt, 2 vols. (Oxford: Clarendon, 1944), II 398.

2. Cf. John Keats, *Hyperion* I.339.

3. See my forthcoming book *The Dance of Being: Man's Labyrinthine Rhythms* (New York: Fordham University Press, 1979).

4. See the discussion of the theme of ontologic parity, reiterated in various ways throughout Justus Buchler's *The Concept of Method* (New York: Columbia University Press, 1961).

5. See the discussion of *Dasein* in Martin Heidegger, *An Introduction to Metaphysics*, trans. Ralph Manheim (New Haven: Yale University Press, 1959), under index references to "Being-There."

6. See my "Toward a Concept of Integrity," *Annals of Psychotherapy*, Monograph Nos. 3 & 4, Vols. 1 & 2 (1961), 70; emphasis deleted.

7. See the discussion by Justus Buchler, *Concept of Method*, p. 7, as well as his examination of "natural complexes" in *Metaphysics of Natural Complexes* (New York: Columbia University Press, 1966), pp. 1–51.

8. Buchler, *Concept of Method*, p. 160.

9. Alfred North Whitehead, *Science and the Modern World* (New York: Macmillan, 1941), chap. 3.

3

THE SECOND PHASE OF
METHOD: LISTENING

PREAMBLE

In this chapter, I depict the act of listening to the flow of responses to questions methodically directed toward the person, an act constituted by three interdependent moments: attending, gathering, transforming. In attending, the inquirer so sensitizes his faculties, his sensibilities, and his conceptual resources as to fill himself with the presence of the other; he places himself in a state of heightened receptivity. Beyond this, he attends his own attending, and thereby analogously receives the compresence of himself with the one into whose nature he is inquiring. Accordingly, a complex set of reflections mirrors to the investigator the variegated aspects of his (interpersonal) relationships with the "object" of search. Layered one upon the other but, so layered, interacting one with the other, these reflections are transmitted as encounterable symbols to a community which bears witness to the inquiry. In the final phase of Method—namely, interpreting —a matrix of intelligible symbols, expressing the essential being of the one searched, is systematically woven into a unitary fabric. Prior to such coordination, seeker and sought are brought into mutual attunement. In this context, both participants are significantly transfigured. Indeed, a kind of parity reigns between the two. For, in reality, each is searching the other. What from the point of view of the investigatory process had been an asymmetric relationship is now converted to a symmetric relationship. Inverting circumstances which hitherto had prevailed, my proposed method allows the very one whose nature had been sought to be revealed as a unified manifold of activities. In both cases, the dialogists are revealed as constituted by sharply etched and intensely luminous foci, a highly differentiated texture, conditioned by and originating within a labyrinth of concealed and haunting depths. In the search, the mysteries resident within the person are progressively illumined, etched against this enveloping background.

Thus gathering together what had been diversely attended—the different facets of the person—the inquirer apprehends the veridical unity of his substance. Upon superficial inspection, psyche and soma are distinguished as intrinsically bifurcated; within each "realm," moreover, especially when pathology prevails but also when either "realm" is insufficiently scrutinized, its characteristic ingredients are often seen as incongruous and disconnected. Yet, upon more sustained attending, and consequent upon the process of gathering in those ingredients, a dialectical play among them unfolds; mutual transformation accordingly supervenes. Indeed, far from being a precariously constituted and merely correlated pair of parallel ontologic processes, the person, I argue, reveals himself, in methodic inquiry, to be but one substance, integral and indivisible. An orchestrated complex, a person is constituted by his manifold rhythms, which are called forth within inquiry and enter into the very composition of the investigator, by a series of intentional acts. Reciprocally, the rhythms of the inquirer are analogously drawn into the one investigated by *his* intentional acts. For each person imprints himself profoundly within the other. In consequence, the substance of no person is radically isolated and distinct from the substance of all persons whom he actually encounters. It follows that every person is, in effect, an agent of those sectors of the community by which he has been personally affected.

In principle, if one were to integrate the numberless increments of encounter over the *entire* community, that (ideal) community, in its entirety, would be disclosed as embedded within its every member. Therein dwelling, the community would reveal itself via the collective symbolisms—the archetypal structures—

of its variegated depositions. Through methodic inquiry, these symbolisms themselves are inquired into. Their diverse *modi operandi* are revealed; the principles in accordance with which they unfold and disperse themselves within the community are articulated. Modified by the special character of each individual, the independent personal centers incorporated within him are themselves internally linked; collectively, they are the manifestation of mutually linked searchers. In its phase of *listening*, Method discerns both the uniqueness and the universality of these indwelling dynamisms. Many laminae of existence—infrapersonal, personal, suprapersonal—are thus gathered into the inquirer (and, reciprocally, into the one investigated). In their interconnections, these laminae disclose the interwoven essence of multitudinous centers of particular existents. Moreover, every person, himself an orchestration of such internalized centers, stands in relationship to the whole cosmos. In effect, his own centricity is realized, and concretized, only in the context of this relationship—namely, how he is linked to the entire configuration of events, personal and non-personal, a configuration whose own "center" transcends that of every particular event composing it.

A complex of comportment, subtly modulated, and spirit, woven of ethereal rhythms, the former manifests the latter as a kaleidoscopic unfolding of mosaics of symbols. Yet, at bottom, comportment and spirit are one and the same. For the person, so my method reveals, is a single and singular substance. At the same time, this very singularity is revealed by that method to be composed of a multitude of analogous singularities. Within this context, the self-identity of every individual is revealed as, in effect, the synthesis of the numberless identifications he establishes with others, and the syncretistic joining of this synthesis with factors already indigenous to his own being. Moreover, spirit, I repeat, is externalized as comportmental symbols; in turn, the latter is interiorized as part of the evolving stuff of spirit. This comportmental–spiritual unity which is the person further discloses itself, by deeper inquiry into his being, to be one who gives—a donor, so to speak, of *data* to another; a donor whose gifts are reciprocated by another who is analogously constituted. In sum, an egalitarian relationship prevails between seeker and the one sought. Both emerge from methodic inquiry transformed, and transformed in a double sense: universally and generally, concretely and particularly. For the essential human substance of each is, in this process, more fully manifested; correlatively, the specific individual potentialities of each are more consummately actualized. In oscillating attachment and detachment—a drawing apart in circumspect surveying of the other and a coming together in empathic union and sympathy—Method proceeds; in so proceeding, it reveals that the person himself alternates between self-surrender in mutuality and self-possession in individual solitude.

A • THE FIRST MOMENT: ATTENDING

(a) The Person as Method Incarnate

In a desultory way, certain reflections have been brought together under the rubric of interrogation; the new questions immediately raised by these reflections suggest a need to rethink the problematic of my inquiry. For this rethinking effectively to be carried through, I must return to the substantive focus of my search: namely, the person himself. In the light of the deliberations of the first phase, I interrogate, not simply, as before, the customary ways of interrogating him, but I actually reopen the issues previously treated by now interrogating the person anew. Accordingly, I again *listen* to him, but now my listening is at once purer and deeper yet throughout informed by the methodological dicta already acknowledged. Before turning to this new phase of method, I first recapitulate, in broadest terms, the general approach here adopted; next, I summarize the conclusions thus far drawn, restating them as basic injunctions to the investigator.

Whatever the class of entities investigated, every inquiry consists of two parts: the systematic working out of a theory, and an exposé of its root assumptions, predilections, and implications. The weighting accorded these parts determines whether the inquiry is designated scientific or philosophic. Stress upon the former suggests a scientific account; stress upon the latter, a philosophic account. How-

ever, when the class of entities is sufficiently general, and especially when no entities are presumed excluded from that class (leaving aside the issue of whether,
under these circumstances, the term "class" can properly be used), the two parts
may not be distinguished; we always speak of a philosophic inquiry. On the other
hand, when the class is sufficiently restricted, the second part becomes trivial or
irrelevant, and the inquiry is deemed categorically scientific. In between, in "mid-
dle-range" classes, science and philosophy jointly reign.

When I speak of the maximal class of entities, I am, in effect, referring to being
qua being. When I speak of a class of entities which excludes some set, no matter
how small or insignificant that set, I am in actuality prescinding from some group
of properties of being qua being, deliberately excluding those properties from
systematic consideration. Thus I am already implying an ontology in which the
notions of the plenitude of being and the emptiness of being are each assigned
meanings, albeit as upper and lower limits, respectively, to a spectrum of instances of "being"—instances ranging from inanimate events, through living
organisms, and culminating (as far as direct knowledge reveals) in persons.
Whether a special intuitive faculty enables me to apprehend either limit (i.e., of
maximal and minimal being), and indeed the character of the inner relationship
between these limits, is not for the moment under consideration. But surely it is
the case that any "object" qua object (be it an event, organism, or person) appears, in some manner, within my experience; surely, moreover, my experience is,
in some manner, haunted by those limits—conditioned, in effect, by that which
is, by definition, unconditioned.

By intention—overt or implicit—or by contingency, or by necessity, certain
traits of any object are assigned a focal role in my perception or in my ratiocination; other traits are dismissed into the background as a vague context the relevance of which to my perception is but dimly perceived. Under one perspective,
a tree exhibits properties which may be conceptualized in a single schema, a
schema which also includes stones, bits of metal, and so forth; under another
perspective, the tree may be brought into juxtaposition only with plants; under
still another, with plants and animals; under yet another, not with stones or plants
or animals but only with persons. Depending upon the makeup of the perspective
—the horizon of objects it is allowed to include and it is required to exclude—
a particular theory, trivial or consequential, is implied. An act of abstraction is
performed with respect to each of these types of objects; a further act of abstraction is performed in bringing together objects of this or that kind. The different
possible horizons, each entailing its own set of acts of abstraction, are, in effect,
classified—with respect, always, to some underlying metaphysical perspective. By
a criterion, whether or not acknowledged, deriving from that perspective, certain
horizons are selectively discriminated as important and, in some sense, "natural";
others are dismissed as artifacts. Thus the horizons of physical events, biological
events, and personal events are usually acknowledged as, in each case, cohering
internally in reasonable fashion. But strata of objects inhering within each of
these horizons criss-cross in often strange ways back and forth from one horizon
to another. With respect to things, or the class of aspects of things, conceptualized
according to some chapter of physical theory, these immanent connections are
usually deemed of no consequence—though a later physical theory may actually

acknowledge as consequential what, relative to an earlier theory, had been dismissed into irrelevancy. With respect to organisms, certain connections between the things characterized by physics are relevant; other connections are irrelevant. Like things (physical events) and (biological) organisms, persons, too, may be conceptualized by effecting the appropriate abstraction. But complications, beyond the kind pertinent to things and organisms, arise. It is to these that we now turn.

On the one hand, a person has an event aspect; by the same token, he has an organism aspect. Surely, both aspects are relevant to the person*hood* of the person —as far as, by this designation, I refer to the full, concrete entity which is the subject of my most empathic and integral encounters. This entity is so constituted that if I squint in one way it reveals itself to me as a mere thing, in another, as a living body, and in yet another, as a mind at work. On the other hand, the term "person" in one sense also implies that I am squinting at this particular entity in a special way, a way analogous to thing squintings, organism squintings, and mind squintings. Hence, at bottom, I am, as before, performing an abstraction. Yet the person may be thought of in a larger sense. For he is also the matrix— fathomless, concrete, and unique—which now "functions" as thing, now as body, now as mind, now as person in its narrower construal. This double sense of "person" implies an inconsistency in the use of this locution. Yet reflection upon this inconsistency compels reflection upon the distinction between the methods appropriate to conceptualizing the person: now this way, now that.

In my inquiry, I assume that the world revealed within my experience is constituted of more intricately arranged constellations of traits than any given (verbal) language can possibly treat. Accordingly, whatever the investigation, I am to some extent always a prisoner of my language. One language will articulate my experience in one way, another in a different way. Certainly, I may discover (or contrive) a more inclusive language which will enable the relevant correlations to be made; and these correlations may, and normally do, criss-cross in weird patterns between sets of terms occurring in the diverse languages. Indeed, simple one-to-one correlations are probably rare. Perhaps, ultimately to render the distinctive qualities of the person, I may only gesticulate, mutter unintelligible sounds, point toward what I *mean*. For the horizon within which meaning itself emerges always demands some means of communication, if only by gesture, by facial expression, by vocal inflection. In general, the whole being of a person who searches, his every mode of comportment, must be mobilized to designate something which is no *thing*: so elusive yet so concrete, so inclusive yet so utterly simple—as, in the larger sense, a *person*.

Now, the person appears to be that which (or, rather, *who*) presents himself by his own inner dynamism, by his intentionality, and presents himself under many perspectives, both linguistic and non-verbal, and always to *another* person, and yet another—always to another who, as seeker, is so expressing *his* intentionality that the two intentions link and fuse. A *double* intentionality; that of seeker, that of the one who is sought! And since it is a double *intentionality*, there is ever the potential for reversal, for interchange of the roles of seeker and sought! For to define a person I must include in the *definiens*—a person!

From a methodological point of view, this situation is quite unique. True, in a measure though without the drama, to define a tree, a mere flash of thoughtless existence, I do likewise—and yet, quite otherwise. It is peculiar that when the datum of inquiry is a person I must already presuppose something about persons in order to conceptualize that datum. And this "something" involves the notion that the person is both ὄν and ἐπιστήμη. Though distinct, each dimension presupposes the other in such a way that the two are also one and the same. On the other hand, in setting forth the traits, say, of the amoeba, I also refer to acts, procedures, techniques performed by persons, and by persons who orient themselves toward some complex of entities they conventionally designate "amoeba"; and the amoeba must, likewise, make itself present as datum. And yet it cannot, reciprocally and in the same manner, orient itself toward the investigator. Accordingly, there is something quite special about method when it is prescribed by the special entity, person. For, alone in this instance, seeker and sought are conjugately implicated: each is ineluctably interwoven with the other; by the very acts of seeking and being sought—in particular, by their interchangeability—each conditions and transforms the other; together, they constitute a transcendent dyad.

Previously I referred to the constrictions of language. Now I stress its power to liberate. For, by the language he uses, the investigator retextures experience in ways felicitous for further action and deeper understanding: hence, he more powerfully reconstitutes language. The relation between action and understanding is complementary and cyclical. Effective development of one enhances development of the other; the two are continuous phases of a single integral act. And when I treat as my data persons I am concerned pre-eminently with *actors*. It is persons who experiment, comport, orient themselves—in a word: search; and in searching, characteristically use language. *Per definitionem*, the person is the one who, among all the powers of the universe, uses methods—i.e., he thinks and acts *methodically*. His methods are diversified and cumulatively integrating. By their use he reveals, in his every action, who and what he is. In this respect, the person is the one incomplete, radically problematic datum. He is incomplete in a sense incomparably more absolute than, for example, the amoeba. True, for the latter, novel perspectives can endlessly be brought to bear upon the study of *its* behavior. But, ontologically speaking, the person *is* the one who searches, and in his searching seeks to penetrate mystery and to bring it, insofar as he is able, under the rubric of finite, rational, and discursive formulation. *A fortiori*, the person *is* the method which originates all methods; and in his own study of the person he himself, with all his resources—his entire being, his singular power of listening—becomes the instrument, the vehicle, and the agency through which (or *whom*) such search is effectuated.

Method, in its own self-inspecting acts, intentionally and rhythmically executed; Method as conjugate seeking, communing, and reciprocal witnessing: this *is* the essential person. The full ontologic import of this doctrine is the focus of subsequent books. Now, I ask: What happens, from the side of Method, when such beings, *human* beings—each Method incarnate—are assembled, and one by one selected, in actuality or by imagination, for methodic inspection? By this inspection, my ultimate end, from the side of ontology, is, first, to set forth the distinctive traits which confer human character upon these beings and, second, to determine how each being is absolutely unique though but a variation upon a universal theme. The methodological injunctions noted in the first phase, *interrogating*, are intended to facilitate this quest. I wish now succinctly to restate these injunctions as the following five themes.

(*b*) The Community as Method Incarnate

First, the overarching method of (philosophic) inquiry into the person is an organization of phases which exist in a double relationship to one another: temporal, as antecedent, intermediate, and consequent; contemporaneous, as in reciprocal dependence, one upon another. Accordingly, the phases both unfold as discrete foci within a continuum of activities and cooperate in correlative fashion. To reconcile these inconsistent features, sequence and compresence, one has to construe one phase as coming into dominance then receding, without annihilation, as it is displaced by another, yet all phases as germinating ceaselessly within a single configuration. But the deeper meaning of this unity of contradictory features will be disclosed only when I treat the final phase. Suffice it now to say: each phase replicates, though with added import, its predecessor; within each is prefigured, in the latter's broader contours, its successor.

Next, through this "succession" of nonetheless "contemporaneous" phases there occurs a confluence of the special methods for understanding the person. Each method reveals a particular horizon within which a certain class of "objects" pertaining to the nature of man may be discriminated; yet no single method discloses the total relational complex which a more concrete encounter reveals him to be.[1] Nevertheless, though many disparate horizons unfold, in an inchoate texturing of what one intuitively apprehends as a unitary and integral phenomenon, an overview of all the associated methods should be not merely synoptic but, in a more creative sense, syncretistic. For it ought to allow that integration of diverse horizons and that welding of the correlated methods which permit the investigator to discern new meanings within each horizon taken individually. Finally, the new meanings are therein disclosed only when the putative object is taken as the transcendent being of the person, a being upon whom perspectives heretofore concealing more than illuminating were afforded by the actual phenomena studied.

Third, this conversion of seemingly independent phenomena into *symbols* which import, by convergence, a single transcendent reality further suggests that the taxonomy emerging in empirical (viz., primary) inquiry is pervaded by a set of polarities, with respect both to "objects" and to their associated methods. However, these polarities are so to be conceived that, in each case, contradiction between their opposing members conceals a deeper unity—a complementarity and an essential compresence. These polarities may be summarily stated:

  (i)   subject *vs.* object (resolved as "complex with both an interior and an exterior")
 (ii)   abstraction *vs.* concretion
(iii)   association with *vs.* experimentation upon (resolved as "disinterested engaging")
 (iv)   oscillation *vs.* dialectical interplay
  (v)   self-action and interaction *vs.* transaction
 (vi)   recurrence *vs.* uniqueness
(vii)   transformation *vs.* invariancy

(viii) hierarchy *vs.* parity
 (ix) plenitude of being *vs.* privation of being
  (x) context as background *vs.* focal foreground.

Fourth, each polarity expresses a different aspect of the quest to convert an ontic taxonomy of ways of conceptualizing man to an ontological penetration to the essence of man. This quest discloses a progressively more intricate totality (the emergent person) as a field of continually yet purposively and directionally changing *particulate* structures. Pertaining merely to a multitude of partial horizons, obscurely interpreted, the ontic taxonomy is transformed into a labyrinthine texture. In this texture, parts which stand to one another in relations of subordination and superordination are nevertheless always profoundly unified: unity within an hierarchical plurality.

Lastly, the gathering together of diverse primary methods so enriches the content of their collectively emerging object that, at this point, the idea of *a community which employs these methods* must be woven into Method itself. This community is associated with the following traits. First, its members systematically interchange, collate, and synthesize the knowledge (of the person) which they individually acquire. Second, this synthesis itself is the product of the convergence of occasionally identical, often harmonious, but usually disparate and even dissident, opinions; through their interplay, and by use of distinct and often contradictory but nonetheless progressively coalescing methods, the truth of a person's being will tend to emerge. Third, the variety of means by which the community arrives at a determination of its object (the person) is manifold: it may exhibit him in metaphor and by allusion; it may act toward him in gesture, intonation, or some other bodily comportment; it may frame rational and ordered (assertive) judgments about him. For the essential unity of the person is too elusive to permit an exclusively conceptual apprehension. Finally, these varied ways of "reasoning" about his nature suggest that a person is, at one and the same time, a *who* to be encountered and a *what* to be conceptualized; and if the latter, either by science or by history. For these reasons (i.e., the four indicated "traits"), the community may formulate a personology; if so, it then systematically binds together different bodies of knowledge, knowledge based upon the what-ness of the person. Alternatively, it may—and this task is *my* paramount concern—formulate an ontology in which a person's what-ness is subordinate and ancillary yet essential to the conceptualization of his who-ness: in the last analysis, the spheres of the who and the what stand in the relationship of mutual fructification.

In sum, I have dealt with the following issues: the organic unity of a triphasic method, self-corrigible in its progressive application: the intricate unity of the object, person, revealed in stages by that method; the ontic paradoxes inhering within both object and Method; the conversion of an ontic account to an ontologic search through systematic resolution of these paradoxes; a community by its collective acts using this method, drawing upon all its resources—linguistic and non-linguistic—to relate the *who* of the person to his *what*. Organic method, organic object, ontic paradoxes, ontological unity, organic community: all involved in the imaginational, conceptual, and attitudinal apprehension of the person *in concreto*. What is the deeper nature of this organicity? How are the paradoxes converted to unity? Whence arise these three elements of "apprehension," and how are they related? To answer these questions, I must advance Method to its second phase—a phase which, in part, replicates, but, more significantly, further articulates the first phase, and prefigures the final phase.

(c) Attending-in-Depth

By a set of procedures and stratagems, P, a community of seekers, C, uses a set of symbols, S, interpreted by a pattern of meanings, M, to portend an object O, the person. P, C, S, M, and O: each is organically to be understood; furthermore, no P or C or S or M or O may be understood apart from the complex (P, C, S, M, O); finally, every factor, and the totality of factors, are in continual and correlative transformation. By Method, I now mean the "movement," the flow if you will, of this integral assemblage, a flow which preserves intact, as invariant, a certain pattern or "form." How may this *flow* be "heard," and, in the third phase of Method, interpreted? To simplify matters at the outset, take as paradigmatic for the community a *single* seeker, I myself; afterward, complicate this model by substituting a *society* of seekers. Three moments may be distinguished in characterizing the flow: *attending* it; *gathering* it in; dwelling upon the resultant complex with a view, in some significant way, to *transforming* it. But these moments themselves flow, one into another; none can be considered without reference to the remainder.

In the first instance, I merely attend. I attend myself (the minimal community) in symbolic relatedness to an object, using a certain approach, and discerning within my symbols a certain meaning; I attend the changes which occur in the connection between approach, symbol, meaning, my own inner state, and that of the object. At first, however, without discriminating these factors, I simply *stand before* the object. Insofar as I can, I empty myself of all preconceptions regarding its character. I use no symbols; I seek, as yet, no meanings; I do not reflect upon what is occurring within me the observer, nor do I draw inferences concerning what is occurring within the object observed. My approach is merely to *stand before* that object.

Accordingly, I allow my senses, my feelings, my thoughts to be affected, without conscious bias, by what I perceive: this particular individual who himself stands before me. Immediately, this *mere* attending, stripped bare of intent, reveals itself an *attentive* attending. For, in it, I radically give myself up to the multitude of synoptic acts it comprehends; I allow myself to "listen" more fully with all my faculties open to the manifold qualities of the other. Literally, I stretch toward this person; I reach out the more accurately to trace the contours of those qualities; I fill myself with his presence. Just now, I referred to the "synoptic" acts my attending comprehends. By this I mean: I glance at him synoptically, now in this manner, now in that; I move toward him and away from him; I deliberately increase the acuity of my hearing, my sight, my touch; I imagine him to be in circumstances other than those in which I initially discover him; I fantasize about who and what he is.

In this way, I find myself more sharply aware of a gesture of *his*, a facial expression, a vocal inflection, a postural change. The aspect, or part, or dimension of his presence I experience, I now, in a second attending—*an attending to the very process of attending*—also experience standing in a certain relationship to the particular way in which I approach him. My manner of "glancing" at him correlates with his manner of disclosing himself to me. My simple act of attending has now been transformed into an act of my attending myself in relationship to something of him which he reveals to me. In effect, I am attending a field of interpersonal activities, a field in which both he and I are implicated.

In observing this field, I become cognizant of an intricate pattern of factors, mutually intertwined: some derive from my comportment toward him; others derive from his comportment toward me. Moreover, I become aware that just as certain elements of his comportment affect which elements of my comportment will be drawn forth, so, conversely, certain elements of my comportment affect which elements of his comportment will be drawn forth. To put the matter succinctly: the patterning of comportment, his and mine, is a function of the interaction of the two; they are reciprocally determining.

As I attend him, and in the measure that I summon my powers to this act, I reflect into my being an Imago of him in his being; conversely, he reflects into his being an Imago of me in my being. By "Imago" I mean a form or a pattern, an εἶδος, suffused by a specific sensory content—e.g., visual, aural, or even (rarely) olfactory, etc. Beyond this, the Imago I reflect *includes*, as one of its essential components, his reflections of my Imago into him; and conversely. In consequence, an intricate layering of reflections is built up—from his side as well as from mine. What unfolds in the comportment of either profoundly conditions what unfolds in the comportment of both.

Accordingly, the *symbols* by which I express the nature of the object before which I stand, when that object is a person, involve the complicated processes which go on between that object, in *his* self-consciousness as searcher, whether active or potential, and me, in my self-consciousness as seeker—in this instance, active. In effect, we are both "participant observers"[2] within a single matrix. Each reveals himself to the other as a pattern of symbols the meaning of which can only be deciphered by reference to a new and more inclusive "object," the field itself. This pattern expresses the mutual attunement of one to the other. For in order truly for me to know him two conditions must be fulfilled: I must be capable of attuning myself, in my rhythms, to him, in his rhythms, and he must be capable of reciprocating by attuning himself to the rhythms of my searching acts. In this way, we are, as a dyad, "in tune." Clearly, from the ontologic side, the implications of these considerations are enormous. From the methodologic side, they are no less significant.

In this activity, I "fill" myself with the presence of the other; this presence includes, as one factor, my own presence as reflected from its impact on him. In this way, my inner constitution is changed as *pari passu* his inner constitution is changed. But, paradoxically, I (and he, too, insofar as he also is a seeker) "empty" myself of *all* presence. For, by *intending* accuracy in *attending* him, so that my perceptions are adequate to his being, I must convert my customary state of existence from one of fullness with imagery and mental elements of all kinds to one devoid of all fantasy and emotion: at least, all which, as it were, I instinctively deem both irrelevant and inhibiting to my free receptivity. In this process, I myself am changed. In the inmost core of my being, I, the seeker, am transfigured; and, in this instance, transfigured not by the reflected imprints transmitted from him to me but by the very dynamism of my own autonomous searching. Beyond this change, I, the one who searches, thus also change the structure of the searching activity itself—an activity conjugately dependent upon the fact that every search is a double search: to search the other entails, reciprocally, that he in principle is likewise searching me, the searcher.

Indeed, the mind of the seeker pulsates rhythmically from a state of fullness of presence to a state of emptiness of presence. Now it is absolutely receptive, awaiting with dramatic stillness the patterns transmitted to it through the interpersonal field—patterns contributed jointly by seeker and by sought, in perpetually interchanging action and reaction; now it is absolutely active, seeking to impose the patterns of its own polymorphic consciousness upon that field—patterns which flow kaleidoscopically: at one moment, inchoate; at another moment, coherent.

Whether received or imposed, "these patterns alternate; they blend or mix; they can interfere, conflict, lose their way, break down."[3] Searching is *methodic* searching insofar as it applies itself to determining how such patterns may be authentically synthesized and not merely eclectically gathered into a specious unity, yet synthesized in such a way that although their haphazard and spasmodic character is reduced their spontaneity is retained. Protean in its inmost nature, this quality of the searching consciousness must not be violated. On the contrary, a truly methodic search reaffirms it while rendering it more greatly diversified and, at the same time, solid and unitary. What had been a mere polymorphism of techniques is converted to an isomorphism, with respect to the invariant essentials of method, between related sets of acts of knowing and related sets of contents of these acts.

Though initially a disoriented knowing reigns, a knowing in which the many separate glimpses of the object of knowledge are held apart, the quest continues to seek that heuristic, generating, transforming, and unifying principle which alone may direct and guide the process of knowing to its consummate objective. The merely prospective and immanent knowledge of a prereflexive confrontation of the object is negated; a dynamic, spontaneous, integrated, and fully oriented knowing is brought to consummation—the object may now emerge in its fully concrete and transcendent character.

And yet—though I am already acquainted with this schema of Method, and accordingly enriched in my potentialities for apprehending the actuality of both the object of my search and my own self-consciousness (for prior ratiocination has heightened the "tone" of both my receptive powers and my active powers)— I must nonetheless once again approach the person in a renewed attitude of naïveté, of methodic humility. Granted: by the previous considerations, an already enlightened naïveté—a prideful humility! But by this enlightenment, this pride, I mean that naïveté which is instituted, quite deliberately, through *suspension of disbelief*.[4] For, whatever my prior preconceptions, and their abolition by the rational skepticism rooted in interrogations hitherto conducted, I now will to believe again—to believe what I in truth perceive.

Intellectual parity dominates this attitude. Granted: the crassness of original belief must be refined, burnt away, so to speak, by careful and systematic searching, by informed and methodic searching. But reinstatement of naïveté is essential. To see the person in a new light—more accurately: in a *renewed* light—this is the inner truth of the moment of attending! Two inescapable facts impress themselves upon me.

On the one hand, there is the clarity, the immediacy, the crystalline purity, the sharply etched lineaments of what I perceive; there is the luminosity, the sheer externality, the unblurred contours, the uniform and well-articulated visibility, the absolute filling of a present reality; there is the vibrancy without suspense, the utter lack of concealment, the palpable fixity of relationships and actions, the "continuous rhythmic procession of phenomena . . . never . . . a form left fragmentary or half-illuminated, never a lacuna, never a gap, never a glimpse of unplumbed depths; [there is] . . . a local and temporal present which is absolute."[5] Everything is as it is. There are no hidden or secret meanings. On the other hand, a radically different perception haunts me. It is on the periphery of my awareness; suddenly, now and then, it appears in the very center. This is the element of drama, mystery, portent: the sense of emergence from concealed, ineluctably hidden depths, of features standing in solitude against a dark and haunting background, a dim and dark matrix; a labyrinth of dramatic but obscure and unfathomable happenings, a sense of the suspenseful, a foreground of fragmentary phenomena playing themselves out amidst inexorable silences—yet stillness fraught with unknown and impalpable but powerfully intruding tensions.

In the first case, the person simply is *as* he is, existing, phenomenal, simple, lucid; he is a manifold of happenings, a durable and luminous configuration of traits, acts, attitudes. In the second case, the person is entangled and stratified; he is a multilayered constellation of meanings, a portentous efflux from deep and obscure recesses; he is a wellspring of meanings, elusive, perhaps miraculous, elemental in their forebodings. Compare, again, these modalities of experience: a constellation of presences, vivid and fully manifest; a constellation of presentiments, of truncated presences and hidden meanings. Whether one attends another, or, for that matter, one's self alone, both modalities reveal themselves: an exterior foreground, a manifest object; the hint of an interior and latent content, a background which hovers about and is immanent in the former. From this point of view, the presentation of a person may always be understood in a double way: as an existence in and for itself, self-interpreted; as a texture of symbols awaiting decipherment, a finite portrayal of an infinite abyss—the repository of elements sublime or terrible, hence, disclosing themselves as a *sacramental* manifestation.

Throughout this account, I have stressed the extrospective dimension of Method—always, however, conditioned by the sense of an objective presence which behavioristically reveals its inner depths. In penetrating that objectivity, the seeker discerns the other as an analogously intentional creature, one who alike is capable of searching—nay, is under existential obligation to search. Earlier, I spoke of an introspective approach as complementary to the extrospective, as indeed needing to be woven into it. For a person is competent to search himself no less thoroughly than he searches another, and with comparable objectivity. When one turns inward to inspect the contents of his own subjective resonances, he is no less aware of himself as an object which conditions his every self-inspection—as a body external to his psychic being.

Accordingly, as he searches *within* himself, the inquirer becomes aware of a texture of feeling, image, thought—a texture at times durable, at times fleeting. As he attends this texture, reaching out to seize it, it becomes more and more like an inner object to him, resistant, yet, when his exertions are sufficiently vigorous, malleable and penetrable. As soon as he has taken hold of this manifold of internal happenings, an authentically existent complex, he discovers that it portends something beyond; he does not desist from continuing his exploration. Touching now this part of his (inner) being, now that, he in effect caresses the entire manifold that he might discover a path which will lead him beyond the apparent toward that of which it is an appearance. Dimly at the beginning, yet, as he progresses, with increasing clarity, a deeper-lying presence first suggests to him a more solid foundation to his psychic being than what he had thus far discerned. In his attending, he is gripped by this object; now it eludes him, now it reveals its hitherto buried contents.

In dream and fantasy, the seeker gives himself up to the unfolding images of his psychic life, pursuing their byways, compelled by their variety, fascinated by the bizarre and grotesque as by the numinous and lovely. He becomes persuaded that he might be led by them along paths which, as he pursues them, ineluctably draw him toward a single road, as though at the end of the way there lies a magnet which, powerful and autonomous, inexorably works upon him. A more deeply concealed presence opens its content to him, immeasurable depths, innumerable recesses, intricate designs; a presence which, in its very diversification, as he allows himself to pass now through this and now through that cavernous way, reveals an ever more persuasively emerging unity. Memories well up from the grottoes of his mind, a seemingly infinite repository. One by one, he traces these memories. Finally, he perceives what he can only acknowledge as the very ground and *fons et origo* of his being: a ground which, working from within, begins to lead him without—indeed, toward the same cosmos to which his search of the other has also led him. With Jung,[6] I speak of the archetypes of mind; unlike Jung, I cannot assign them merely psychic status. Though initially they reveal themselves as immanent within me, as within another, they are ultimately experienced as transcendent to each, hence inclusive of both. But what these archetypal presences are I must defer answering until, in later books, I treat the ontology of the person.

To summarize: inquiry into the person differs from most inquiry in that, in the former, one may pose the question (concerning Method) in two ways: by reflecting upon one's own nature, or upon that of another, as that nature is lived, from "within" his own experience, or the experience of another, as felt in its ownmost subjectivity; or by reflecting upon the nature either of oneself or of another perceived as an objective datum, a natural complex of activities. In the first instance, I deal with the person as psyche, and this either by introspection or by extrospection, each a form of in-specting, or *seeing within*; in the second, I deal with the person as physis, observable process.

Hence, by Method I mean the employment of reason to discover the reasons for, and operative within as foundational to, the phenomena to which Method is applied. As used here, "phenomenology" refers to preliminary study of the relevant themes. It surveys from the point of view of their initial appearance themes the full delineation of which would constitute an ontology. In both cases, the suffix, logos, is used. By a logos of phenomena, I mean a gathering together of the appearances, the manifest presences of a person, into a coherent unity. By a logos of being (ὄντα), I mean the gathering together of all that these appearances point toward as their inner import and meaning.

From the standpoint of physis, the person is a unity of natural processes, processes the "outside" of which is manifested as the phenomena of simple observation (as well as the focus of scientific study). From the standpoint of psyche, the person is construed in his essence: that which animates and vitalizes him and, thereby, engenders his physis. In the broadest sense, however, a person's essential being is both psyche and physis; they are inseparable aspects of him. By this I mean, the person is, at once, meaning and symbol, inner life and manifestation, essence (in the narrower sense) and existence. Accordingly, an ontology is a gathering into a unified manifold of what under one perspective is subject, under another perspective object; under one, a plurality, under another, a unity; under one, a *relatum*, under another, a matrix of relatings. It is to the methodic activity of *gathering* which, in the previous moment, had merely been attended, that I now turn.

B · THE SECOND MOMENT: GATHERING

(a) The Emerging Manifold

According to my previous account, within the new indwelling presence, a presence *gathered in* by me, the one who searchingly attends, I discern both a vivid play of luminous phenomena and the resonances, perhaps dim but always haunting, of a something beyond the surface texture of the being of him who is sought; but "something" which I cannot yet, in this phase of my search, articulate to myself. Consider the etymology of "attending." To attend is to stretch out toward, and thereby to come close to the other; it is to imprint myself into him as he, reciprocally, imprints himself into me. For, at the very moment of my *renewed* search (i.e., renewed after the phase of interrogation), the element of reciprocity between seeker and sought—a bond intimate and indissoluble—is apprehended as an essential ingredient within what seemed, by superficial observation, to be no reciprocity at all, but an intrinsic *separation* between seeker and sought.

Again I cast a fleeting glance at him. I draw in something, a trace undefinable and obscure—perhaps the hint of a gesture or of a facial movement; and when I step back from him and glance anew, once more there is the deposition within me of something of him. It is thus that I may speak of the multitude of perspectives revealed to me in my every act of attending. Should I desist from further attending while I reflect upon this or that perspective, delineating its constituent elements in a precise and systematic way—fixing that perspective, so to speak, as though it were a genuinely durable pattern—I am again regarding the person merely behavioristically. By extracting such and such a constellation of traits and dwelling upon them, I am again constructing an abstraction, a caricature of the actual person. Accordingly, if I were to arrest the process of attending (and in-gathering), and turn to another "similar" datum, and yet another—until I assemble a class of data, each datum truncated, degraded, privative, and partial—I am in a position to form a theory about a class of data assembled from factors from which certain traits have been systematically, recurrently, and deliberately (i.e., through deliberation) prescinded. Herein lies the kernel of, the germinal basis for, an empirical approach to a partially denatured nature; so that my subsequent attending is to class qua class—to which, of course, I may impute its own reality.

However, when I become aware of my representation as essentially caricatural, I dissolve it and return to dwell with him in his total presence. Once more, my quest is *intentional*—i.e., stretching toward the "within" of the person to apprehend his concrete being. For I again attend his comportment not as composed of discrete elements isolated from one another; on the contrary, my desire is to comprehend him as a whole, to apprehend every element of his being within and in relation to the lineaments of his *entire* being. Thus within the very act of attending (i.e., intensively observing), I am already aware of the method I am "using," a drawing together of parts into a unitary configuration: a more concrete representation than that hitherto framed—one which, again and again, re-presents him to me in the ever-increasing fullness of his presence. That method may be succinctly stated: I, in my total being, *am* in respect to him, in his total being. Here, the "am," a *being with*, conceals facet after facet of subtle implication—the reciprocal implication of him with me, sought and seeker, in a single communion of knowing.

To express the structure of this "being with," whereby seeker and sought are mutually implicated, with intricate reversals of role and relationship as ever present potentialities, I must allude to an earlier distinction between two stages of the moment, attending: attending which is synoptic, attending which is syncretist. By the former, I mean a mode of attending which tends toward the fragmentary, the aspectual, the unintegrated perspectival, the merely incidental manifold. By the latter, I mean a mode of attending which involves the conversion, by accumulation of appropriate insights, of what from a lower viewpoint was merely coincidental to a new pattern which, from the resultant (more inclusive) higher viewpoint is systematic, unified, and coherent.[7] Already, when attending has been transformed from the synoptic stage into the syncretist stage, it has become identical with a new moment of "listening": namely, *gathering*.

By the moment of gathering, I mean: a gathering into a single inclusive manifold what hitherto had been a plurality of disparate manifolds. To effect this transformation, four sets of conditions must be operative: the focus of what has been attended must be sharpened, limited in scope, and precisely delineated, and the several foci thus discriminated brought into systematic relatedness; the total configuration of what has been attended must be broadened to comprehend hitherto undisclosed patterns of relationship between different totalities of analogous kinds; the approach used in attending must be complicated sufficiently to embrace an ever-widening range of diversified techniques, procedures, instruments of observation—in short, extensions of our sensory-perceptive apparatus; the findings consequent upon attending must be shared, interchanged, disputed, collated, deliberated about by a community of seekers, a community using various approaches, choosing different foci, and configuring the objects of their inquiry in idiosyncratic ways.

Compliance with these conditions—namely, *sharpening the focus, broadening the configuration, complicating the approach,* and *sharing the findings* [8]—brings about the convergence of inquiries, originally conducted from many points of view, upon a single, multitextured, intricately constituted manifold of parts, parts arranged hierarchically in patterns of subordination and superordination, parts which as a totality form a concrete entity systematically related to a community of entities of similar composition. Yet a manifold which is not opaque to an integrating, generative, directing, and purposive "center," a potency which actualizes itself by varied means in varied ways! For, on the contrary, the manifold thus constituted is through and through transparent to that potency and, hence, revelatory of the transcendent ground of being: a ground which, though transcendent, dwells immanently within that manifold and, in analogous ways, within analogous manifolds. By "manifold," I here mean the person construed as an activity which, at once, unifies a plurality of elements and diversifies the unity of their combination.

In this moment of gathering, moreover, a number of factors are separately brought to unity: the community, the approaches, the symbols, the meanings these symbols portend, the objects—persons in relation; in short, what previously was designated as the complex (P, C, S, M, O). How does organicity reign with respect to these factors—factors taken both as individual sets and as a single unified set of sets? This is the true problematic of the moment of *gathering*. For, by its symbols, a multiple "joining together" (i.e., συμβάλλειν) occurs. Seekers are brought together as a single all-inclusive communal inquirer. Approaches are brought together in a single, integral communal comportment. Meanings are brought together as the unitary life of the spirit, a life made transcendent and luminous, and replicating itself as thematic variations unfold as one object of the quest after another is surveyed and understood. Persons—to understand whom is the objective itself of my method—are brought together as a community of reciprocating inquirers. Finally, the symbols themselves are coordinated as a unified complex expressing persons-comporting-toward-persons, and, in these comportings, disclosing to one another—exhibitively, attitudinally, and conceptually —the ultimate ground for the possibility of their collective activity: persons who reveal to one another, through the very comportment by which they actualize in each other's presence their powers for reciprocal and mutual benefit—the rhythm, the harmony, the polyphony of their shared existence; the mystery of their collective being. As these communities grow, and novel approaches are cumulatively woven into those approaches already acknowledged, and meanings are enlarged and enriched, the symbology by which those meanings are expressed becomes a veritable sacrament of the collective, ever-evolving, and self-differentiating yet always integral and unified spiritual existence of persons in relation.

(b) The Oscillations of Attachment and Detachment

Searching by diversified means (each an element with a single, integral approach) expressing its findings in a unified pattern of symbols the meaning of which resides in an inclusive spiritual life; informing its every investigatory act by the reflections concerning method already set forth, ceaselessly deliberating over the differential efficacies of means and symbols, the unitary methodic approach may now be viewed as exhibiting two aspects. These aspects manifest themselves under the rubrics of attachment and detachment—a distinction which does not coincide with the contrasting pairs, mentioned earlier, of either introspection and extrospection or subjectivist and objectivist. In each of the latter, what from the standpoint of *interrogation* appears as dichotomous pairs of approaches has, by now, been interpreted in terms of a single concept of two components: person qua manifest (i.e., symbol and existent), person qua latent (i.e., meaning and "inner life"). The integral person must always be conceptualized in terms of both components. To inspect a person by introspection or by extrospection is to apprehend him as a unity of these components. To experience him behavioristically is to experience him dually: now as an observable constellation of existent factors—his manifest aspect or his status as object; now as an hypothecated dynamism by which the former may be explained—his latent aspect to which the status of subject may or may not be assigned (depending upon the degree of philosophic narrowness of the behaviorism).

In both attachment and detachment, duality and unity are each grasped. In the former, unity is usually, but not necessarily, in the foreground of attention while duality is usually, but not necessarily, in the background. In the latter, the converse holds. To approach another detachedly is to remove oneself from him. It is to apprehend him, so to speak, from a distance: as an entity in and for himself, an entity reflexively constituted and composed of "parts" which make their individual contributions to his reflexive makeup—each part functioning both in and for itself and in relatedness to the whole which this reflexive entity constitutes. On the other hand, to approach another attachedly is to join oneself more intimately to him. It is to apprehend him, so to speak, as meshing with oneself. It is to experience him, and oneself as well, in profound interconnectedness with his personal milieu, a milieu which includes my very self, the one who searches. For the essential nature of the person as an entity, insofar as he is experienced by attachment, is to be no entity at all. On the contrary, that person is one whose very identity is profoundly interwoven with his identifyings with others, including me (the seeker); in the final analysis, it is inseparable from the identities of other persons.

Accordingly, what is gathered in, alternately by attachment and by detachment, is, alternately, two Imagos. First, there is the Imago of the person as solitary in his own self-identity, a "center" of activity who, as himself a *searching* center, orients himself toward his circumambient milieu, indeed toward the entire cosmos, as though the cosmos pertained to him alone—indeed, as though it were, in effect, centered in him and even, in a certain sense, reciprocally oriented toward him as he is toward it. From his standpoint, he methodically investigates the cosmos. He extracts and focuses systematically upon the objects he discriminates within it—insofar, I stress, as this manifold alone is relevant to his own existence. Further, the solitary seeker experiences this context of his existence in relationships of co-dependence, and interdependence, with his own being. His very body is felt as his possession, together with the cosmos to which it is (corporeally) linked. The inquiring self is never disembodied. On the contrary, that self is actually incarnate in the system of observations body makes through the agency of its own senses. As body, the inquirer is physically connected to his instruments of observation and experimentation. Moreover, the seeker thus embodied may be extended or contracted. As he journeys about this cosmos with which he, as body, is so intimately conjoined, the seeker may assume a variety of corporeal shapes. Indeed, he may, as body, be so shrunken or deformed as to reside "beneath" the skin of his own organic makeup. Analogously, these considerations apply when, from the standpoint of *my* solitary character, I inquire into myself.

From these considerations, it follows that the general character of the cosmos revealed by detachment is of a constellation of personal centers, each framing a cosmology—always, of course, from within its own perspective. As embodied, each "center" intentionally reaches out, draws back, projects diverse horizons, integrates some and dismembers others, stresses some and dismisses others. A principle of cosmic relativity reigns. Yet the intent is always to conceive a cosmology as expressing a pattern of relations—persistent and durable—between the ever-fluctuating multitude of personal centers. For the seeker strives to know (in terms of space, time, and matter) the non-personal invariants which persist unchanged despite transformation from one cosmic outlook to another. He seeks the *form* of the cosmic laws pertaining to each individual cosmology that he might represent one permissible transformation or another within a whole (invariant) scheme of possible transformations.

Actually, two sets of invariant relations express the character of this generalized cosmology: one, objective; the other, subjective. Most generally, the former invariants are specified in theoretical physics, with the relevant parametric specializations for biological phenomena. I do not here rule out the possibility that such fundamental heuristic devices as "organism," germane to understanding biology, might not, indeed, be foundational to devices like "mechanism," implying that the latter might be explainable in terms of restricting the scope of the former—hence, either making biology in some sense a more fundamental science than physics or necessitating (a position I shall adopt) the translation of the key concepts of both into a more inclusive conceptual frame. In any case, the latter invariants refer to the system of personal bonds relating the members of the society of personal centers. But since these centers are, by definition, solitary, the laws (like Kant's *synthetic a priori*) have formal status alone; their ontologic content cannot be specified. By *transcendental* naturalism, I mean the methodological position which a community of such (potential) searchers into one another prescribes to itself when its *special* methods are subsumed under the approach of detachment. The term "transcendental" suggests that the cosmologies framed under this rubric are by no means denuded of the quality of mystery and hidden depths which might be imputed to the spatio-temporal-material invariants. Quite the contrary. These invariants affirm, in effect, that, at any finite stage in the progress of inquiry, more is concealed by these physical invariants than is revealed. Under *interpreting*, the third phase of Method, I set forth the main tenets of this position.

Second, there is the Imago transmitted by the approach of "attachment," the portrait of reciprocal bonds linking seeker and sought in an inherent and indissoluble solidarity, and, in turn, linking both to the entire community. Previously, each personal center was conceived as intrinsically isolated from the other; in consequence, each personal center conceives himself, and himself alone (and only the other in a Pickwickian sense), as transcendental center of the cosmos. From his point of view, he looks out upon the cosmos, framing its constitutive laws, as though it were purely external to him. Now, however, the very same personal centers conceive themselves as interwoven with one another, and interwoven so profoundly and so empathically that the self-identity of each can be specified only by reference to the self-identities of all. Yet not as merely conditioning one another *ab extra* but as constitutive of one another *in se*! Hence, not only does each person "know" his fellows as merely distinct and independent *I's* implicated in the same interpersonal field, conceptualizing this knowledge as the processes characteristic of that field; but, in addition, and more deeply, they "know" each other as indeed essential ingredients within their own beings.

(c) Perspectival Levels

A consequence of this doctrine, expressed under the rubric of what has already been designated transcendental personalism, is the fact that all personal centers themselves are but perspectives upon a more generalized personal center of centers: a Center immanent within each subordinate center yet transcending all as their ground and source; further, a Center which allows all subordinate centers to be immanent within all while transcending each. According to this doctrine, the tenets of which—complementary to those of transcendental naturalism—are also set forth in the chapter entitled "The Third Phase of Method: Interpreting," each person grasps his own identity in and through the identities of all persons whom he encounters. In consequence, he is able to experience his own being as, so to speak, transparent to the being of the suprapersonal Center which grounds his strictly private being—as, indeed, it grounds the beings of all personal centers; and of which he himself, analogously as for others, is medium, agent, and instrument. The more one meditates upon oneself, or upon another, the more he is (passively) moved to his own center by the gentle and activating presence of this ground: a ground which benignly beckons him and summons him as he, reciprocally, bears witness to its call. By thus giving oneself up to this Center, as a beneficent plenitude, an inner order, an indefeasible unity, one is transported by its radiance, and "ecstatically" lifted out of customary "stasis," or immobility, into the inmost recesses of the self.

Moreover, according to this doctrine, the principle expressing in the mode of naturalism the invariant structure of the cosmos must, despite its transcendental character, be transformed into a richer and more inclusive principle. For, now, the cosmos is conceived as suffused with personality—a universal presence pervading all, reaching to the inmost recesses of the inorganic as well as the organic, of the merely living as well as the personal. The principle of naturalism is modified by the addition of a component which takes cognizance of this experience. For, in addition to the strictly physical element, an invariant pattern is stipulated which links the panoply of personal centers. Whatever transformations of personality are undergone by these centers, they remain—as a totality—unchanged in their most private and inward character. Transcending the merely formal status which this component exhibits under the perspective of the less comprehensive doctrine, transcendental naturalism, the intrinsic structure of personality (as a universal "form") first acquires substantive and ontological status. Now two principles of invariancy reign, two principles which, at bottom, are ingredients in a single overarching *imperium*! One expresses the solidarity of the physical cosmos, under the rule for allowable physical transformations; the other expresses the solidarity of the personal, under the rule of *its* allowable, but as yet unspecified, transformations.

When one joins the perspectives these principles entail—and I merely anticipate a view to be made explicit, from a methodologic standpoint, in the following pages—the vision of a cosmos of four interrelated textures opens before one. First, I distinguish an infrapersonal "center," expressing the objective (physical) cosmos—the cosmos of physis or of intertwined processes, processes which as a whole may be conceived as cyclic or progressive. Embracing all the separate horizons opening up to the numberless personal centers, this physical cosmos is, as it were, external to the community of seekers, a community which experiences it only in their mutual detachment from one another. Next, I distinguish the matrix of solitary personal centers. From within their private and privative "subjectivities," these diverse "centers" look out upon the sweep and the grandeur of an infinite and awesome world. Individually felt as radically separate worlds, merely coincidentally related to one another, they are nonetheless synthesized to a single, integral world. For, despite their solitude and essential detachment from one another, the "centers," embodied as persons, are empowered contingently to join these worlds to a unified cosmos—at least asymptotically, as converging upon a limiting ideal; and these acts are effected by experiments executed, deliberated about, and collated. Third, I distinguish a matrix of personal centers in solidarity, experiencing communion and relating empathically to one another. From this standpoint, all persons dwell within a shared world; and they represent that world through diversified patterns of symbols—art, science, religion, myth, language, dream. Constituted in accordance with its own unique distinctive set of generative principles, each symbolic "form" progressively unfolds its hitherto compressed and hidden content. Thereby, as a totality, these forms disclosed a unified world of increasing variety and wealth. Lastly, I distinguish a suprapersonal Center which constitutes an objective interior realm. Animating the person from within, this Center grounds his being as, likewise, and in the same manner, it grounds the being of the community of persons. At the same time, this ultimate personal ground is absolute psyche; it is the authentically subjective element of the (larger) cosmos. For, literally, it is a Center of "centers." *Thrust beneath* personality as immanent within it and foundational to it, the Center is the essential ingredient of its every manifestation, its every aspect, and its every instance.

Clearly, in this schema, the second and third textures—namely, the matrix of solitary personal centers and the matrix of personal centers in solidarity—are themselves conjoined as one texture. Dialectically, in oscillating detachment and attachment, persons relate to one another; and in their interpersonal relatings, they mutually relate to the world—a world within and a world without. Two seemingly distinct manifolds collapse into one. Dialectically, their solitary and their solidarity aspects fuse in a kind of intimate cohesiveness. The inner connection between these aspects, the dynamics by which two matrices are united as one: consideration of these issues is the central problematic of the next moment, *transforming*. For, having gathered these images of the person into concrete juxtaposition, every member of the community—and all equally are seekers—is enjoined to ask, from the standpoint of Method as well as ontology: How may their dual character be reduced to the character of unity?

A second question arises, one, however, not within the direct scope of this inquiry—though, surely in the long run, deeply relevant to it: How are the *two* centers, infrapersonal and suprapersonal—each of which is associated with both exteriority and interiority—themselves related? To deal with this question (essentially, the α and the ω of metaphysics), the problematic of an altogether new inquiry reveals itself: an inquiry which, going beyond the quest for an ontological account of the person, falls within the province of a united ontology, theology, cosmology, and eschatology. Though this inquiry cannot be conducted in the present investigation, some main lines for its approach are indicated briefly in my final chapter and epilogue. For, in spite of the fact that the topic is largely excluded from my account, its deeper relevance to a speculative theory of the person is profound. A less generalized but equally significant topic is of immediate concern. What has been gathered in as an Imago of the person in the preceding account is, surely, quite changed from what was originally simply attended. It is the specification of this transformed Imago, from a methodologic standpoint, to which I now turn.

C · THE THIRD MOMENT: TRANSFORMING

(a) Subject–Object Metamorphoses

Having first made its appearance, in primary interrogation, as a set of disparate procedures, each suitable to its particular objective—determining an object and, in turn, determined by that (emerging) object—Method then seeks, in primordial interrogation, to simplify itself; but, always, framing *in abstracto* and formally the norms to which it ought to conform—unity, order, comprehensiveness, systematicness. Under the succeeding phase, listening, Method next sought to convert this purely formal unity to a concrete unity, by *attending* once again the object of its quest—but now within a focus both sharp and comprehensive. Having then *gathered* together a single, coherent Imago of the person by specifying the complicated nature of his essential dynamism, and having (normally) anticipated the dialectical character of the interplay of the two fundamental approaches, attachment and detachment, to studying this dynamism, Method is now prepared to transform its image of the person by joining these approaches to a concrete dialectical unity.

In the beginning, Method is prereflexive. What we observe, judge, and imagine is already conditioned by innumerable preconceptions, substantive and methodologic. To begin with, the searching mind is a vast storehouse of (preliminary) knowledge. By virtue of this already acquired familiarity with the object of inquiry, the person, certain of his characteristics are already known. As he alternately attaches himself to and detaches himself from that object, in the manner previously indicated, this knowledge is significantly increased. From a methodologic point of view, (secondary) reflection upon what has been, in the dialectical interplay of these approaches, gathered together reveals a *transformation* in the very concepts of subject and object.

To the inquiring mind, the object constitutes the firm and unalterable facts of the case. Within its already *pre*sensed presence, the intrusive character of the object presents itself for selective discrimination of further significant factors. A *something else*, objective and solid, emerges from concealment into focal awareness, a "something" even less evanescent than what had originally been discerned as object. This novel element reveals itself as truly invariant amidst the (merely subjective) transformations to which it is subjected. Subsequently, this invariant itself will burst asunder; the complex thereby released will then be scrutinized as problematic. Thenceforth, a new and even more durable configuration of elements will emerge. In this fashion, the searcher moves from an empirical orientation toward his object to a transcendental orientation. By this transition, I mean he now penetrates the inner core of the person, a core of which the empirical is but the fleeting and variable manifestation.

Emerging correlatively with this (transcendental) object, in the searcher's experience of the person, is his perception of a double subjectivity as source and ground of action. On the one hand, there is the subjectivity of the seeker; on the other, the subjectivity of the object sought. In the context of methodic investigation of the person, each—the one employing Method and the one to whom Method is applied—is an actor within a complex field of (objective) processes; each stands in a certain determinate relationship to that field. As actor, the seeker imprints an image of his subjectivity into the one sought; that image becomes part of the latter's own subjective makeup. By virtue of this imprinting, the sought one—now perforce changed in his subjective constitution—reciprocally imprints himself into the searcher. Owing to this reciprocity of influence, the respective subjectivities of seeker and sought are constantly changing. Yet a core of (invariant) self-identity remains; indeed, by the interaction of seeker and sought, this core is—in its very intricacy—solidified as the increasingly dependable ground of the relationship. The relationship itself now emerges as the object (and objective) of the seeker's quest. At the same time, as each acts, seeker and sought, each becomes aware of himself as actor. In this capacity, each becomes an object to himself. Inspection of this objectified self, explicitly by seeker and implicitly by the one sought, reveals a pattern of significant relationships between the emergent self and what hitherto had been experienced as external object—explicitly by the first, as the one sought; implicitly by the second, as the seeker himself.

Accordingly, from the standpoint of the seeker, the more truly he experiences himself as actor, the more he extrudes from his own actings an Imago of himself as actor. In this connection, he deploys certain techniques, procedures, and approaches; in short, he applies his method to the one sought. However, what he now studies is not simply another person isolated from the method applied to him. What, indeed, he is studying is a compound of his actings and that person: namely, an actor orienting himself toward the person and, in this process, changing him. A new object complex is created for the seeker, a complex which, prior to their synthesis, consisted of two ingredients: the original object under study, and the seeker himself in his application of a method to that object in that study. Indeed, the seeker has created something new; and this by virtue of a *doubly* creative act. For, first, he gave birth to a product; then he synthesized that product with something else already there, another human being.

By my argument, the object of search has truly been altered (from O to O'). For, now, that object is *the one sought in his relationship to a seeker using a method with respect to him.* Moreover, by this alteration, the subjectivity of the seeker is itself altered (from S to S'). In effect, his original subjective status has been converted to a new subjective status. For in the seeker's latter (subjective) capacity, he is now conducting a new and more comprehensive search. In the original methodic orientation, O correlates with S; correspondingly, in the new methodic orientation, O' correlates with S'. In general, therefore, a series of O's, namely (O, O', O'', . . .) correlates, in one-to-one fashion, with a series of S's, namely (S, S', S'', . . .). As an alternative locution to new, in the expressions *new subject* and *new object*, one might propose "different states" of the same subject and object. But, strictly speaking, the two formulations are not equivalent. For, as we see later, the latter suggests a too *passively* changing subject and object; here I am stressing the genuine transformation which occurs in both.

When I say that there has been not a mere alteration of state, in S and in O, but an actual transformation, I mean the following. From the original subjectivity of the seeker, something has actually been extruded. By this extrusion, what had had merely subjective status acquires objective status. For the extruded factor is newly joined to the original object: the person sought. By virtue of this joining, a veridical transfiguration has occurred in the object. In consequence, novel comportment of the seeker, now in altered subjectivity, arises with respect to the one sought, now in altered objectivity.

In one sense, the new seeker, S', is more complex than the former seeker, S; in another sense, S' is simpler than S. In one sense, S' is an authentically new seeker; in another, S' is the same seeker as S except that he searches differently. S' is simpler than S, for his searching has been purified and clarified: the seeker is closer to his own "internal objectivity" than he had previously been. He has achieved a deeper unity of his being as seeker. He knows more correctly what he is about. On the other hand, S' is more complicated than S, for he is the (subjective) outcome of a series of extrusions. As terminal member of this series, he is empowered to review not only how it stands with respect to his current relation with the object sought, O', but also he can survey the entire process. Reconstructing each of its stages, he experiences them all as implicated, though in integrated and coordinated fashion, in the terminal stage: namely, for a two-stage process, the relationship between S' and O'. A more complex yet more united seeker, S', *attends* a more complex, but, by argument analogous to that for the (S, S', S'', . . .) series, more unified object—the *terminus ad quem* of an analogous series, namely (O, O', O'', . . .).

Throughout these transformations in his own subjective makeup, the seeker preserves his self-identity; he discloses himself as, at bottom, invariant. An analogous argument holds for the object of his search. For, the succession of (new) comportments of the seeker toward his object has through the relevant syntheses progressively changed it; yet, despite this multitude of transformations, something invariant remains in the one sought: his self-identity persists. For the most part, this topic will be taken up under the heading (set forth in a later book) Ontology. Nevertheless, some clarification from the methodologic point of view is in order.

(b) The Transformations of Person qua *Datio* and Person qua Datum

Extending the preceding argument, I note that I, the seeker, receive certain impressions from the one sought. Quite literally, these impressions *press* themselves *into* me. In consequence, they are (synthetically) woven into the constitution of my own (thereby changing) subjectivity. By way of *re*orienting myself toward the one sought, a reorienting compelled by the momentum of the synthesis occurring within me, I express myself in some new way with respect to him. Quite literally, I *press out* from this synthesized product which I have now become a certain attitude toward the object of my inquiry. My expressions are embodied as my changed comportment toward him—they are my attitude incarnate. As such, these expressions impinge substantively upon him, the one sought, as impressions which he receives; the latter, in turn, are woven into the constitution of *his* subjectivity. Through the alteration thereby induced within him, he constitutes a more complex (new) object of my study. Yet, insofar as he effects a veridical synthesis of his received impressions with the already solidified content of his subjective makeup, he himself is, at the same time, more unified. This more complex yet more unified object sought is, precisely, the one sought as he himself has been changed by the impact of his perceptions of me upon him in relationship to the system of my methodic quest to understand him.

Surely, as I claimed earlier, both seeker and the one sought may be said to preserve their own self-identities; and this despite alterations and transformations through the interplay of expressions transmitted and impressions received. This persistence of self-identity consists in certain powers which inhere in every person: the power to collect relevant impressions; the power to synthesize these impressions; the power to *re*collect the factors synthesized; the power to send forth, in manifold ways, these elements as transmuted into expression. Accordingly self-identity resides in a double power: the set of powers just indicated, considered as jointly actualizable; the power to (self-)activate those powers, translating them into the force of expression. The precise specification of this (double) power requires an account of the reflexive makeup of the person; this account properly belongs to an account of his ontology.

I have been considering the methodological situation from the standpoint of the seeker. Turning now to the one sought: he himself is (as is, likewise, the seeker in his searching acts) a donor, a donor of *data* transmitted to and conceptualized by the searcher. Recollect that the datum *par excellence* (and to begin with)— namely, the object inquired into—is the very donor of that datum, whether or not that donor is conscious of what he is giving. Moreover, the more intensively, directly, purposively, systematically, and comprehensively the seeker searches for data from the donor the more the donor is, in the total configuration of his being and in all its constituent parts, affected by that seeking; and affected in such wise that either he will yield or he will withhold those data and, if the former, he will yield truly or distortedly.

When I say that the donor is affected in all his parts by the "request" for the "gift" of his data, I mean: the request, insofar as it is a powerful one, is transmitted to his every part, each in accordance with its capacity to receive; in turn, each part transmits the impact of this "affection" to other parts; in consequence, all parts functioning conjointly and working from within the donor communicate to him an interior (conventionally, through the sympathetic and the parasympathetic nervous systems) of what is being requested (or demanded). Registering upon the donor from within him as an Imago of processes internal to his (bodily) makeup, this Imago sets in motion (within the subjectivity of the donor) its own peculiar resonances; these are joined synthetically to those resonances which work through him by the impressions received from without (and transmitted by means of his sensory receptor organs and his peripheral nervous system). My point is: from both within his being, by inducing the relevant alterations in its parts, and from without by working upon him, so to speak, as a whole, the orientation of the seeker to the one sought so affects the latter as veritably to transfigure his very being, in its every aspect. But this process, too, must await its fuller delineation until I treat (in a later book) the ontology of the person.

The data "proffered" by the donor to the seeker are given for his reflection. Modified by the subjectivity of the latter, they are nonetheless reflected back to the former. In turn, the donor experiences himself as in a "mirror" provided by the seeker: he is reflected in the image of himself entertained by the seeker—an image, of course, continually reshaped by the seeker's mode of recipiency of the data; and this self-experience (of the donor) as an image in the mind of the seeker once more becomes, for the latter, another datum. Analogously, as reflected back to the donor, the expressions by the seeker of this self-experience become for the former, likewise, a significant datum. The process of transmitting such derived data back and forth from seeker, now the donor, to the one sought and from the one sought, again the donor, continues. Insofar as methodicity holds sway, awareness of its *modus operandi* is heightened to particular acuity for the seeker; nonetheless, the germ of methodicity with respect to the sought one's relationship to the seeker always immanently conditions their interaction.

In consequence, it is the perception of this egalitarian relationship between seeker and sought which constitutes, in the final analysis, the field of objective inquiry of the seeker. Moreover, it is through the approach of detachment that this new object is inspected, appraised, evaluated, and conceptualized. Yet, when the seeker surrenders himself to his quest, allowing his subjectivity to be filled and transformed through its reception of impressions transmitted by the object sought, the approach of attachment is surely being adopted. Accordingly, the dialectical relationship between these approaches is complicated. For, in order for the seeker to focus upon a field composed of ingredients derived from inter-action between himself and the one sought, he must detach himself from an "objective state of affairs." It is within this field that he transactionally discriminates certain components—i.e., components each active and together interactive; yet, components the matrix of interaction and self-action of which is itself trans-formable, in the process of inquiry, to a new matrix. After such discrimination, the inquirer draws certain inferences from the patterning of these components, or —more precisely—from the succession of patterns which unfold as the methodic quest continues. These inferences concern the complicated makeup of the person. This complexity derives from the fact that the person is a shifting focal point, with (by my previous account) a nevertheless constant synthesizing dynamism within a structure of ever-changing relationships; hence a pattern (or a set of patterns) which is fluent and evolving.

In short, by the approach of *de*tachment, the seeker discerns the intrinsically *at*tached character of the person: namely, the person not merely embedded within but, indeed, constituted by, a field of relationships, cumulatively evolving. But, note, the seeker encounters the person *directly* in two ways: as agent through whom the transmission of impressions occurs—since the impressions are embedded within a field the influences of which pervade him, are transformed within him, and are sent forth by him—i.e., him in his status as medium more or less transparent to those influences; as actor who, by his synthesizing and originative acts, initiates the transmission of impressions. For this doubly constituted encounter to occur, the seeker must now encounter in the mode of *at*tachment: a direct encounter of one who is, dually, agent and actor. Yet, what—more correctly, *whom*—he encounters attachedly must, so to speak, be conceived *as* abstracted from the field within which he acts and, accordingly, *as* constituted as an entity sui generis; hence, *de*tachment from the congeries of interpersonal processes. In effect, attachment and detachment are biphasic moments of an oscillating process.

By the foregoing reasoning, the dialectic of attachment and detachment involves the following considerations. Through the method of detachment, an ontology of attachment is constituted; through the method of attachment, an ontology of detachment is constituted. Moreover, the inquiring subject must transform part of his own subjectivity—i.e., detach that subjective element from himself; he must transform it into an object which, then, is wedded to the object the character of which he is investigating. On the other hand, insofar as the object sought has attached to it another object—namely, what had hitherto been part of the subjectivity of the seeker—that (sought) object, a person, responds to this attaching act. He responds to the comportment of the seeker who is, in the indicated manner, orienting himself to the former; as respondent, the sought one himself is converted to a subject who inspects this activity of searching into himself. A fortiori, he inspects the constitution of the very seeker; hence, he—the former object sought—himself is now converted to seeker. Indeed, by the dialectic, this complicated entanglement between seeker and sought is alternately raveled and unraveled. For the same considerations previously applied to the seeker must now, anew yet in similar fashion, be applied to the very one who, having been sought, is now seeker. By these reflections, I am affirming the (methodologic) principle of the conversion of subject to object and, conversely, of object to subject.

By this argument, the method for inquiring into the person, unique in the respects indicated, involves several related factors: double intentionality, multiple reflexivity, oscillation of detachment and attachment, reciprocal conversions of subject and object. Each of these factors has its correlative ontologic import. Only (later) when I treat that import may their deeper bearing on methodology be disclosed.

For the moment, I merely summarize. Two donors give, as data, themselves, each to the other in a mutuality of self-surrender. In this act, which may be generalized over the entire community of persons, a systematic, cohesive, and integral manifold of the diverse facets of the gifts donated, in acts of continual reciprocity, is integrated to unity, unity amidst the very plurality of interchangings which perpetually occur. Emptied of preconceptions, the self studied surrenders himself to the self who studies; and reciprocally. In harmony, both give themselves up to what continually unfolds. Like a compressed spring, the labyrinthine depths of persons-in-relation, hitherto condensed and undisclosed, uncoil to reveal their contents. From a philosophic point of view, the true object in the quest to understand the person *in concreto* emerges in the context of such dialectically attuned searchers.

(c) The Way from Transforming to Interpreting

In this activity of what has now been transformed into mutual searching, I begin to discern myself, the inquirer, as in my very essence implicated in the community of persons, all of whom are searchers: they search the shared cosmos; they search one another. Its members are in varying stages of methodic quest. As it evolves, the community itself, as a whole, passes through various stages of methodic quest. These two sets of stages replicate one another. Some members search consciously; others search unconsciously. But, as a collectivity, all progressively work out—in argument and in collaboration—the norms, operations, and procedural rules for responsible inquiry.

In this process, I, like every seeker, experience myself as a responsible agent. This responsibility is constituted by my responsiveness to the inner attunings of seeker to seeker. Insight is gained by steps. Initially, there is mere *pretending*— informed fantasy *tentatively* groping toward the truth. This stage gives way to *attending*, a stretching toward the sought object—first synoptically, then syncretistically. In turn, attending is superseded by *intending*: here true intentionality emerges; the seeker seeks the inner and generative (dynamic) principle governing the action of the object sought. Next, there is *"re-tending,"* as in *retentive*, where what is grasped is absorbed and retained. Following this stage, there is *"obtending,"* in which the true object, so to speak—or, what is equivalent, the object in its inner truth—is *obtained* and fully comprehended—i.e. (in Whitehead's language), *totally* "prehended." Finally, the process culminates in *"trans-tending"*; a glimpse is had of mysteries lying beyond the object, the matrix from which it emerges and to which it will return: the origin and the destiny of the person.

By thus playing with the stem "-tend," and affixing the succession of prefixes (namely, *pre-*, *at-*, *in-*, *re-*, *ob-*, and *trans-*), I direct attention to the fact that methodic quest for the person is a continual exercise of powers, an effort sustained, systematic, comprehensive, and precise: one reaches out toward the person; one reaches deeply into his constituent elements and dynamism; one draws in a knowledge of these factors, absorbing and fixing them in inner attention; one holds fast to him, in his essential, concrete core and identity; one acknowledges his embeddedness within a manifold of activities which—surrounding him, going beyond him, pervading him—ground his being. For the ultimate goal of *trans-tending* (the culmination of this searching process) is to apprehend the person in these ways: as a harmonizing of his constituent parts; as a coordinating of their rhythmical unfoldings; as a discerning of the broader lineaments of the person; as an experiencing of his rhythmical enmeshing with the larger cosmos, a cosmos from which he ceaselessly draws sustenance.

To achieve this end, all the inquirer's senses, his every mode of judgment, comportment, and discrimination, must be integrated into an informed apprehension. He must grasp the nature of the person under the perspective of a plurality of "forms," all interwoven as an architectonic complex of patterns; denying no subtle nuance, he must yet affirm an inner unity. For what is but *ap*prehended must also be *com*prehended. The inquirer is enjoined to bind to a concrete and unified discernment all the various prehendings (or sensings) of the person; these diverse prehensions are drawn into harmonious balance and proportionality. In this way, the methodic consciousness truly crystallizes; further, it is heightened and objectified.

Now, I pass to the third phase of Method, *interpreting*. In this phase, three moments will unfold as constitutive of Method. First, in a revised taxonomy of the person, his *integrality*—expressing the inner unity of mind and body—will be stressed; the various levels of behavior of the parts of his being will be systematically ordered. Next, by *encounter* of the person with all one's senses and empathic capabilities, two leading tenets of Method will be disclosed: encounter by way of transcendental naturalism; encounter by way of transcendental personalism. Through encounter appropriately executed, integrality is authentically disclosed. Finally, the *integrity* of the person, his essential wholeness and uniqueness, is grasped by a true discernment of his inmost being: a discernment which is constituted reflexively, rhythmically, and proportionately.

I have already mentioned being as reflexively understood and being as rhythmically understood. Method also requires the idea of being "proportionately" understood—i.e., the notion of "proportionate being." For each person, and each part, dimension, or aspect of each person, is articulated *in proportion to* (i.e., in a way commensurate with) certain specific forms of inquiry: namely, those the horizons of which comprehend the objects belonging to classes of which these parts, dimensions, or aspects are instances. Moreover, I previously alluded to the upper and lower bounds of being, namely *absolute plenitude* and *absolute privation*. Each is likewise associated with its own method of inquiry. Under the phase *interpreting*, specification of these bounds in their relevance, first, to the idea of proportionate being and, derivatively, to the ideas of reflexive being and rhythmic being will illuminate the concept of *integrity*. For, as I note, this concept, in the final analysis, embraces the ideas both of integrality and of encounter. Its clarification leads to the core of Method; afterward, it will also lead to the core of Ontology.[9]

NOTES

1. See Bernard V. Lonergan, S.J., *Insight: A Study of Human Understanding* (New York: Philosophical Library, 1970), pp. 415–30.

2. A term which Harry Stack Sullivan used throughout his psychiatric writings;

see, in particular, his *Conceptions of Modern Psychiatry* (Washington, D.C.: The William Alanson White Psychiatric Foundation, 1947).

3. Lonergan, *Insight*, pp. 385.

4. Charles Sanders Peirce, "The Fixation of Belief," in *Collected Papers of Charles Sanders Peirce. V. Pragmatism and Pragmaticism*, edd. Charles Hartshorne and Paul Weiss (Cambridge: The Belknap Press of Harvard University Press, 1934), pp. 223–47.

5. Erich Auerbach, *Mimesis: The Representation of Reality in Western Literature*, trans. W. R. Trask (Princeton: Princeton University Press, 1959), pp. 6, 7.

6. Carl G. Jung, *The Archetypes and the Collective Unconscious*, trans. R. F. C. Hull (New York: Pantheon, 1959), pp. 3–41.

7. A point which Lonergan stresses frequently in *Insight*. See esp. pp. xxiii–xxvi.

8. Ibid., esp. pp. 401–23.

9. Ibid., pp. 444–46.

4

THE THIRD PHASE OF
METHOD: INTERPRETING

In this chapter, I show how the inquirer reflects methodically upon the meaning of the data he has through appropriate questions elicited, then systematically attended in their variegated facets, and finally gathered together and assimilated to his own prior experience. In reflecting, the inquirer mirrors to himself the significant traits of the "object" of his inquiry, as that "object" unfolds its contents before his discerning eye. Interpreting the characteristic activity of this "object," *the person*, the inquirer, in effect, acts as an agent through whom the responses of the one investigated pass and, in reflective meditation, are transformed into a symbolic manifold. Within this manifold, the person reveals himself to be a single, indiscerptible substance, a veridical unity. Grasped as an orchestration of symbols—not abstract symbols, but symbols incarnate, living symbols of the substantive presence of the person—the latter presents himself under the double rubric of mental activity and physical activity. However, these complementary and seemingly dichotomous loci of relatively autonomous activity are but focal regions within a more inclusive and unified comportment–spiritual complex. Qua integral, the person is revealed to the methodic interpreter of his being as exhibiting labyrinthine depths into which he is empowered to reach and explore. As he freely searches the interior recesses of his being, the person (in self-determination) delineates his own self as an assemblage of factors, pluralistically dispersed and expressed yet internally unified and grounding those expressions as a unity. Within this manifold, the physicality, the organicity, and the spirituality of man are revealed as significant dimensions of his existence. For each is shown to constitute an essential part of his essential being, yet all are shown to be interwoven in the concrete reality which is the person—a concrete being, the unique and nonduplicative embodiment of universal man.

The more the inquirer methodically penetrates this concrete universality, the more he becomes cognizant of the very substance of man as woven of his encounters with others. In my exposition, I declare the person both a substantive unity who is functionally diversified and a functional unity who is substantively diversified. For he is an integral structure of variegated processes and a unitary activity engendering a multitude of structures. Under both perspectives, the unity of the person is, nonetheless, revealed as constituted, when he is understood in his individuality, of the unities of numberless persons. Accordingly, with respect to the person, unity is complex rather than simple. For unity refers to complicated actions and intentions. Hence, this concept applies both to the person *in solitudine* and to the person *in communitate*. To inquire into this unity, a double route of methodic investigation is requisite: transcendental naturalism, which exposes the first mode of unity; transcendental personalism, which exposes the second. By "transcendental naturalism" I mean the methodic disclosure of the "natural" substance of the person in its hidden content. By "transcendental personalism" I mean the methodic disclosure of the substantive *relationship* between person and person in *its* hidden content. Moreover, in mere naturalism, the "outside" of the person is investigated—his behavior in a strictly empirical sense; in mere personalism, the "inside" of a person is investigated—an empathic apprehension of his internal being. Since these approaches are complementary, the designation "transcendental," attached to both naturalism and personalism, implies that, when its foundations are exposed, each approach entails a quest which penetrates the foundations of the other.

In sum, methodic inquiry involves a dialectical interplay between transcendental naturalism and transcendental personalism. Jointly, these positions explore two sets of dichotomies: internal personal being and external (behavioral) personal being; the sphere of the personal qua individual and the sphere of the interpersonal. A more inclusive doctrine incorporates both these positions: namely, transcendental substantialism. According to this synthetic approach, I propose three tenets as significant to methodic inquiry into the person: the substantive makeup of the person is interwoven with that of all persons; the interpersonal field is one substance; every person is, at one and the same time, spirit naturalized and nature spiritualized. By these tenets, which themselves must be placed within a larger metaphysical context in order to reveal their fullest import, the integrity of the person is disclosed, through methodic inquiry, to be a unified plurality, but one which is embedded within the unified plurality which is the interpersonal matrix. In both instances, diverse elements are so attuned to one another, and constellated into such re-

lationships of subordination and superordination, as to comprise a unified pattern, a rhythmic complex of attunements. In this context, each person, inquirer and subject of inquiry, is construed as seeker, and by their mutual interplay and resistance, the two are conceived as seekers, who catalyze further search, each from the other and each from within himself. In this reciprocal searching, distorted data initially received from the other, deformed replicas of reality, are progressively emended in the direction of integration of data, and their harmonization. Throughout this process, seeker and the one who is sought, reveal themselves to be not only self-initiating and intentional centers of action, but, in addition, *agents* who transmit to one another the depositions of other persons hitherto encountered in the metamorphoses of life—depositions which form layers of constellated imprints within each person, layers which are stratified, one upon another.

A · THE FIRST MOMENT: INTEGRALITY

(a) The Thesis of Body–Mind Reductionism

In the culminating phase of Method—namely, interpreting—the seeker must frame a generalized methodologic response to what he has heard in reply to the questions originally "put" to the object of his search. This response unfolds in three moments. In the moment of *integrality*, the diverse methods are shown to be so interwoven that the objective of inquiry, the person as intrinsically unified and concrete, emerges as a single, indiscerptible "substance" of which his mental and his physical sides are but perspectives, attributes, and aspects. In the moment of *encounter*, these methods are exhibited as pervaded by a sense of two mysteries, themselves interwoven and joined: mystery residing within his infrapersonal dimension (which is, nonetheless, constitutive of his personal being), mystery of his personal dimension proper. In the moment of *integrity*, the methods are disclosed as ordered in such a way that they will conform to three conditions: commensurability with the "proportions" which the elements constitutive of the person exhibit in their mutual relations; competency to detect the more subtle rhythms, flowings, and harmonies which bind these elements into a unified plurality; disclosure of the pervasion of the person by the factor of reflexivity—a *trans*-biological organism, the person is thereby shown, in his origins, in his constitution, and in his destiny, to be implicated profoundly with other persons in a communal field.

In this chapter (interpreting), I proceed seriatim to treat these unfoldings of Method. As I note, in the final chapter, "Method as Organon," the moments herein treated are themselves the "natural" evolute of the preceding phases, and the moments of *these* phases. First, I turn to the idea of integrality.

Traditional philosophic reflection upon our primary datum, the person, discloses not a simple reality but two heterogeneous components, irreconcilable in their essential characteristics. "How," as Hartmann puts it, "a process can begin as a bodily process and end as a psychic process is absolutely incomprehensible. We can well understand *in abstracto* that this can be so, but not *in concreto*."[1] Mind and body, the realm of the psychic and the realm of the physical, are therefore conceived as distinct and antithetical entities, each to be comprehended in terms of principles governing its realm alone. Nevertheless, it is conceded, a certain mysterious parallelism obtains between these components: alterations in one often appear to induce alterations in the other; correlations may thereby be observed between processes constituting the one and those constituting the other. Given the complicated body and mind of a person, these apparently independent structures, though neither is fully explainable in terms of the other, appear to presuppose one another as necessary conditions for their respective activities.

Many attempts have been made in the history of philosophy to resolve, or else to justify, this dualistic conception of the "substance" of a person. Prominent among these attempts are those of Plato, Descartes, Spinoza, and Lucretius. For Plato, the physical is a degraded manifestation of certain configurations of mental elements, which endure permanently in a higher realm of existence than is open to the ken of ordinary human perception, but a realm which nonetheless may be grasped by intuition or by intellect, depending upon the epistemological status accorded it, as ineffable essences or as abstract ideas. Alternatively, in the Cartesian dualism, the physical and the psychic are independent entities joined by a mysterious bridge composed of still a third but entirely unknowable substance, residing, Descartes speculated, in the pineal gland. Or, as in Spinoza's philosophy, mind and body can be regarded as parallel manifestations of a substratum, a neutral substance which has a structure and exhibits a dynamic which may be grasped by pure intellect. And, finally, the spiritual realm may, as for Lucretius, be understood as expressing the behavior of material particles distributed into certain constellations. These proposed resolutions of the mind–body dilemma are of two kinds: reduction of one member of the pair to the other and reduction of both members to a third term.

The first kind of reduction has achieved, in its Lucretian version, special prominence in contemporary times. Freud, for example, stands out among those who have sought to articulate the causal texture of the psyche. Hypothecating mechanisms by which this texture is formed, and reconstructing it, for a given individual, as the narrative of his psychic life, he regarded the psyche, for purposes of treatment and the theory of psychoanalysis, as an autonomous entity governed by its own laws of growth and decay. But he believed, with prevailing scientific opinion, that mind, though not simply an illusory "appearance," is nevertheless a "function" of body. It emerges as a unique phenomenon in the evolution of the cosmos; for mind, so the argument runs, is a manifestation of a peculiarly complex arrangement of matter. How, Freud wondered, does biological energy get "translated" into its psychosexual form?

According to this biologistic view, mental behavior is, at bottom, constituted by the specific potentiations of certain nerve structures through interactions of their "containing" organism with its environment. This environment includes other organisms within which analogous structures are likewise potentiated. Interplay of these mutually activating configurations of material elements is conceptualized as a fabric of social laws expressing, in effect, the "collective" mental states of many organisms. A person, as crystallizing out of a matrix of interpersonal processes is, therefore, ultimately the actualization of potentialities which inhere within a *physical* system activated by the impact of its relevant physical environment. True, laws characterizing different "phenomenological levels" (e.g., the social nexus of relationships) are explicitly acknowledged as formulating necessary conditions for behavior. But in actuality, proponents of this view imply, these laws merely constitute, in the final analysis, statements concerning a distribution of organisms in a field of neuronal potentiations. Though one may state laws expressing its causal texture, mind is, in principle if never in fact, explainable by reference to, because it is a manifestation of, body.

The claims that mind is *explainable* in terms of body and that mind is a *function* or potentiation of body are not, however, identical. The first, as a methodological assertion, may be given an unimpeachable scientific interpretation. The second, as an ontological assertion, raises perplexing philosophic difficulties.

Attempts to "reduce" mind to body (or, among philosophical idealists, the converse) fill the history of philosophy, psychology, and biology. Whatever value these enterprises have, clearly the reduction is, if legitimate, methodological and never ontological (or existential). For it has to do only with the *conceptual* correlation of two causal series and the explanation, by reference to abstract principles, of one series in terms of the other. But the very preoccupation with a methodological reduction often leads to unwarranted (if tacit) commitment to some notion of ontological priority—a priority which, indeed, assigns, in the final analysis, the status of fiction to one series and of reality to the other.

To be genuinely empirical, we must, when we inquire into the constitutive properties of an object, attend to every aspect and subtlety of that object. So a circumspect glance at a person discloses not a mind *and* a body, mysteriously conjoined as independent structures, not a mind which is an evanescent product of body, but a gesture, an expression, a gait, a sign of his intellectual acuity, his physique, his physiognomy. We experience that person as an integrated agency, a living, breathing, moving, joyous, and sorrowing whole. Whether in dignity, defiance, or wretchedness, he declares himself before us to be *himself*. When he acts and when he thinks, he expresses a single dynamic of existence.

The biologic and the psychic, indeed every part of a person's being which we may discern with any of our senses, are only (parallel) aspects or dimensions of this existence. They are areas within which the person as *agent*, as a focus and a center of intentionality, manifests his essential powers; and biologic and psychic energies are abstractions from these powers. The stuff of which a person is made, I am suggesting (and here I declare myself a Spinozist), is not primarily material or spiritual. We must confront him with all our senses and feelings, our intuitions and our intellect, to grasp his nature. And even then, we have not exhaustively apprehended him.

My body and my mind are mine as my possessions as well as of my very substance; they constitute me a person, unified and indiscerptible. Nowhere has the substantive priority of personhood over bodyhood or mindhood been so dramatically stated as when Job declares to God:

Thou hast made *me* as the clay ... clothed *me* with skin and flesh ... fenced *me*
with bones and sinews. ... Terrors are turned upon *me*: they pursue *my* soul as
the wind ... yet ... I will maintain mine own ways before him. ... 'til I die I will
not remove mine integrity from me [Job 10:9, 11; 30:15; 13:15; 27:5].

But my ownership of body and mind is not passive; for they are possessed in use
and in enjoyment. They are ceaselessly in flux, amidst their permanences, as an
unfolding and a becoming. A system of organic processes, my body is always in
motion, whether of its parts with respect to one another or of these parts as
configurated into my gait, physique, gesture, or physiognomy. A mosaic of elements in perpetual interplay and transfiguration, my mind is a coming-to-aware-
ness in thought, perception, feeling, volition, and intention.

Each series, physical and mental, is a continuum of structures, generated by the
activity of the person; and each structure may be isolated by that person—in effect,
disconnected from the activity which transforms it into the next structure and, as
such, contemplated as inert and self-alienated. When I touch my leg, Sartre writes,
"what I cause to exist here is the *thing* 'leg'; it is not the leg as the *possibility* I
am of walking. ... To the extent that my body indicates my possibilities in the
world, seeing my body or touching it is to transform these possibilities of mine
into dead-possibilities."[2] By analogy, the activity of mind terminates from moment to moment in patterns of ideas of fixed and determinate logical structure.
My integral person, accordingly, is a movement and a flow; a field of possibilities
actualized in the realms of body and mind. And the agent by which these possibilities are translated into specific corporeal or mental occurrences is, when I am
in full self-awareness, my "I," my very destiny.

"I am lived," Groddeck declared, basically "by the It" which

accomplishes everything that happens with and through and in the man; it is
responsible for his existence and gives him all his organs and functions, helps him
out of his mother's body into the light of day, does everything which the man appears to do. In accordance with its own infallible purpose it creates speech, breathing, sleeping, work and joy and rest and love and grief, always with correct
judgment, always, purposefully, and almost always with full success, and finally,
when he has lived long enough, it kills him.[3]

Groddeck's "It"—i.e., my unconscious and "interior" determinants—is the prime
impetus of my being, in its physical and its mental dimensions. The "I," on the
other hand, is a conscious exertion, an explicating, searching and focusing upon
specific elements within the processes initiated and sustained by the "It," re-
directing its activities and reshaping its powers. Together—the first blending
into its derivative, the second—"It" and "I" constitute the essence of the person;
and this essence is an "indissoluble correlation," in Cassirer's words, a "structure
sui generis ... concrete synthesis ... and unity" which, in spite of "inner antith-
eses,"[4] may only *in abstracto* be split into the contrasting tensions of mind and
body. This phenomenal entity, in its facticity and givenness, reveals itself to be
"inwardly animated" by the energies of "It" and "I": its every facet glows with
their vitality.

The power which thus inwardly animates, and which we discern under the perspectives of body and mind, is a blend of traits which, separately, are universally present in man, so that when each is perceived by him as truly belonging to him he is joined more intimately, more inextricably, to his human heritage, but which together constitute an absolutely and indefeasibly unique whole. This autonomous *vis vitae*, Groddeck's "It," *lives us*; but it is transformed by its own issue, the "I," from *my being lived by* to a *living of my being*. And in the metamorphosis, I may fulfill, or strive to fulfill, what, by the utterly idiosyncratic yet transcendently and universally human organizing center of my being, I was meant to become. Within us, indeed, is, as Fromm writes, a

> universal man, the whole man, rooted in the Cosmos . . . the plant . . . the animal . . . the spirit . . . his past down to the dawn of human existence . . . his future to the day when man will have become fully human, and when nature will be humanized as man will be "naturalized."[5]

But within us, too, is *this particular* plant, animal, and spirit, this particular way of being in the world. And each of us from his inmost depths, in silence or revolt, persists without ceasing in his demand to be heard, to be seen, to be known as uncompromisingly unique, to experience what he, as universal *and* special man, is *intended* by his particular endowment to experience, to experience himself "more deeply in touch with humanity"[6] without constrictions imposed by that "social filter"[7] which blots out experience uncongenial to society.

I have referred to the "It" as the *interior* determinant of the person, the *vis a tergo* of human existence, that which both propels and becomes the blossoming of the person as unequivocally distinctive, as unconditionally singular. But, naturally, human impulses, tendencies, and gifts are not recalcitrant to shaping, or even engendering, by environment. A person is intrinsically plastic—indeed, this is one of his most characteristically human qualities—and so our actions, beliefs, and feelings are conditioned or altered by the forces of nature and society which surround us: the *exterior* determinants of what we shall become. Surely, it is only by reference to an Other than ourselves that we can emerge as true and fulfilled men. Nevertheless, there inheres within each person an irreducible surd, a seed which *can* contain essentials of a man's future in it; and only should he recognize, if not indeed overcome, by that very "I" which has, through his numberless encounters, been fashioned from the "It," what threatens or thwarts its unfolding can he become spontaneous and autonomous. Only thus can he become self-determining, choosing for himself what, within the limits of his plasticity, is congruent with his essential and novel endowment.

In its engagements with other bodies and in the dynamic equilibria obtaining between its parts, my body "presents" itself to my "I" in terms of factors which Allport calls the "proprium"[8]—the durable, unique central core of the personality: its coenesthetic components and its adaptive, self-preservative, and self-perfecting tendencies. This presentation, which is primordial mind, occurs within a *person*; and as the person, an entity which apprehends its own movements and activities, encounters others, its "I"—that power which executes the moving *and* the apprehending—expands the scope of perception and feeling to include the new impingements. No longer a passive "me" who merely receives mental impressions from the "interior" of the person, the "I" is strengthened in active capacity to select those elements from all it experiences as cognitively and affectively the most interesting; it thereby shapes that person into a more fully volitional, self-affirming, and self-determining agency. So, in every encounter with another, one's very being is shaken and reconstituted. One's "center" is transferred from self-referential status as *mere* apprehension to a point which permits enjoyment of the other in reciprocity and selflessness, a consummate enjoyment which not only does not entail sacrifice but, indeed, enhances self-interest.

(b) The Thesis of Body–Mind Unity

In sum, body is the extended correlate of mind, paralleling mind insofar as mind is construed as mere apprehension. Thought (as the process of apprehending) and action (as the moving of body into a nexus of physical relationships with other bodies) are correlative activities executed by the "It" flowing into the "I." Mental and physical occurrences, the aggregations of which form mind and body, respectively, in their static dimensions are termini, mere products, of these activities. And in their active dimensions mind and body are complementary, indeed integrated, aspects of the same dynamism. They cannot be isolated from one another and still retain their true character. Each is "implicated in the changes of the other . . . ; the soul," as Bradley declares, "is never mere soul, and the body, as soon as ever the soul has emerged, is no longer bare body." [9]

This dynamism cannot be identified as either physical or mental, for it is the power which determines and potentiates both spheres. The bifurcation of the person into mind and body, indeed, becomes possible only when I conceive the person as purely self-existent, as an organism contemplating and enjoying itself alone. Then only may I discriminate two self-contained and apparently autonomous structures: body, the object; mind, the subject. But when I observe that the encounter of one person by another is truly gripping, that it mobilizes all energies, physical and psychic, in one self-transcending act of meeting, then I recognize that these energies must be mere abstractions from a drive which itself is neither physical nor psychic—an orientation and a commitment which derive from the depths of the being as unifying and animating all its parts and aspects.

When I confront myself I apprehend the parts of my being to be informed by certain pervasive qualities, suggestions of this inward animation: a brittleness, resiliency, solidity, pliability, constrictedness, vitality. This is, indeed, my unique and special world—projected as the space, the time, the matter, in which I dwell. All my senses, feelings, intellect, and volitions join in the full impact of self-encounter to disclose these qualities as expressions of an integrated agency of many aspects. And mind and body are but conventional ways of classifying these aspects. The diversity of my moods and movements, the subtle ramifications and many layers of my being all elude definite categorization—whether in their evanescence or in their permanence. I only *extract* from myself what may suit my purpose—a structure of elements analyzable as my "anatomy," a constellation of traits analyzable as my "personality," a system of processes analyzable as my "physiology"—and so I may proceed to focus upon and systematically to articulate the multifarious dimensions of my being. For, depending on this purpose, I am oriented toward myself in an indefinite number of ways, experiencing myself in many modes, such as the cognitive, the sensuous, the affective.

In this reflexive act of self-orientation, I perceive myself under one or another perspective, revealing some aspect of my being: a trait of mind or of body. Each aspect appears to me as something, once perceived, alien rather than integral to my person. It is, indeed, only the *act of orienting* which constitutes my self in its essential dynamic. To touch a part of my body, to take note of a particular thought, is—in Sartre's words—to transform a possibility of action into a "dead-possibility" —into something completed and therefore apart from myself. It is I who think, touch, move, withdraw; and as I act, whether toward myself or toward another, I encounter something which in *its* essence lies outside of me in *my* essence.

Self-encounter and other encounter, I want now to stress, are only apparently of different orders of experience. At first sight, it would appear, as Alexander has proposed, that the mental is the person "from the point of view of the experient or enjoyer," whereas the physical is the person "from the point of view of the on-looker or, if of the experient himself, not in his character of experiencing the mental process but of reflecting on its basis in neural process." [10] These dual modes of encountering—i.e., by enjoyment and by contemplation—are not, however, truly discontinuous; nor are they mutually exclusive. For we can perceive both ourselves and another equally by the outer senses, such as sight, touch, and odor, or by the inner senses, such as feeling, empathy, intuition, which grasp the "core" of the person.

Indeed, the boundaries between self and other are not so sharp as to require the notion of an authentic separation between inner and outer sense. For self and other, as MacMurray has proposed, "are correlatives discriminated together by their opposition; and this opposition constitutes the unity of the experience." [11] To be fully aware of one's own existence *means* to be equally aware of the exist-ence of the other, and this awareness is not, in the one case, an "enjoyment" and, in the other, a "contemplation." It is, in both instances, a deep, a full awareness; for neither self nor other may be posited separately. Man, as Bone has suggested, "needs an other to achieve the uniquely human kind of awareness . . . to select among, and organize, his polymorphous possibilities . . . that his autism may be-come autonomy and his impulsivity, spontaneity." [12] By the resistance one feels in one's actions "against," or with reference to, another, by the utilization of one's power to encounter another, one shapes and defines, on equal terms, one's own existence and that of the other. To be fully alert to what goes on between oneself and another, one must experience one's relationship, the matrix of reciprocal ac-tivities, as real, and, hence, the *relata* themselves as real.

A person, according to my conception, is at once the source of his actions, a free creative being, and their sign or indication. For he is, as Cassirer writes, an "expressive phenomenon"; he "represents a particularization and embodiment, a manifestation and incarnation of meaning." [13] By this is meant, he shapes himself into something which, in Hegel's language, "bears the lineaments and forms of his spontaneously active being," disclosing only "what is actually implied by his setting his original nature to work." [14] Each movement, as of Sartre's limb, con-stitutes an enactment and a deed, distinct from the person, a symbol which ex-presses the *fact* of his action; but as symbol it partakes of the character of what is symbolized, rendering the inner life directly and immediately. It reveals the fate of an individual, correctly embodying his "inner determinate constitution."[15] This contrast between the "outer" and the "inner," symbol and meaning, expression and inward animation, is in actuality a distinction between what is integral to one's being and what, having once been integral, has become alienated.

In the flux of life, the integral and the alien do not remain fixed in status. "Living possibilities" and "dead-possibilities" undergo endless metamorphoses in the dialectic of life. For as much as he is manifested by the acts, the person is reconstituted by them to act anew. The "inner" becomes the "outer"; what is now "outer" enters into the constituency of the "inner" of the next moment. The inwardness of an individual is revealed by his entire achievement; and his essence is, in consequence, cumulative. Summed up in the present, and disclosed from moment to moment as a completion and a finality, this essence is nevertheless open, in the sense of being reconstructable, to the future.

Man, I am suggesting, is at once a many-faceted entity, with various modes of action and responsivity, and a unitary focus of movement, the communality of these modes—a *center* of activity and orientation of which his special powers are partial expressions. This "center" is the composite, cumulative result of all his activities and commitments: moral, intellectual, manipulative, sensuous, affective. Each person, moreover, has a direction or, better, an integration (at every point of his growth) of directions—a vector whose origin *is* the "center." This direction acts as a "filter" sifting certain experiences from others, determining which will be absorbed, which modified and which eliminated.

Yet a person, in his centricity, is not rendered opaque by the complexity of his manifestations and aspects. For each person reveals himself, with varying luminosities, in every one of his acts and judgments. Both mind and body, through perspectives upon the person, grasp him entirely as well as, at one and the same time, perspectively. Indeed, the totality of what one is manifests itself, in the ideal case, in every particularity of one's existence.

(c) The Pluralistically Unified Person

Though each person is integral and indiscerptible, he must also be conceived as a plurality of factors. A method of investigation appropriate to the disclosure of each factor must involve these criteria: the plurality of factors may be subsumed under, hence his nature illuminated in the context of, five distinct perspectives; these perspectives, each overlapping with the remainder, are themselves inclusive of all that pertains to his being; the lack of their mutual exclusivity in no way obscures the essential focus upon the integral person they collectively afford. I affirm this principle: sufficiently probed, each perspective reveals *all* that man is; no single perspective may be sufficiently probed unless complemented by all perspectives. For in their complementarity they constitute a focus which brings together in a *special* way themes which, considered in their assemblage, lead directly to the *fons et origo* of his being.

These perspectives I designate as follows. First, there is "nullity," "non-being," or the radical annihilation of anything which is an instance or a dimension of man's actual being—in effect, the lower bound or limit to every imaginable specimen of existence. Second, the chain of being proper begins with "physicality," or all that pertains to man's status as a strictly physical event, a spatio-temporal-material entity without thought or life or perfectibility, yet an entity vibrant with energies and movement. Next, the chain of being reveals "organicity," or everything which belongs to his "nature" as a living, metabolizing, and self-replicating creature, a creature unified amidst the vastly diversified manifestations of its existence, and a being of appetite and desire though these—on the level of the strictly organic—are but immanently operative and never consummately realized. Fourth, there is the perspective of "intelligibility," or man's character as an *explicitly* sensing, willing, believing, feeling, and, pre-eminently, *thinking* being—where by "thinking" I mean an activity which is not merely cognitive but passionate, engaged, and committed: a consummatory thinking in which sensing, willing, believing, and feeling are subordinate yet necessary constituents (subsumed yet not obliterated) of a self-conscious *reflecting into* man's being of an "Imago" of how it stands between Man and Other than Man, the personal and the non-personal. Finally, the chain of being culminates in "spirituality," or man construed in the fullness of his being: the upper bound or limit to any specimen of existence, man qua spiritual worshipfully sings in unison with his fellows of the glory of creation and of its creator; yet this fullness paradoxically includes, even as it dramatically transcends, the absolute emptiness and privation of being. Indeed, the most consummate mode of being enters into a strange but conceptualizable dialectical relationship with non-being, a kind of ultimate dialogue which ceaselessly unfolds (within man and cosmos) in an eternally evolving spiral of thesis, antithesis, synthesis. In a later book, especially in my comments on eschatology, this dialectic will be treated. For the moment, though reference will be made to both the upper and the lower bounds of being, stress will be on the second, third, and fourth modalities—namely, *event, organism,* and *person.*

The enumerated perspectives, each a mode of being save for that which is deficient in all being, express facets of existence which are constitutive of man. Moreover, each facet, while transcending that which, in the schema, is antecedent to it, is itself immanent within all consequent facets. An idiosyncratic rhythm typifies each, even, indeed, the ineffable rhythms of the absolute stillness of non-being; but though independently conceptualizable as relatively autonomous and complementary to one another, all these rhythms are nonetheless reciprocally interpenetrating in, precisely, the relationship of transcendence and immanence. By "transcendence" I mean, first, a gathering together into a unified assemblage of all relevant resonances on any rhythmic "level"; secondly, a transformation of this assemblage into a novel scheme of resonances; and, lastly, a new diversification of this metamorphosed product as the rhythms typical of (and archetypal to) the succeeding (and adjacent) level. By "immanence" I mean the myriad fragmented nuances inscribed as not yet articulated or clearly perceptible overtones and undertones—subtle vibrations beneath the threshold of potent rhythms, ineffable and subterranean yet conditioning and thereby significantly (though subliminally) altering the primary resonances; vibrations which gently yet surely leap into consummate actuality in the succeeding levels, thence to perish anew as powerful but subliminal factors in yet another level.

I am proposing that in the primordial "content" of his being, the person is an intricate texture of rhythms, now surging into dominance, now ebbing into hidden recesses, now strong and durable, now fragile and evanescent. Further, he is a texture woven of reverberations derivable as seemingly distinct systems from each level of his "being" yet reverberations which, in the final analysis, are so constituted that this perspectival view of man itself becomes subsumable under a transcendental overview which is paradoxically both non-perspectival and never completed. To conceptualize this consummate perspective which in its very inclusivity negates its own perspectival character is to show how the indicated "great chain of being" is, from the point of view of a personology, constitutive of man as well as cosmos. This ontologic dictum has a methodologic implication. Thus, in methodically treating the person qua integral, in the senses just defined, a new taxonomy replaces the one introduced earlier. Now, five horizons of objects are distinguished, all relevant to inquiry into the person. These horizons are hierarchically ordered, the seemingly more complex subsuming the seemingly less complex. No judgment is made here concerning the issue either of *actual* complexity of horizon, or, for that matter, of "degrees" of *reality* associated with each horizon—though, clearly, an implicit commitment to the indicated order of being is made.[16]

In this scheme, man is conceived as *multiply* a unity: he is a unity of nullity; he is a unity of physicality; he is a unity of organicity; he is a unity of spirituality. At bottom, what or who he is as any of these unities will reveal itself as identical with what or who he is as all these unities. Insofar as it is construed as integral, Method must comprehend man as participating, at one and the same time, in five realms: mystery as absolute privation (the realm which is *no* realm), physical events; living organisms; intelligent creatures; mystery as absolute plenitude—an order perfect, eternal, and infinite, and hence (as in the first realm), defying specification as a realm. In each of the (three) intermediate realms, a characteristic species of communion prevails between entities of the same kind—even though the latter may not be woven into the fuller being of man, but might "function" independently of the personal context. Ultimately, the authentic nature of these realms (treated under Ontology) will be conceived as *mediated* by the two limiting realms, in *their* intimate yet unspecifiable relatedness.

What an entity *is*, in and for itself or exclusively in its relations with like entities, differs, often strikingly, from what that entity is—its *modus operandi* and even its inner constitution—when it functions within as contributing to the being of the person. Moreover, I stress (the ontologic principle) that the upper and lower bounds in this chain of being are, respectively, a wonder of such emptiness and a wonder of such fullness that both involve and transcend the finite, negating infinity—so to speak—in opposite directions that they may also be conceived, mysteriously, as the *no*-realms between "which" a transcendental communion holds, hence, an inner unity.

Between these diverse realms of being, insofar as they pertain to man, there is, paradoxically, a sense in which parity holds and a sense in which hierarchy holds —i.e., an ordering of subordinate and superordinate parts. Moreover, if one were a biological vitalist, one would ground the second realm in the third; if a mechanist, one would reverse these assignations (of substructure and superstructure). A spiritualist or a mystic, on the other hand, would, surely, assign priority to the fifth and the fourth over the third and the second—though among those committed to such points of view, there would be differences of opinion concerning the role of the first, or, for that matter, the relationship between the fourth and the fifth. Lastly, the skeptic might join forces with one species of the mystic, holding to the thesis that the first alone is ground and import of (whatever could be called) "existence," and that anything else which is designated "reality" is but fancy and deception. On the other hand, he might—and most likely would—simply declare the entire enterprise irrelevant and absurd. For my part, the reader has already been given a glimpse at my position, though he could hardly yet be expected to embrace it.

To anticipate this position, I note: first, I stubbornly use the terms "being," "essentiality," "realm," though shortly I shall assume the obligation to clarify my use of each term; next, I deny that, as applied to a concept of the person, the notions of physicality, organicity, and intelligence can fully be separated from one another; nor do I believe that, in their reciprocal interpenetratings and mutual conditionings, the realms these notions indicate can (in the long run) be construed in the customary manner of scientists—in their fullest import, they transcend usual scientific usage. Finally, I presume that, despite their paradoxicality and their obscurity, the ideas of the emptiness and the fullness of the being of man are themselves essential for inquiry into his own essentiality. These contrasting poles haunt any philosophic account of man: his fragility, his evanescence, his ultimate dissolution; his incomparable vitality, his ecstasies, his capacity for transcendence.

The "chain of being" I have outlined in this revised taxonomy of "objects" is associated with revision in the taxonomy of methods. Reflection upon fully integrated inquiry into the person requires explicit statement of this taxonomy. To this task, I now turn.

B · THE SECOND MOMENT: ENCOUNTER

(a) Naturalism and Personalism

One of the significant and recurrent doctrines of this investigation has been a twofold claim. Under one perspective, a person is encountered as a unity, integral, indiscerptible, and, however elusive, primordial and absolute. Under another perspective of encounter, he is a diversity, a plurality of parts, and of parts of parts, each relatively autonomous, each sui generis a potential focus of study. What follows is a commentary upon this doctrine from the point of view of Method.

Granted: as an intrinsically unified activity, a multiphasic but singular process, a unique and unrepeatable event, the person is, nevertheless, the locus of diversified acts, roles, functions, experiences of varying grades of intensity, depth, and scope. But the locus itself is unitary and indivisible. In a phrase, a meaning may be assigned to the formula: every person "has" an essence—more properly: exhibits (or presents) an essence; this essence is (ontologically) antecedent to his existence. The designations "essence" and "existence" need clarification. For, in another sense, it may validly be argued that essence is posterior to existence. According to that interpretation, only through specific, identifiable acts may a person's essence be not only disclosed, but, what is more significant, concretely "worked out" in practice.

The topics suggested by these words ought not to be abandoned. For they may be construed as referring to complementary rather than inconsistent themes. Reflection upon these themes leads to the question: How can it be that a single action, man in his essentiality, manifests itself as a plurality of acts, specific and perceptible modes or instances of existence? From the standpoint of understanding the person, this is a problem of momentous import, ontological and methodological. It is the dominant problem of this phase of my inquiry. Moreover, it is a problem which cannot be separated from considerations of both a cosmological and a theological nature.

On other hand, I have designated the person a multitude of constituent factors, and this intrinsically. In this instance, he is a "society"[17] of body parts, parts which may or may not be associated with mentation, feeling, or, in general, some psychic element; but parts which, in their total configuration, are ineluctably so associated; and parts which, in their isolation from one another, make with varying grades of relevance their particular contributions to the psychic.

By "society" I mean an assemblage of factors which fulfills the following criteria. (i) No specification can be made regarding a putative lower limit to the elementarity of the texture of a person's parts. For that texture may, in principle, be indefinitely refined, but only as far as the rubric "society" is applicable without further stricture. Either the texture is bounded by the limiting infinitesimal, or there may be a finite lower limit which inquiry asymptotically approaches. (ii) No commitment may be made—without introducing other considerations of a *general* metaphysical nature—to a supposition that the context, within which the entirety functions as a single unit, sets an upper limit to the constituency of that unity. Either through appropriation of parts from that context or through extrusion of parts into it, the unit, a person, may (possibly) be indefinitely enlarged; though it may also be contracted, clearly it may not indefinitely be contracted. (iii) All parts are co-dependent. Reciprocally influencing one another, these parts are governed, in this joint functioning, by a principle of dynamic reciprocity. (iv) Every part is in active relation to the remainder, which is construed both distributively and collectively—i.e., individually and as a totality. (v) Each part transmits its individual impact along some route of influence, or along some network of routes of influence. (vi) The totality is ordered in accordance with some hierarchical law. Certain constellations of parts dominate other constellations: an elaborate scheme of subordination and superordination prevails. (vii) The entire arrangement is so contrived that the resultant potency —immanent within the combined activities of all parts—is actualized as a *behavioral* unification of diverse regions. For potency is manifested as behavings specific and diverse yet integrated as one and indivisible. (viii) This unity amidst a diversity and this diversification of a unity exhibit the character of a system the components of which are dynamically equilibrated; and equilibrated in such a way that when equilibria are shattered, new equilibria tend to form. I assume here that amplification of these criteria is required for an understanding of the focal issue of this investigation: namely, the person's essential unity.

In a formula: the person is both a substantive unity, functionally diversified, and a functional unity, substantively diversified. For the modern world, the first notion was worked out, in different ways and with varying success, by the genius of Spinoza, Kant, and Hegel. Heidegger, in particular, continues this tradition. The second notion was imaginatively conceptualized by Whitehead, Dewey and, by implication, the collective research of natural science as it bears upon the illumination of human behavior. My intent is, first, to sharpen the distinctions between these positions, treating them as contrasting and in some respects frankly contradictory. But, secondly, I seek to articulate a perspective inclusive of both while ignoring no paradox their joint affirmation entails. Indeed, the perspective itself may be designated a perspective of paradoxicality. It is the purpose of this section to indicate the main tenets of this perspective from the methodological point of view (prescinding from its ontologic import).

An approximate statement of the first perspective I term a philosophy of personalism; here, the unity of the interior life of the person is stressed, though it is construed as a unity simpliciter. The person is experienced qua *res cogitans*, though in a broad construal of *cogitans*. In this construal, all mentation is held to be symbolized by some bodily manifestation. But interest lies not so much in the manifestation itself as in what the manifestation symbolizes: its inner meaning, import, and intentionality. But the latter is more postulated than articulated. Moreover, though the diversity of manifestations of this unity of the person is respected, it is not conceptualized. An approximate statement of the second perspective I term a philosophy of naturalism; here, the exteriority of the person is stressed, the diverse but coordinate parts of his factual existence. The person is regarded as an assemblage of behavings, and of behaving components which contribute to these behavings. He is a plurality of interwoven natural complexes, though a plurality simpliciter. The person is experienced qua *res extensa*, though a different treatment of space, time, and matter from that proposed by the classical philosophers is here presupposed. *Extensa* is so construed that, though a restricted class of bodily functions is termed mental or psychic, a larger class than is customarily acknowledged is conceived as implicitly or immanently psychic. Nonetheless, the psychic principle of animation of parts, animation which also effects their unity, is essentially formally construed.

Yet these "approximate" statements of the two perspectives upon the person—namely, the perspective construing him a unity and the perspective construing him a plurality—do not refer (strictly speaking) to complementary aspects of his being which are, in effect, equivalent. What I mean is that philosophic naturalism, as the philosophic expression of an essentially scientific outlook on the person, tends to treat him from the standpoint of his membership in a class—i.e., from a scientific point of view. Though its ontologic implications are manifold, and it surely inspects the person—within the frame of naturalism—in his *uniquely* natural status, its emphasis is upon collating data obtained by the study of innumerable persons, or of selected persons deemed paradigmatic of the class, and of parts and aspects of persons. On the other hand, philosophic personalism treats the person *par excellence* in his uniqueness and in his individuality; whatever its flaws, it is an exclusively philosophic doctrine. Though personalism draws upon the natural sciences, it endeavors only to illuminate its main focus by what it finds there. On the whole, it does not seek to integrate, in a unitary conceptual scheme, those findings with what its own particular style of reflection yields it.

(b) The Doctrine of Transcendental Naturalism

Nevertheless, a philosophic doctrine may be extracted from the approach of naturalism, a doctrine which penetrates to the inner content, and the hidden suppositions, which a *mere* naturalism might postulate but does not (sufficiently) explore. For this new doctrine, which I designate *transcendental* naturalism, explicitly acknowledges that, sufficiently explored, the pluralistic array of natural complexes converges upon structures and functions quite different from, often indeed inconsistent with, what those complexes *seem* to portend. Space, time, and matter mean different things on the level of gross observation of phenomena from what they are revealed to mean, by their deeper examination in the contexts, say, of general relativity theory or quantum theory. What constitute, from the standpoint of customary experience, strange paradoxes and bizarre notions emerge when one reflects upon the import, scientific as well as speculatively philosophic, of those theories.

In its approach to man, transcendental naturalism is both an interdisciplinary and a synthetic doctrine. It is an attempt to extract a set of ideas as, immanently, the ingredient common to the different perspectives afforded by the multitude of scientific outlooks upon man. Treating him as an existential complex of behavings, it aims at discursive articulation of the root notions shared by these varied approaches as their presupposed elements. More than mere naturalism—i.e., naturalism simpliciter—it acknowledges the mystery, the elusiveness, of man. At the same time, it seeks to construct an inclusive rational scheme for articulating the relationships between his "parts"—organic and inorganic—to constitute an intricate, pluralistic configuration: a configuration which functions *as though* it were an indefeasible unity. The method of transcendental naturalism is dialectical. For different contexts of inquiry into man's "nature" are allowed, by this method, to engage one another in a kind of contrapuntal analysis and synthesis. The doctrine expresses the endeavor to cut across discipline barriers, going beyond customary distinctions; it encourages and promotes reciprocal interplay of the empirical contexts for investigating the person.

The doctrine of transcendental naturalism involves several phases of methodic inquiry. First, the investigator accepts a naturalistic account of the person in its own (scientific) terms, though not in certain philosophic implications which may be drawn from it. For the limits within which a pure naturalism functions effectively are themselves defined by this doctrine. He seeks to correlate the perspectives upon the person disclosed by (natural) science and thereby to frame a more inclusive perspective. In particular, he conceptualizes in their mutual relations the event aspect of the person and his organism aspect. In turn, he weds these aspects to a naturalistic account of his overall behavior, psychologically speaking.

Secondly, the investigator seeks to penetrate to the fundamental substantive ideas which organize each of these perspectives; he welds these root notions to a unitary approach to the *infra*personal aspect of the person, an aspect which, indeed, he later postulates as exhibiting a *quasi*-personal character in certain significant respects. I use the term "personal" to refer to a person as "a self with a perception of himself." By this self-consciousness, I mean a polyadic reflexivity in which every act of self-consciousness is constituted, first, by the mirroring of innumerable self-consciousnesses to one another and, secondly, by the reciprocal transformations thereby induced within each. These transformations occur (and here I accept an Hegelian account) in stages of successive moments: each moment is a symbolic objectification (and expression) of the person in some significant dimension of his existence. Clearly, a psychological behaviorism *as such* is not competent to treat the person in this sense—i.e., in the richness of his interiority. For, by its own governing methodology, behaviorism (quite literally and exclusively) concerns *behavior*, what is externally available as data to scientists using the experimental tools of natural science.

Finally, the investigator accordingly treats essentially the intrapersonal dimension of the person: his exteriority construed both as a constellation of parts and as these parts are configured to a whole. Nevertheless, he regards this aspect to be of profound relevance to understanding the person qua person—i.e., in the fullness of his internal existence. However, such relevance holds, according to this doctrine, only if several crucial methodological principles are adopted. Moreover, ontology and methodology are so interwoven here that the deeper import of these principles and a justification for their application in this context may be discerned only when a systematic ontology of the person is set forth.

In their methodological status, these principles are as follows. First, the context within which an entity functions contributes significantly to the character of that entity; "metabolic"-like interchange of contents occurs: accordingly these contents are dynamically equilibrated. Next, when a coherent locus of activity has crystallized, a context itself may be regarded as an entity embedded within its own (more inclusive) context. Third, the first and second principles jointly imply (*a*) that contexts and entities are, in principle, interchangeable and (*b*) that context-entity "complexes" are mutually enclosed within one another, like so many Chinese boxes or concentric spheres. Fourth, depending upon its particular character, every entity is to be understood in a *simply* reflexive way; it stands in a certain determinate relationship to itself. This relationship is so to be understood that that entity is, in some definable sense, oriented toward itself.

Next, and particularly germane to a philosophy of the person, reflexivity as applied to infrapersonal beings is, as for persons, bound up with the following ideas: self-identity, self-generation, self-transformation, self-interiorization. These ideas assign to events and organisms a character of (partly) self-induced growth amidst preservation of an invariant property. Methodologic justification for this imputation of the character of agency to non-persons will be treated under the third moment, integrity. For the former—namely, events—reflexivity concerns the notion of an inwardly coiled space, a space non-Euclidean, non-Archimedean, non-asymmetric, and non–three-dimensional, a space which—so to speak—turns in upon itself; a matter involving quanta energy fields interchanging with particles, a deep, indeed labyrinthine, intricacy of structure; a time involving a matrix of coordinations of different cyclical patterns, the possibility of time reversals, and relativity of congruency with respect to time intervals. In general, the doctrine of transcendental naturalism stresses the mutual dependency of space, time, and matter: trajectories are complicatedly constituted and interwoven. For the latter —namely, organisms—reflexivity concerns the notions of replication, transmission with minimal change of a set of characteristics from one generation to another with, however, the inherent possibility of mutant forms; the doctrine of transcendental naturalism incorporates the (Darwinian) theory of accumulation of small variations with adaptation to favorable circumstances, destruction of forms not so adapted, and selected patterns surviving with increasing potency and quantity. According to my view, events and organisms share the character of growth and evolution through transmission of invariant factors which, under variable circumstances and by specifiable dynamisms, so eject certain elements and so absorb others with respect to a context of functioning that former patterns of constancy break down and hitherto concealed patterns (newly) emerge or are newly shaped. Progressive but often imperceptible uncoiling of an inner content, seemingly invariant over certain time increments but actually evolving through accretion of novel variations, leads to novel forms.

Sixthly, as an addendum to the fifth point, the contributions of an assemblage of entities to the total configuration of these entities consists of the imprinting of the reflexive character of each entity upon the entire configuration. This transmission of reflexivity (by convergence of parts on a whole) exhibits a cumulative and synergistic character. One contribution activates another; pervasive catalysis effects creation of a general reflexive pattern which is not a merely mechanistic summation of the separate contributions. Under the third moment, integrity, this concept of synergism will be taken up; for, as I then note, it is closely related to the character of agency.

Finally, the principles set forth are so to be construed that they apply to the person in a threefold way: a set of influences is so coordinated as to function from "within" the person, naturalistically speaking; another set of influences is so coordinated as to function from "without" the person, naturalistically speaking; these two sets of influences interact, at the *boundary* of the person, to create in a special way a new influence. The concept of person as both bounded entity and centered entity, with a complicated meshwork of converging channels of influence upon his boundary—itself an often elaborate structure—(channels both internal and external), will be treated in its methodologic import, in the third moment, integrity, but primarily in later books concerned more directly with ontology.

Taken together, these principles suggest, as the root methodologic injunction of transcendental naturalism, the following. To conceptualize the infrapersonal aspect of the person, seek an assemblage of context entities forming varying patterns of inclusion and exclusion, of overlap and concentricity, and all functioning in homologous ways but on varying levels of intricacy. Further, seek the immanent isomorphism which expresses the invariant factors with respect to the phenomenon of reflexivity, in ways appropriate to the levels of organization of these patterns. Next, seek the structure of influences transmitted throughout the organism constituted by this assemblage as they impinge upon one another so as to issue in two sets of "resonances": the set working from within the person, organically conceived; the set working from without the person, organically conceived. Finally, exhibit these resonances as correlative with a state of *infra*subjectivity, for, belonging neither to pure subjectivity nor to pure non-subjectivity, they nonethe-less *mediate* both; a mediation which occurs by virtue of a common character shared by events, organisms, and persons: namely, invariance of reflexivity in the form appropriate to the type of entity under consideration. What these *resonances* are can be clarified only by ontologic inquiry. Prior to disclosure of their actual im-port as the objective of my inquiry, they can only as yet be mentioned as an intui-tive apprehension. Here, I am imputing without philosophic justification a radical interiority, the primordium of what in man will become self-consciousness, to all actual metaphysical entities. My characterization of this reflexive self-orienta-tion, even where an entity as it were "possesses" no self, will progressively unfold, in an increasingly systematic fashion, within the succeeding books.

According to the preceding considerations, the doctrine of transcendental natu-ralism examines what naturalism discloses as sheer externality as, more deeply, the self-interiorizing ground of externality. Within the diverse phenomena con-stituting the external, a pattern of "horizontal" relationships may be extracted. By homology with the personal, this pattern further reveals to our methodic quest the external as governed by, and the manifestation of, an inner and covertly operative unifying principle. A new pattern of relationships "vertically" binds the external domain to the dynamism to which this principle refers. From this standpoint, the inquirer journeys deeply into the womb of the nature of man. There he finds, resident within as animating and unifying natural processes, a quasi-subjective element.

(c) From Transcendental Personalism to Transcendental Substantialism

On the other hand, I am affirming the doctrine of transcendental personalism. According to this doctrine, what from the standpoint of personalism is the unity of sheer interiority is transmuted, by methodic quest, into an objective manifold of diversified content which works from within man. Under this perspective, the inquirer journeys deeply into the womb of the spirit of man; a journey which discloses, as though in miraculous vision, an interior phenomenal realm; a realm of endless wealth of shape and movement; a realm kaleidoscopic and archetypal. Through intense inward focusing upon image after image, as it now flows past the inner gaze, or now hovers in transitory fixity, now evanescing, now crystallizing as a relatively durable configuration, this inner realm progres-sively unfolds its hidden content. As one allows oneself to be gripped by these images, to dwell with one, another, and yet another, each is transmitted—by gradual self-disclosure or by a sudden bursting asunder—into yet new elements; and one is drawn toward an inner world of marvelous design, a veritable second cosmos as compelling and luminous as the starry heavens without. In effect, symbols are layered upon symbols; they point, not toward some abstract and formal "meaning," but toward one another. An endlessly rich and varied texture of symbols, laminated and multifaceted, is revealed by my inner journey. What these symbols portend is, not an isolated and solitary element, but the very configuration which they blend and intermix to form. Yet the fuller import of this glowing assemblage of inner symbols—the connection of the fabric of psychic images which it constitutes with the cosmos without, the translucent but cryptic character of each as it shapes itself before the inner eye as, paradoxically, both in and for itself *and* pointing beyond itself—must be deferred until later books.

In a formula: transcendental naturalism exhibits an external diversity animated by an interiorly subjective unifying principle; transcendental personalism exhibits an internal unity as ruled by an (interiorly) objective diversifying principle. But the modifier "interiorly" has a different meaning for each principle. In the former case, it refers to the inner life simpliciter. In the latter, it is a strange kind of exteriority. For it enters man, so to speak, from *within* his spirituality, as though from an altogether new realm. With this difference established, the two doctrines may be regarded, if not as equivalent, at least as having parity; they are complementary and mutually presupposing.

In another sense, transcendental personalism subsumes transcendental naturalism. For, unlike the latter, the former is pre-eminently a doctrine of the person. Inquiring into the mysterious relations joining the "interiority" of the *infra-naturality*" of the person with his strictly personal aspect, this doctrine never departs from the level of the personal. As a focal problem, it treats the curious mediation between the infrapersonal and the personal effected by the "resonances" to which I alluded earlier. It treats the inner connection—substantive, dynamic, concrete—between the naturalist image of man and the personalist image. Seeking to join the archetypal structure of the person to his organicity, transcendental personalism endeavors to unite the body Imago with the world Imago. Synthesizing these Imagos, each transmitted to him in an organic way, this doctrine weaves them to man's subjectivity. From these points of view, transcendental naturalism is an essential ingredient of transcendental personalism, which, including it, nonetheless transcends it.

Yet, from a certain point of view, these doctrines may indeed be deemed equivalent. By reference to an inner reflexive dynamism, one doctrine unifies a diversified exterior phenomenal manifold. By reference to an internal objective suprapersonal manifold, the other diversifies a felt unity of subjectivity. The first concerns nature; the second, spirit. Together, they may be subsumed under a third, more inclusive doctrine. According to this construal, when these doctrines engage one another, each is compelled to transfigure itself; jointly, they converge upon the same transcendent point. For, whereas the one spiritualizes nature, the other naturalizes spirit. By spiritualizing nature, I mean imputing to nature the character of interiority. By naturalizing spirit, I mean subjecting spirit, an inner phenomenal realm, to reason; hence, bringing spirit under the aegis of law. Thus complementing one another, in dialectical fashion, they themselves are sublated in a new doctrine: *transcendental substantialism.* I am using the word "substantialism" to refer to an Hegelian construal of Spinoza's "substance." To *substance*, Spinozistically interpreted, one may impute infinite attributes in an infinity of ways (modes); of these, only two—mind and body—are known. In my study, transcendental naturalism studies body in its consummate form; transcendental personalism studies mind in its consummate form; transcendental substantialism penetrates each to reveal a third domain which lies beyond both: a comprehensive view which includes both. When I speak of an Hegelian construal of substance, I mean: as far as "substance" pertains to the person, he is construed as a radically self-metamorphosing creature within, and oriented toward, a cosmos construed as itself radically self-metamorphosing.

In my first chapter, I stated that, sufficiently probed, the approximate statement of transcendental personalism—namely, personalism simpliciter—and the reinterpretation of naturalism as transcendental naturalism are, in effect, equivalent; through adequate search, each leads to the other. A seemingly double doctrine of tenets in opposition becomes, so I stated, a single doctrine of tenets which are mutually complementary. From this standpoint, I further mentioned that the essential unity of the two doctrines constituted the third doctrine: namely, transcendental personalism. The axiom of parity, or (ultimately) equivalence, between transcendental naturalism and personalism affirms the following: when body evolves to a certain state of complexity, it "functions" as mind; as such, it "releases," by the synergistic effect of its natural parts upon it, something new and quite unique—indeed, the very same factor which at the outset is postulated, and by different means sought, by *personalism*. Yet, in the light of my preceding statements, I now suggest that it is more accurate to affirm parity between a more deeply probed transcendental naturalism than hitherto alluded to and no longer a mere personalism but, at this point, actually a *transcendental* personalism. Thus, I may now speak of an evolving doctrine of transcendental naturalism. In its earlier stage, it *is* equivalent to personalism. In its advanced stage, it is equivalent to transcendental personalism. On the latter interpretation, I have argued the need for a transcendence with respect to both transcendental naturalism and transcendental personalism.

Analogously, transcendental personalism exhibits both an earlier and a later stage. The later stage subsumes both transcendental naturalism, in all its unfoldings, and its equivalent, the *earlier* stage of transcendental personalism. For clarity, I rename this *now* distinguished (later) stage transcendental substantialism. With regard to this now *most* inclusive doctrine of the person, I must at this time affirm that it, too, unfolds in stages. These stages I designate the stages of *integrity*: namely, *proportionate* being (of the person), *rhythmic* being, *reflexive* being. To this final moment, integrity, of the final phase of Method—namely, interpreting—I now turn.

C • THE THIRD MOMENT: INTEGRITY

(a) The Doctrine of Transcendental Substantialism

According to the doctrine of transcendental substantialism, disclosure of the person *in his integrity* is the objective of philosophic inquiry into the person. By "integrity" I mean the unique quality of a person's life as constituted by four sets of factors: the quality of relatedness between him *and* things and non-personal creatures, those about him and those within him which constitute his body—the infrapersonal cosmos; the quality of relatedness between him and other persons—interpersonal solidarity; the quality of relatedness between him and himself—personal solitude; the quality of relatedness between him and the inner ground of his existence—the suprapersonal theos.

By this classification of modes of relatedness, every person has being in four realms of being: the (infrapersonal) cosmos, the human community, his own self-in-solitude, the (suprapersonal) theos. How these specific realms—namely, *cosmos, community, self,* and *theos*—themselves interrelate is a problem for general metaphysics. Here, they are significant only insofar as they possess aspects to which the person himself is related. Hence, my investigation focuses upon four modalities of *the-being-of-a-person-in-relation-to-the-being-of-an-Other,* including the relation of self-identity. In each instance, an Imago of the Other imprints itself into the person, including the (self-)imprinting of himself into himself. These imprints are intricately interwoven: distinct imprints of analogous kinds are interwoven; the four assemblages of imprints, as a totality, in their mutual relations, are interwoven. How the four modalities themselves interrelate constitutes the problematic of the integrity of the person.

In my analysis, I am concerned with what I designate the three moments of integrity: the style of ordering the elements which constitute the whole pattern of relations—the constellating of these assemblages into a unitary complex; the style of the attuning of the assemblages, considered individually and considered as a totality; the style of incorporating (or internalizing) these assemblages— the dynamics of the process whereby imprints are absorbed, synthesized, and expressed. Ordering concerns proportionate being, the relative weighting of one factor with respect to another and the structure of relations they sustain to one another as constitutive of the person. Attuning concerns rhythmic being, the interplay of the resonances these factors set up within the person. Incorporating (internalizing) concerns reflexive being, the analyses and the syntheses of the images associated with these factors, images which themselves constitute a pattern distinctive for each person.

To formulate a theory of integrity, one must frame a systematic account, from the standpoint not of general metaphysics but of the metaphysics of the person, of these qualities of relatedness, these modes of being, and these styles of organizing imprints. The three moments of integrity—namely, proportionality, rhythm, and reflexivity—are, accordingly, treated in succeeding parts of this book; the general outline of a theory of their nature and interconnections is set forth in subsequent books on ontology. Nevertheless, a few comments are in order from the methodological point of view.

The doctrine of transcendental substantialism concerns, essentially, the relationship between ontology per se and an ontology of the person. Accordingly, some remarks of a general metaphysical nature are appropriate. A metaphysical schema may concern entities in general, formulating the ways in which they are immanent within, and hence constitutive of, one another or the manner in which they transcend one another and thereby preserve their individualities. Or it may concern a particular class of entities, analogously exhibiting their own distinctive modes of immanence and transcendence. In this investigation, the entities examined are restricted to persons; indeed, it is my supposition that an adequate and coherent account of entities in general requires as a prolegomenon (though not necessarily as a conclusive metaphysical scheme) a philosophic characterization of persons. Two reasons suggest this view.

First, inferences from the character of more complex entities (like persons) to the character of the less complex, suppressing such traits as are present only in the former though they may be germinal in the latter, render experience more reliably than the converse inferences, which regard the more complex as *nothing but* the summation of the less complex. For the unwarranted temptation to dismiss a striking feature of experience—to preserve conceptual economy or some arbitrary notion of priority—as the mere "appearance" of a composite of traits predicable of simple entities may thereby readily be recognized. The danger of radical reduction which does violence to experience is greater than the danger of falsely imputing to simpler entities such primordia of traits as are found in the more complex. It is less risky thus to attend to the variety of experience, even though one might unwittingly produce a fallaciously animistic or personalist account of the cosmos. The notions comprehending less complex entities should be derivative from the notions interpreting the more complex. In so doing, the principle which advocates minimizing superfluous fundamental ideas need not, moreover, be violated. For both reductionist schemes and such systems as presuppose parity among all facets of experience will require in their final systematic elaboration an equivalent number of ideas. It is a matter of indifference to Occam's razor whether these ideas appear in the list of basic notions or are introduced somewhere into the inferential structure as statements correlating basic notions, which purport to express "ultimate" realities, with empirically ascertainable but conceptually designated "appearances" or artifacts. I am simply maintaining that a principle of parity between diversified items of given experience ought to assume priority over a principle for economizing the primitives of the theory comprehending those items. In the final analysis, I find no other basis for supporting this contention than that of respect for the fullness of experience, and my conviction that the primary metaphysical notions ought to express this fullness. This assumption, implicit in these pages, I amplify in my final chapter, "Method as Organon." It is, in effect, a principle of plenitude, and of parity between the diverse items of this plenitude: nature has vast amplitude, a multifarious character. There exists no *a priori* rationale for dismissing any of these items into the oblivion either of metaphysical irrelevancy or of metaphysical artificiality.

But a more compelling reason for choosing the person as a privileged focus (perhaps among other privileged foci) for metaphysical investigation may be found. Alone among entities, it is the person for whom his own "being," and that of entities within his world, are an issue. The quest to understand that "being" is indeed itself part of his own character *as* "being." Only as one makes explicit one's manner of comportment toward such entities as command one's interest may the "being" of *any* entity emerge with clarity. Conversely, prior to interrogating objects within one's world in order to disclose their *particular* qualities of "being," one must understand the matrix within which these objects appear. This matrix *is* the primordial objective of interrogation leading to ontologic portrayal of the objects which constitute that objective—the ultimate "object" sought. The matrix *is* our very selves comporting us toward the objects discriminated within the activities of searching—and searching is really directed, systematic comportment; the comportment itself is a component of the "being" of the one who by his nature *must* comport himself toward "being," the one who, in fact, is under metaphysical compulsion so to search. From a metaphysical point of view, the object and the attitude of the seeker toward it cannot be separated; to effect separation entails the splitting of a single metaphysical inquiry into several scientific inquiries. For, as I have proposed, metaphysics endeavors to discern the qualities of an "object" in its full concreteness. It specifies these qualities prior to extraction from them of those constellations hypostatized by "common" sense, and by common sense made available for comprehension by special theories.

(b) Transcendental Method as Agents-in-Relation

In the disciplined interrogation which constitutes metaphysical inquiry, one presupposes the availability of the object being sought; and the "structure" of one's inquiry will in part determine the "responses" that object will yield to its interrogator. In the appraisal of these responses, the object becomes accessible. What at the outset is obscure becomes luminous; what had been hidden is uncovered. But, in the final analysis, disclosures of the "being" of him who is seeking and of the "being" of what is sought presuppose each other. Both seeker and sought present themselves to *each*, who, qua seeker, presents to himself the structure of his comportment toward those objects. As a foundation upon which he stands to extend his horizon, each "correct" appraisal increases the adequacy of a subsequent appraisal. The true idea of the object sought is self-certifying as true. It is not ascertained as true independently of its quest by reference to some "evidential base." On the contrary, its truth becomes apparent *within* that quest; it announces itself in the frame of inquiry. For as one inquires, one witnesses the truth emerging. Self-certification *is* this process of emerging truth. Having thus certified itself, truth proclaims itself as self-evident. To understand the object of an inquiry one must understand the inquiry itself, in its actual unfolding. The "relative" truths of the sequence of ideas "produced" within inquiry are but reflections, and momentary consummations, of stages, themselves acts, in the act of inquiry.

By metaphysics, I mean the systematic rendition of the results of ontologic inquiry with a view to framing a generalized theory of experience. Contrary to the "neutral" attitude I assumed earlier, I am now proposing (for the purpose of this inquiry alone) the absolute priority in the enterprise of ontology, and hence of metaphysics, of the clarification of the "being" whose "essence" it is to clarify. To elucidate *what* that "being" seeks to clarify, one must elucidate the "essence" of the nature of the search itself, a search of which there are such specific modalities as scientific searching, artistic searching, ethical searching. Both *this* "essence" and that of the "being" *who* searches are mutually implicated. Through existing, which in itself is a comportment toward "being" and a clarifying of comportment *in* searching, "being in general" strips away the veils by which it is concealed in ordinary experience. I am simply proposing that persons are those entities who characteristically, and by their essences, clarify, and *as* they clarify make accessible, non-persons. By the latter, I mean those entities whose "being" consists in their intrinsic incapability of clarifying, entities which are themselves only in the context of the activities of persons. Further to elaborate the connection between things and persons requires the laying of the foundations for the elucidation of "being in general."

The character of the one who inquires is thereby laid bare. In the inner reality of his existence, man becomes accessible to himself, and hence to others. For to exist is, at bottom, to *coexist* in self-disclosure *with* another. Existence itself is constituted by a primordial sharing, even indeed through the interpenetration of existences. In this sharing, man reaches toward a future replete with possibilities; he aims to make these *his* actualities. Surely, man's freedom *is* this power ceaselessly to appropriate and uniquely to absorb into his own existence these possibilities for action which he perceives as lying in the future. By decisions, he flings himself into what nevertheless is unknown save as mere possibility. In the loneliness which comes upon him as he momentarily dwells in a realm in which he has lost all footing a miracle may befall him; for when he thus opens himself to receive whatever this future holds, he draws himself into a double relatedness: internal, as an interweaving of his roots with those of another, each reaching toward his freedom from common soil; external, for in a world which unfolds itself to both as a great and shared spectacle each attains in this very communion an intensified individuality. The "being" of that which lies beyond, the beyond of the within and the beyond of the without, discloses itself as a living presence; its essential nature is unconcealed. For, indeed, all existence is a groping, a searching toward that which flickers as a distant star which, as one approaches it, grows to the dimensions of the sun; but a sun which so illuminates the "within" and the "without" that the boundaries between them dissolve and the person stands forth aglow in his integrity.

Conversion of *mere* comportment toward "being" into search for "being" involves deliberative endeavor. In the frame of the appraisals to which endeavor leads, the entities which had constituted the veiled objects of comportment acquire a luminosity which is self-certifying. Their qualities reveal themselves to one in the very acts by which one inquires into them. But this endeavor is no mere reflective activity. For the deliberations are woven into a fabric of receptivity in which all senses are mobilized to enable the inquirer to respond appropriately to the objects of his quest as they imprint themselves upon him. As he, in his searching, "moves" toward them, drawing them from concealment, they in turn present themselves to him. Indeed, endeavor consists of *resistance in a striving to come into touch*. There is a mutual impact of seeker and sought which expresses itself as quality—the data of experience. Thus what is sought impresses its potency into the "substance" of the seeker whereupon the latter expresses by *his* potency, activated by the former, *its* distinctive qualities. If what is sought were intrinsically impotent, mere shadowy data, it would be but a phantasmagoria the nature of which is not per se determinate but the fanciful concoction of the one who searches, images of a passive mind from which the corporeal had been stripped away.

Accordingly, there is a kind of mutual comporting in which seeker and sought each presents "himself" as agent, the actualization of some power which through meetings is again and again potentiated. Both are entities which in some manner "strive." I am denying here the doctrine of a radical distinction between the person, whose "being" consists in its being an issue for itself, and the nonperson. Moreover, I am presuming that the "data" of experience are the registrations of "meetings" of seeker with sought. Granted: the greater perfection of the agential character of the former, expressed as superior efficacy of endeavor, confers upon him the status of "luminator"[18] of the latter. Nevertheless, I am proposing the doctrine that the searcher does not simply *re*present his object to his "mind" as though he moves in a sphere of insubstantial "existents," emanations of an ineluctably concealed reality. He *pre*sents himself *to* that object *as* it presents itself to him. Two entities are already there as existing in the sense of having potency and hence offering resistance. By touching one another, they reciprocally impress themselves into one another. Each reconstitutes the other while retaining its own distinctive individuality. It is because these entities make themselves present *within* each other without "essentially" altering their respective characters that knowledge of the "being" of each becomes possible. But the exemplar of the agent, who can both impress and express, is the person who therefore serves as prototype for all metaphysical entities.

(c) The Concept of the Person as Agent

In this view, the philosophic enterprise, and particularly a metaphysics of the person intended as prolegomenon to a general metaphysics, proceeds by three complementary methods, all constituents of the method of transcendental substantialism: emendation, systematization, and analogy woven with deduction.[19] This enterprise presumes that the data of experience, as initially encountered, require analysis into their authentic import and patterning prior to investigation's framing a generalized schema. For crude data are but distorted reflections of reality, reflections which for everyday purposes—embodied in the conventions of daily life—one assumes to be reality. But to claim that these truncated facts constitute reality rather than simply the shadows which reality informs with its presence is to succumb to incorrigible illusion. For they are a privative presentation of a concealed and indeed partly transcendent reality from which by the stereotypy of custom they had been extracted. Their emendation consists in discerning such agencies (i.e., organizations of self-actualizing potency) as may be correlated with the appropriate data to which, in their interplay and reciprocal influencing, they give rise. Inapposite collation of data with imperfect agencies, rather than their inspection under such perspectives as will rectify cognition of imperfection, leads to this phantasmagoria of an unrecognized but always vaguely felt reality. Accordingly, data are not mere indiscerptible facts to be aggregated, explained, and used as evidential bases for vindicating theories derived from their inspection; they are fragmented, inchoate, and isolated manifestations of a reality immanent within them and, as such, pose problems regarding the character of that reality. And reality is a system of relatively autonomous agents-in-relation with these properties: each agent actualizes its potency under conditions set both by the remainder and by its intrinsic limitations as a finite "mode"; its strivings toward self-realization are a privative expression of an eternal order of agents in that community which while constitutive of these agents requires no sacrifice of their individuality; agents are hierarchically ordered according to such criteria as their intricacy, their unity, the inclusiveness of the perspective of objects they entertain, the subtlety of their rhythms, the intensity and the scope of these reflective acts.

A partially effective agent within the world rather than a spectator *ab extra*, a person is so constituted that his cognitions are invariably tainted with distortions reflecting the defection of his agency by the reciprocal privations of other agencies. Through interplay of these agencies, more or less powerful and in mutual resistance or harmony, arises the human predicament. Ontology rectifies our privative idea of "being" by revealing that mutual thwarting of agencies which "produces" deceptive data. Immanent within ontologic inquiry, and emerging as inquiry progresses, is "truth," the clarified idea of reality which guides it toward its objective: to disclose its own character while acknowledging the residual mystery, stemming from our finite durational status as participants within the cosmos, into which the "periphery" of truth ineluctably fades. Analysis of a pulverulent datum to ascertain the forces which have rendered it illusory discloses *authentic* reality. It points toward contrasts of that reality with the illusion which emanates from it.

Accordingly, illusion arises from the limited perspective under which one experiences the cosmos as referred to oneself, witnessing it from without rather than experiencing oneself as an interactive agency participating within it. Systematic coordination of analyzed data as the basis for a metaphysical schema leads to "derivation," both by strict deduction and by analogy, of such specific constellations of crude data as will, by thus placing them in a new light, remedy initial perspectives upon defective data. By emendation, one proceeds from an impoverished, fragmentary world to a more integrated and concrete world. However, the principle of parity which prescribes respect for all aspects of experience is not violated. For "illusory" data are nonetheless real; they simply constitute one's naïve and unclarified but experientially compelling perspective of the world. Philosophy renders this fabric of reality by the emendation of these merely received perspectives, systematically interweaving them into a structure which compels by its clarity. Wherein consists this clarity? It is that which affords a measure of philosophic satisfaction to the community of informed seekers after truth. Here, I recur to such criteria, implicitly specified in my first chapter, as coherence, adequacy, scope, consistency.

Transcendental substantialism is the doctrine which holds that the person is through and through an agency. Composed of an intricate pattern of agencies and embedded within a matrix which itself is an intricate pattern of agencies, he actualizes *his* powers by synergistically actualizing the powers of the members of the hierarchical manifold of agencies to which he internally and externally relates. From the collective impact of the influences transmitted by these agencies, as they converge upon him, he renews his own potency, adding to it new elements, that it might be potentiated anew. This vastly complex configuration—the person—imprints himself into each of his constituents and, likewise, into the context of his own functioning; analogously, every constituent imprints itself into every other. Cumulatively, this imprinting gathers momentum until, in effect, both the internal constitution of the person and the constitution of his matrix, reciprocally, imprint themselves into him. Accordingly, his parts internally relate to one another with systematic coordination; the configuration of these parts relates both to its own components and to analogous configurations with systematic coordination.

Whatever specific procedures of investigation are appropriate to any agencies extracted from this complex are to be employed, within the prescribed limits of a procedure, with precision and adequacy. Insofar as it pertains to illuminating the person as an integrity, Method is the integral of all specific procedures. It is summed over these procedures in a manner which assigns to each its appropriate locus within the entire manifold of procedures. Accordingly, Method should be adequate for conceptualizing the particular rhythmic patterns and the particular reflexive patterns associated with the *modus operandi* of each agential complex. Further, it should comprehend the dynamisms by which these patterns, rhythmic or reflexive, synergize one another to constitute the full wealth and diversity of the person's existence and, at the same time, his absolutely concrete unity.

Finally, Method should comprise all techniques for understanding the genesis of the person—the metamorphoses and the transfigurations he undergoes. By "metamorphosis" I mean a leap from one state of existence, one manner of functioning, to another. By "transfiguration" I mean a radical alteration in the arrangement of the elements constituting a given stage, an alteration so dramatic that a person's very self-identity must be redefined. From the person's first coming into existence until his passing out of existence, new sets of powers within him and about him are continually potentiated. The pattern of his makeup, as that of his milieu, is ever changing, and changing in accordance with the specific principles which govern all transformations: those in parts and those in wholes, those with respect to his interior composition and those with respect to the composition of the context of his activities. A chronological sequence of diverse patterns of relatedness lawfully unfolds.

The different stages of the life of man alike requires delineation in terms of the specific arrangement of powers characteristic of that stage. Spatially considered, each configuration imprints itself into each of its parts; each constituent is indelibly altered by the form of the unity of the whole of which it is a part; reciprocally, every constituent makes its own unique contribution to the unity of the configuration. Analogously, to speak temporally, each stage not only prefigures its successor—the unity of the latter, so to speak, anticipated as an ingredient in the unity of the former—but, in addition, stamps that successor with something of its own character. The form of the unity of any stage is indelibly altered by the character of each of its antecedent stages. Accordingly, the succession of antecedent stages cumulatively contributes to the form of the unity of every successor. In turn, this evolving of a person's manifold aspects indelibly imprints the person's existence into the rhythmic–reflexive makeup of cosmos wedded to theos: World in its mysterious reciprocity with God.

NOTES

1. Nicolai Hartmann, *Grundzüge einer Metaphysik der Erkenntnis* (Berlin & Leipzig: de Gruyter, 1925), p. 322.

2. Jean-Paul Sartre, *Being and Nothingness*, trans. Hazel E. Barnes (New York: Philosophical Library, 1956), pp. 304, 305.

3. Georg Groddeck, *The Unknown Self* (New York: Funk & Wagnall, 1951), pp. 39–41.

4. Ernst Cassirer, *The Philosophy of Symbolic Forms*. III. *The Phenomenology of Knowledge*, trans. Ralph Manheim (New Haven: Yale University Press, 1957), pp. 92, 93.

5. Erich Fromm, "Psychoanalysis and Zen Buddhism," in D. T. Suzuki, Erich

Fromm, and Richard De Martino, *Zen Buddhism and Psychoanalysis* (New York, Evanston, & London: Harper & Row, 1960), p. 106.

6. Ibid., p. 139.

7. Ibid., p. 99.

8. Gordon Allport, *Becoming* (New Haven: Yale University Press, 1955), pp. 40, 62.

9. *Appearance and Reality*, pp. 296, 299.

10. Samuel Alexander, *Space, Time, and Deity*, 2 vols. (New York: Humanities Press, 1950), II 9, 11.

11. John MacMurray, *The Self as Agent* (New York: Harper, 1956), p. 109. This volume contains a fine discussion of the relationship between thought and action, self and other.

12. Harry Bone, "The Inter-Personal and the Intra-Psychic," unpublished presidential address delivered before The William Alanson White Society, May 26, 1959; p. 7.

13. *Philosophy of Symbolic Forms*, III 92, 93.

14. G. W. F. Hegel, *The Phenomenology of Mind*, trans. J. B. Baillie (New York: Humanities Press, 1949), pp. 339, 338.

15. Ibid., p. 342.

16. See Lonergan, *Insight*, pp. 444–46.

17. In the following paragraph, I am adapting Whitehead's idea of the person as a society, presented in *Process and Reality*.

18. Hallett, *Creation, Emanation, and Salvation*, p. 279. See index for various discussions of "agency," esp. pp. 22–34.

19. Ibid., pp. 23–24. See also H. F. Hallett, *Benedict de Spinoza* (London: Athene, 1957), esp. Part II. My discussion in this and the following two paragraphs is indebted to Hallett's writings on Spinoza, especially to his *Creation, Emanation, and Salvation*.

III

The Word Illumined:
Man Resolute Yet Unresolved

METHOD AS ORGANON

PREAMBLE

In my final chapter, I show how the phases of Method—namely, interrogating, listening, and interpreting—are interwoven and interdependent. By interrogation, the inquirer questions the person again and again, weaving a multi-perspectival approach to his being by focusing in diverse ways on the variegated facets of his existence. By listening, he becomes aware of the unity of the person as doubly constituted: a manifest aspect, comportment, which symbolizes; a latent aspect, his spiritual being, which is symbolized. By more intent listening, he becomes increasingly cognizant of the subjectivity of the one attended as operative within himself, the investigator; hence, he holds a kind of interior dialogue with that internalized deposition. In this process, wherein inquirer and the one investigated become coeval in status, an interpersonal "field" is created. Transmitted back and forth, impressions of seeker and sought are so meshed with one another, affecting both in analogous ways, that a veridical mutual compresence supervenes. Since each dwells within the other, parity holds between the two. By interpretation, the inquirer conceptualizes the full organicity of the person as unitary, relational, and authentic. For, first, he is conceived as one substance, integral and indivisible, a substance of which mind and body are aspects. Next, he is conceived as constituted by successive encounters. Finally, as the imprints of the other perish within both him and the one he investigates, the essential being of each is revealed as both autonomous, each in and for himself, and empathically receptive, each constituted by the other; authenticity is the interplay of these seemingly paradoxical components.

Furthermore, methodic inquiry into the person is exhibited as one species of philosophic inquiry in general. Like the former in its more restricted task, the latter discerns the most inclusive perspective upon all objects of *its* quest—namely, any entity whatsoever. It regards every scheme cast in the wake of inquiry as but a limited perspective, a subordinate moment, valid sui generis as long as its limits are correctly specified, yet requiring emendation should it illicitly seek to comprehend phenomena beyond those limits. Not only are the presuppositions of any topic of investi-gation exposed by the philosophic quest, but these presuppositions are deliberately converted to problems which themselves are to be probed. For truth is construed as a limiting ideal which no finite inquiry may more than approximate.

The means by which truth may thus be asymptotically approached are essentially three-fold: by assertive judgment, wherein it is determined what statements conform to the pre-existing structure of the object; by active judgment, wherein it is determined what objects conform to pre-existing norms and values, and how objects may be reshaped so to conform; by exhibitive judgment, wherein it is determined how norms and objects must be mutually changed in coadaptation to one another. Accordingly, philosophic judgment possesses a complex intentional structure. In assertive judgment, a cognitively systematic matrix of ideas emerges; assertions are coordinated and organized. In active judgment, the shifting attitudes of the inquirer both express his valuation of that object and constitute an implicit comment upon its nature under the perspective of those values. In exhibitive judgment, the object is constantly held up for inspection and encounter; thereby it is apprehended through an essentially aesthetic attitude. For such factors as unity, harmony, economy, symmetry, and elegance of design are as important for discerning its constituent properties as verification of specific assertions or, for that matter, evaluations which incorporate the attitudes a philosopher assumes toward the object. Indeed, from the standpoint of methodic study of the person, the ever-changing texture of his being provokes ever new appraisals of the essential character of that being. Hence, in symbolizing himself to the inquirer, the person, via the medium of that symbology, reveals his own immanent content. Accordingly, for this species of philosophy—namely, philosophic inquiry into the person—assertive judgment and active judgment are, in fact, ancillary to exhibitive judgment.

In general, whether philosophy is general metaphysics or the specific metaphysics of the person, it is a *universal* adventure, an adventure incorporating in varying proportions the indicated kinds of philosophic judgment. As universal, even a particular philosophic system or mode of inquiry validates itself by reference to a warrant the efficacy of which is determined by appeal to standards formulated by the community of philosophers. By collating diverse perspectives, either by specific decree or through the sanction of their actual activities, this community creates complicated normative schemes to which every philosophy must be submitted for determination of its worth. In effect, by appeal to those differential schemes, the community deliberates regarding that worth. But, in addition, the philosophic enterprise is ineradicably personal. Ultimately, it is grounded in the unique values and predilections of each inquirer. Hence, the community to which a specimen of philosophizing is submitted for judgment must be construed as indefinitely large, extending endlessly into the future.

To apply general philosophy to a philosophy of the person means to meditate the person. It is to place oneself at the center of *his* being again and again, and to call forth from within oneself (namely, the inquirer) one's own inner reality. It is to inspect that inner reality from within as constituted in a fashion analogous to the composition of the inner world of the "object" of inquiry. It is profoundly to identify oneself with the other, to feel the rhythms of his existence within oneself, creatively to experience the fathom-less depths of self and others. Finally, it is to grasp the person as an intentional being, inwardly free, yet always expressing his freedom within specified horizons. By discerning the many laminae and significations embedded within the interplay of questions and responses between seeker and sought—in a word: by inspecting deeply the speech and the comportment of the one investigated—the subject of investigation is revealed in his inmost being. Thereby the organic character of dialogue is apprehended, and the authentic creativity and indefeasibly volitional character of man are disclosed. Method grasps the shared meanings of sender and receiver, a system of communication and action. Encoding hidden portent, a prestructural message the meaning of which awaits deciphering, this system incorporates the actual forms of seeker and sought. Each thus in-forms the other with the veridical forms of his own being. Each imbued with his own distinctive preferences, values, and ends, seeker and sought alike interpret the import of the deliberations of the other—in both instances shaped by the "form" of the other. Yet, always, both are enclosed, despite their idiosyncratic differences, within transcendent concerns pertinent to each. Hence, one may truly assert: no self-actualization is independent of the activities of both parties; the intentions and actions of each ground those of the other.

A · THE INTERWOVENNESS OF THE PHASES OF METHOD

(a) Sketch of Phases Already Set Forth

The phases of Method, like, indeed, the respective moments of each phase, are profoundly interwoven. In any inquiry, the first step is *to question*. It is to question the (putative) direct object of inquiry; it is to question the questioning of that object. In this process of questioning, new questions always suggest themselves. As this multitude of questions is posed and posed again, it takes shape as a cumulatively evolving pattern. The structure of this pattern was the topic of Chapter 2. Two primary concerns emerged from that investigation: the issue of taxonomy, and the issue of repetition. In the first case, Method enjoins the principle that inherent in the act of posing questions is the progressive emergence of classifications of questions, classifications of *increasing* relevance to the object being considered. From this standpoint, the objective of inquiry is to ascertain an order of relevancy with respect to the factors implicated in the object under investigation. In the second case, Method enjoins, whether one deals, as object of search, with a single factor or with a class of similar factors, that questions must be put to that object, or to the class of like objects, in such a way that it will be inspected again and again, from many points of view and in many contexts. In this way, the taxonomy initially proposed is secured as a significant taxonomy.

The second step of any inquiry is *to listen*. It is to listen to the responses "given" by the object of search to the questions put to it. In listening, one must first attend, filling oneself with the presence of the object, in its manifold aspects and dimensions, by emptying oneself of preconceptions. As the object is apprehended, its manifest content, those vividly perceptible foci, is distinguished from its latent content, the haunting background of concealed interior depths which, at one time, reveal themselves within the phenomena attended and, at another time, recede into obscurity. Finally, what in this activity presents itself, insofar as presence is construed as existing in and for itself, is deemed physis: a natural and corporeal process; what (secondly) presents itself, insofar as presence is construed as the symbol of an inner content, is deemed the embodiment or incarnation of an animating psyche.

After attending, one must gather in what had been attended. This gathering activity is either synoptic or syncretistic. In the former instance, the activity reveals a manifold of fragmented or perfunctory incorporatings (within the person) of what was attended; in the latter instance, the activity reveals the disparate elements of this manifold to be woven to unity. Moreover, the gathering activity is so constituted that syncretistic unification is effected by dialectical interplay between two orientations toward the manifold: attachment to that manifold, experiencing it as intimately conjoined with one's methodic acts; detachment from that manifold, in which it is—so to speak—held at a distance and surveyed as it is in and for itself. Further, detachment essentially implies a thoroughgoing orientation of detachment in which the community of seekers is conceived as persons seeking in mutual detachment from one another, and, by this quality of their seeking, disclosing themselves to one another as mere objects. From this point of view, these objects are construed as functioning within a multitude of disconnected horizons separately and individualistically related to an *infra*cosmic center, a center upon which converge disparate envisagements of the cosmos entertained by mutually detached persons. On the other hand, attachment essentially implies a community of persons bound together, *in solitudine* and *in communitate*: an orientation of attachment embodied in persons empathically related to one another; and, in their collective searching, disclosing the archetypal ground of their mutually enmeshed interior beings to be, in reality, a suprapersonal center.

Accordingly, now that what had been attended has been gathered in, the conceptual scheme for understanding the person must be transformed into a new scheme, a scheme in which different facets and elements are emphasized. In the latter scheme, the fully concrete nature of the person is finally—though in its earliest stage—grasped and conceptualized. For an understanding of that nature, two principles must be affirmed. First, the concrete character of the dialectic of subject and object must truly be experienced: subject becomes object to himself. Yet this object is so joined to the object of his study that the latter is thereby compounded and enriched. At the same time, the object, qua person, is *himself* immanently a subject who is altered *from within* his own objectivity; thereby, he provides a new datum for the inquirer. Secondly, the dialectic between subject and object unfolds in an intricate way. In its unfoldings, it reveals that each person, the one who seeks to know and the one who is to be known, transmits impressions of himself to the other; these transmissions proceed back and forth within an interpersonal field in oscillating detachment and attachment. In analogous fashion, each person expresses to the other what he has "received"; in consequence, an egalitarian relationship is established between the two: a relationship which so allows for complete interchange of the roles of seeker and sought that the community of persons becomes a veridical community of inquirers, each into the other.

This schematization of the process of inquiry reveals it as truly organic; it exhibits interwoven phases and interwoven moments of phases. Concretely though systematically, it reveals the dialectical and intricate relationship between the diverse elements to which I alluded in my predelineation. However, only in the final phase, *interpreting*, does Method become fully explicit. For, following the question put to the object of inquiry and the listening to *its* response, *the one who* thus methodically questions and listens must himself explicitly respond. The pattern of *his* response is already prefigured in the first two phases of inquiry, just summarized. Reflection on the structure of this response reveals it, too, to be organically constituted. Indeed, the first moment of interpreting—namely, integrality—replicates, but on a higher and more unified level, the first phase of Method; the second moment analogously replicates the second phase of Method. Just as the first two phases dialectically engender the third, so the first two moments of the third phase dialectically engender the third moment of *that* phase: namely, integrity.

(b) Schemata of Method

I have designated the moments of interpreting as integrality, encounter, and integrity. I wish now, in diagrammatic form, to sketch the correlations and interdependencies to which I have just referred.

*First, Second, and Third Stages
of Third Phase*

1	2
INTEGRALITY	ENCOUNTER
Monad: Mind–Body Aspects	Dyad: Antithesis of Integrality
⟨⟩	⟨⟩
Attending: First Moment of Second Phase	Gathering: Second Moment of Second Phase

3
INTEGRITY
Triad: Synthesis of Integrality and Encounter
⟨⟩
Transforming: Third Moment of Second Phase

The Unfolding Phases of Method

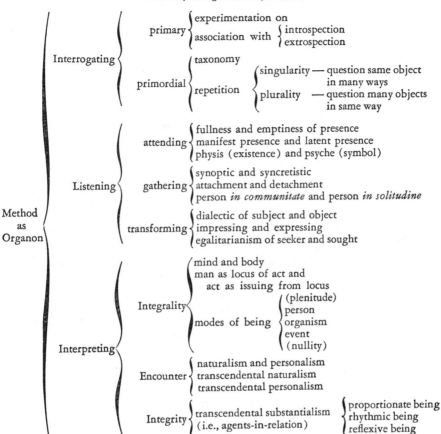

I *Master Plan: organicity of Method*

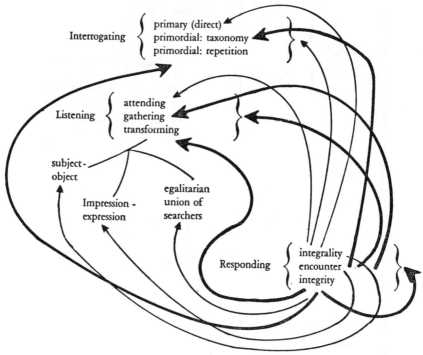

II *Additional Connections: Superimpose on Master Plan*

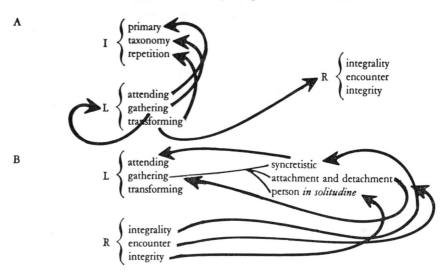

III *Relationships*

A (*a*) horizontal pattern of manifest phenomena, naturalistically speaking

$$\infty \ldots \longleftrightarrow \alpha \longleftrightarrow \beta \longleftrightarrow \gamma \longleftrightarrow \ldots \infty$$

   (*b*) vertical pattern of latent contents toward which (α) points, as a symbolic manifold

B

experiential manifold:
A ≡ external object — physis
Ω ≡ internal object — psyche

C

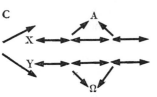

The double search of the person as he receives patterned images of natural phenomena, in series X and Y

{ searching, expressed as external symbols of X, leading toward A, the mystery of physis.

searching, expressed as internal symbols of Y, leading toward Ω, the mystery of psyche.

Ultimately, A ⇌ Ω
As conjoined, A and Ω ground the person

D Naturalism (abstract plurality) ⇌ Personalism (formal unity)

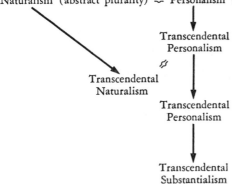

Transcendental Personalism   { first stage of unfolding: concretely diversified unity

Transcendental Naturalism

Transcendental Personalism   { second state of unfolding: union of Transcendental Naturalism and Transcendental Personalism

Transcendental Substantialism

Hence, Transcendental Substantialism subsumes (1) Transcendental Personalism (first stage) and Transcendental Naturalism
      (2) Personalism and Naturalism

E Patterns of organization emerging in transcendental inquiry:

Each pattern (p) of structures, associated with a set of phenomenal functions (f), is transformed into a new pattern. Any given pattern, p_i, equals $p_i\{p^1(f_1{}^1, \ldots, f_n{}^1), \ldots, p^k(f_1{}^k, \ldots, f_n{}^k\}$, $p^1, \ldots, p^k$ representing all antecedent patterns and $f_i{}^j$ representing specific natural activities, forces, properties, or events. In general, p expresses the dynamic evolving of $p^1 \rightarrow p^2 \rightarrow \ldots \rightarrow p^k$.

(c) The Generalized Frame of Method

The three phases of Method have been treated seriatim. This manner of presentation suggests that, in practice, the phases unfold sequentially; that they are
employed, item by item, in temporal order. Actually, the matter is not that simple.
For the phases, and their constitutive moments, weave in and out; they form no
definitive pattern of sequence. The correlations I have diagrammatically indicated
are only specimens of formalizations of what, in fact, is a fluent structure. They
do not exhaust all possible arrangements.

Consider the matter from this point of view. Questioning, listening, responding: these are essentially the phases. But are not these phases, at bottom, contemporaneous rather than sequential? For each phase actually implies, and indeed
presupposes, the remainder! To question is already to be guided by an interpretive
scheme; when made explicit, this scheme is a response. Furthermore, in order to
question, one must, as a prelude to query, have listened. Surely, one should be in
that state of receptivity which allows the object of query already to have impressed
itself upon one. Accordingly, one must, in effect (in preliminary fashion), have
mapped out the routes along which and by the determining contours of which
questions are put to the object. Moreover, an authentic listening requires a universe of discourse, a frame of reference, one already adopted as immanent within
query. In effect, this "universe," this "frame," is implicit response. But, clearly, as
my own sequence of presentation shows, listening involves prior questioning;
responding involves prior listening and, a fortiori, prior questioning.

What I am stressing is the organic character of query; and Method is but query
systematically articulated, its tenets laid bare in their structure and import. From
this point of view, my manner of setting forth Method was chosen more for
convenience than by necessity. Alternative modes of presentation might have been
chosen. Yet the manner selected permits analysis of the fuller import of each
major component of query: namely, questioning, listening, responding. Accordingly, the stipulations and the strictures regarding overall governance of query by
a principle of the organicity of Method should correct any misimpression of a
simplistic construal of my intent.

The general frame of reference presupposed throughout but made explicit only
in the final phase—interpreting—involves two basic sets of suppositions. The
first set, outlined in my account of that phase, refers to (substantive) metaphysical
presuppositions providing an essential background to an ontology of the person.
At this time, I shall not further develop my line of thinking as it pertains to this
issue. Reference will be made to these presuppositions at appropriate places in the
working out of my philosophic theory; a theory I begin to develop, though sections
have already been sketched, in subsequent books treating the theme Ontology.
In particular, the moments of integrity, previously mentioned but not elaborated,
will be systematically treated there. The three moments of integrity—namely,
proportionate being, rhythmic being, reflexive being—will be shown to be germinal notions. The second set of suppositions, not yet mentioned in my account,
concerns my view of the philosophic enterprise as that enterprise bears upon a
generalized theory of the person. I turn now to this theme.

(*a*) The Abstract and the Concrete

Wherein consists the distinctive character of a *philosophic* inquiry into the person? Why do I not—and I raise this question again—speak, rather, of a scientific inquiry? My comments are intended to be applicable to the general philosophic adventure. The theory I am presenting is but a limited instance of that adventure. Much of what I say here I have already said. However, in considering my method as an organon, it is appropriate that I collect, in a single presentation and at this point of my inquiry, my earlier, more desultory remarks concerning my conception of the philosophic enterprise as a whole.

Many specific theories have been proposed, some with considerable predictive power, to comprehend the different aspects of human behavior. A welter of *personally* significant details may be discerned as characterizing every person. Each theory abstracts from these details certain recurrent patterns. It seeks the reasons for recurrence in principles which are presumed to express basic tendencies and pervasive activities of men. The value of such special theories derives from their power to yield consequences which reveal novel modes of interconnectedness between the elements composing these patterns. The variety of compositions is, in principle, unlimited. An inexhaustible wealth of deductions can be drawn from any theory, provided its fundamental tenets are formulated with consistency and precision. A theory is fruitful when these deductions correspond to what observation (to which theory has led) suggests as striking, interesting, or significant facts about the entities it concerns.

But lurking in every theory is a danger for the enterprise of knowledge. The impact upon the inquirer of its fruitfulness often obscures his acknowledgment of its fragmentary character. The scope of its central notions is sharply limited. Even in the infinitude of their possible interweavings, these notions constitute but a single perspective upon a phenomenon. For they have been extracted from a more inclusive universe of meaningful discourse about the person. Irreducible factors originally excluded from this perspective may intrude. There is an inescapable risk that these factors will be deemed resolvable into the elements or patterns of elements which the theory presupposes. Thus a theory of economic behavior might unquestioningly seek to comprehend under the laws governing the quest for profit the religious impulse. Again, the cultural life of man might be accounted a sublimation of sexual instincts. Or, more generally, the phenomenon of mentality might be presumed a manifestation of a certain constellation of material particles.

"The topic of every science," Whitehead wrote,

> is an abstraction from the full concrete happenings of nature. But every abstraction neglects the influx of factors omitted into the factors retained. Thus a single pattern determined by vision limited to the abstractions within a special science differentiates itself into a subordinate factor in an indefinite number of wider patterns when we consider its possibilities of relatedness to the omitted universe.[1]

Moreover, these "possibilities of relatedness" are not merely tantamount to the generalizations of that science, as where Newton's laws apply to a special case of

Einstein's theory. Widely diversified and methodologically unrelated realms of inquiry may be relevant to one another in a larger view of some entity which independent investigation discloses them jointly to concern. Indeed, it is an additional task of philosophy to search for such common entities as are differential-ly understood by scattered foci of inquiry. The body of a person is not one entity and his mind another, though the theoretical suppositions of physiology and psychology are such as, despite disclaimers by their respective researchers, to imply this division. It is yet a third of philosophy's tasks to suggest a larger frame of reference for comprehending a phenomenon, pointing beyond to the unfathomable immensity of relevant circumstances. Philosophy seeks to penetrate unknown depths in the characterization of an entity. By the novelty of its formulations, it aims at fusing perspectives revealed by special modes of inquiry. The aesthetic dimension of a man's life, his religious yearnings, the practical frustrations he endures in his daily existence may each be isolated, probed, and understood by particular disciplines. A philosophy, however, would entertain notions germane to all these activities. A man also craves a unity in the manifold character of his life. Philosophy is the quest for that unity. What religion celebrates in prayer and worship—the harmony, the vivacity, the complexities, the unboundedness, the integratedness, the sheer concreteness of all things and the intensely personal character of our relationship to them—philosophy formulates in rational dis-course. Where the religious man consecrates himself in contrition or exuberance, the philosophical man dedicates himself to deliberate with humility or daring. He systematically renders meanings which dawn upon him as he experiences reality to become luminous. This unveiling of reality is achieved by its continual interrogation from every point of view *conceivable* to the philosopher so that distortions inhering in its initial confrontation are progressively rectified. The philosophic enterprise is one of gradual emendation of error haunting immediate observation. The philosopher ruthlessly probes his experience in all its qualities. Of what emerges in philosophic retrospection as but a specious reality, because of uncritically adopted conventions of science and practical life, man ascertains the factual scientific basis.

The emphases in philosophy may be critical or speculative, though in either case both strains are found. It is the proportion which determines how a specimen of philosophy is to be designated. In the former, the presuppositions of a science or of a mode of experience are made explicit. Contradictions and verbal ambigui-ties are disclosed. Critical philosophy aids the inquirer to clarify, articulate, and systematize his intuitions, to evaluate his tacit preconceptions. It alerts him to his substantive and methodological assumptions. The logical structure of a dis-cipline is laid bare. Methodicity of a prescribed and unquestioned kind prevails. The aim is clarity, order, rigor, conformity to customary usage, systematic critique of that usage. More susceptible to quixotism because of the boldness of its imaginative deliberations, though it does not neglect the factors upon which critical philosophy lays stress, speculative philosophy—of which this book is in-tended as a limited example—delineates comprehensive notions which sweep the range of human experience, gathering under their purview its multifarious aspects, depths, and nuances. It aims, as Whitehead said, at "disclosure beyond explicit presuppositions,"[2] at, indeed, the critique of all method, though it perforce must always employ in its particular searches, with notable flexibility, a single method. Philosophic reflection which constitutes a metaphysical inquiry, whether its end is system or that assemblage of important notions which precedes system, is vital to the human adventure. Its essential characteristic is inventive generalization. As long as its notions are formed as systematic responses to questions posed by experience, and insofar as the implications which issue from their explication and interweaving succeed in further illuminating experience, a philosophic exploration, carrying the inquirer over whatever seas the winds of thought drive him, is warranted and, indeed, for those of a certain disposition, mandatory.

(b) Speculative Philosophy and Science

This is an essay in metaphysics. Connections between the notions I shall introduce and concrete matters of fact cannot be exhibited with the rigor, the explicitness, the precision, the completeness to which science aspires and accustoms us. The referents of those notions will nonetheless always be experience. Indeed, if they are philosophically meaningful, they should accord more closely with a larger experience, plumbing its deeper and more intimate realms, and disclosing hitherto impenetrable depths, than science the power of which depends upon a capacity to abstract a significant sector from phenomena, exhibiting the details of its texture but suppressing its relationships to other fragments and a fortiori to the whole of experience. Assisted by metaphor and hints, by anticipations of ever broader but as yet unformulable perspectives, by strategic incorporation of selected insights from particular fields, philosophic notions vindicate themselves in the sporadic flashes of illumination they momentarily or unexpectedly shed upon shifting but interconnected foci of experience, revealing its vastness, its unboundedness, its wholeness. They are daring in that they purport to compress, in their modes of formulation, endless possibilities for disclosing novel aspects of reality. They are humble in that they invite the philosopher further to explicate and elaborate their contents or, indeed, to negate their validity. For if one feature be chosen to express the essence of philosophy, it is its reflexive character: alone among disciplines, a philosophic doctrine relentlessly ponders even while it uses its own presuppositions.

Speculative philosophy interprets consistently and on a high level of generality experiential data thought to be disparate, systematically relating them to the extant fabric of knowledge. In this respect, it resembles science the leading principles of which, provisionally unchallengeable owing to their capacity to organize theoretical foci over a wide range of inquiries, thereby integrate what have hitherto appeared as qualitatively dissimilar and prima facie unconnected phenomena. But its comprehensiveness, as I have noted, greatly exceeds that of science. For it extracts its concepts from widely separated disciplines of thought; and with categories fashioned from these concepts it daringly roams the entire range of experience.

Though it may build a labyrinthine architectonic and render its findings with logical adroitness, philosophy lacks the explicitness and precision, hence the predictive power, of a scientific formulation. An immense wealth of its significant consequences must be suppressed, and for them substituted concise summations, epigrams, mere clues. Since, accordingly, a philosophy cannot command the evidential certainty of science, it may only be sanctioned by its appeal—in terms of coherence, reasonability, the sense of "philosophic satisfaction" it affords—to the specifically philosophic and, ultimately, the larger human, community. However, philosophic inquiry is not a vaguer species of scientific inquiry. It need not therefore apologize for its failure to conform to standards of science. For, unlike science, it seeks, in the final analysis, to articulate and authenticate deep feelings and abiding convictions concerning the character of a man's experience as a unified and value-charged whole. And peculiar among all disciplines, I repeat, it strives candidly to expose wherever possible its own methodological, valuational, and factual assumptions. It compels by its power to strike chords of assent, on profound levels of human existence, in *others* whom it may likewise have stirred into intensive scrutiny of their intuitions. It does not veil the object of its investigation with a fabric of symbols which owes its explanatory power to its success in abstracting the common traits from a multiplicity of objects. Unlike science, speculative philosophy seeks to comprehend its object in its full concreteness and multifarious character. It does not (as does science when its abstractions are confusedly taken for the realities from which they have been extracted) imperil the aliveness, the subtleties, the many facets, of its object. Indeed, the lure of philosophy is that, while daring to unveil a reality it presumes a *distorted* experience to conceal, it never purports to go beyond what a clarified intellect or spirit *could*, were its prescriptions heeded, enjoy and from which take its point of departure for yet further philosophic adventure. In its ultimate aim, philosophy strives to clarify experience, and to deepen and extend the range of our understanding of experience.

I do not mean to imply that philosophy sustains no reciprocal ties to science, ties in which each activity fructifies the other. In a philosophic schema science appears as a derivate. The objects comprehended are restricted to a particular class; their myriad traits are confined to a salient few. By "derivate" I do not suggest the logical compulsion of deduction. Rather, I mean a special clustering woven into the more complex but less precisely rendered pattern of ideas delineated by philosophy. And philosophy, in turn, gains new images from science; its notions are shaped in response to experience therein illuminated anew. But it does not gain its wisdom from science. The cumulative impact of science provokes modification of philosophic notions; it poses a continual challenge. For philosophy must be vigilant lest an archaic experience, untouched by science, is made the basis for its conceptualizations. But in its foundations, philosophy remains an autonomous activity which takes account of all special experiences in the frame of notions not beholden to any allegedly *privileged class* of special experiences. Analogous considerations hold for art, that concrete re-presentation of experience to which philosophic patterns allude; for the novel experiences afforded by art in the continual re-creation of the world by man must themselves be woven into any philosophic scheme which claims coherence and adequacy. The singular ways in which a Rilke, a Cézanne, or a Bartók "saw" the world inspire within those affected by their work the quest for its *justification* under a truly adequate philosophic perspective.

A philosophic scheme, whether systematically rendered or a fortuitous assemblage of notions ordered with vague methodicity, is a portrayal of the universe, depicting its drama, illuminating its recesses, linking the diverse modes by which it may be experienced. It is a portrayal, however, under a perspective, a perspective of threefold character: unique as expressing the texture of experience of a particular philosopher; both general and unique as mirroring through him the attitude of a culture or an epoch, attachment to a special philosophic method, a substantive preconception regarding the qualities of the ultimate entities into which the universe is deemed divisible and by which, purportedly, it may be understood; potentially generalizable as eliciting imaginative assent, supplementation, or frank negation from the community of its competent assimilators.

(c) Philosophic Reason

The "natural complexes" ordered by a philosophic scheme compel that scheme to conform to their character. But they compel within a range of possible modes of ordering. Though they resist arbitrary proposals, mere whims of speculative fancy, for rendering them intelligible, they tolerate—indeed, solicit—many points of view in available or prospective accounts of their nature. For it is of their essence to stand in specific relationship to their possible experiencers; their content is defined, in part, by reference to that relationship. The complexities of nature, inexhaustible in the wealth of their elements and the modes of interconnectedness between these elements, may be extracted in innumerable ways. Each way reveals, when methodically ordered and the order is explicated, a *novel* philosophic orientation.

Though it solicits verification for its conclusions, vindication of its premisses, and validation of inferential links between conclusions and premisses—in short, a *warrant* in the ultimate experience of the many—a philosophic account of nature not only affirms or explains. Depicting by vivid tropes and exhibiting these to the beholder, it discloses what a philosopher has newly discerned. It discriminates from the massive impact of fact upon *him* those factors most relevant and valuable for him. The spectacle of the universe is revealed in a new light. Like works of art, authentic philosophic orientations (i.e., those in which comprehensiveness and methodicity prevail) revivify their contemplators, stirring discontent with desiccated and habitual modes of experiencing, inspiring a quest for fresh experience, shaping new attitudes—as well as compelling revaluation of belief.

As a system of assertions, organized judgments upon the real character of real things, divergent philosophies invite comparison, synthesis, extension, rejection, and extraction of elements pertinent to a new system.[3] Each philosophic perspective results from the application to an "object" of a method more or less powerfully designed, more or less emendable or transmutable by the product it fashions, more or less explicitly formulable. Meaningful collation of philosophic perspectives is grounded upon fertile deployment of an overarching method—elusive and vague, but always felt as pervasive background in authentic philosophic search. This generalized method includes as its specializations and refinements particular methods which shape definite constellations of ideas into philosophically persuasive schemes. It is through the success of its instances as fruitfully bearing the germ of philosophic method that the core and spirit of philosophy vindicates, clarifies, and perpetuates itself.

It is either by indirect reference to that method by invoking one of its instantial methods or by direct reference that a philosopher may evaluate his own speculations—or test those of another. It is by collation of numerous philosophic perspectives that he may, in extracting felicitous elements from each and in formulating cogent reasons against utilization of other elements, further those speculations. It is, however, only by attending to the universe as it speaks to him, from far reaches and almost concealed depths, by feeling its message and rendering those feelings vividly, intelligibly, and genuinely, that the integrity of the philosophic adventure is preserved and its kernel nourished for its subsequent growth.

The dominant theme of these reflections on the philosophic adventure is its ineradicably personal character. In the case of science, the reasonableness of a single scientist flows from the reasonableness of the entire community of scientists. Reason is quite precisely institutionalized as a set of norms and principles to which its members subscribe; indeed, are compelled to subscribe if they would practice science. However, this dictum does not negate the role of idiosyncratically imaginative deviations from these norms and principles. In their cumulative effects, such deviations may be of great significance in effecting revision of what had been institutionalized.

But philosophic reason, on the other hand, is ineluctably grounded, by its essential character, in personal commitment, personal value, personal knowledge. For the scientist, evidence, by and large, is external to his own personality; for the philosopher, evidence lies *within* him. Save in the measure in which evidence derives from his re-collecting experiences formed in his encounters with other philosophies, evidence *is* the philosopher's own self making explicit the (evidential) consequences and import of his privately executed acts. Philosophic insight arises from and is constituted by the philosopher's disinterested desire to know; it is "his *own* advertence to the polymorphism of his *own* consciousness."[4]

True, the individual element is, quite often, undoubtedly of crucial importance for science. Indeed, in its critical periods, the advance of science depends upon defiance! Perhaps a single scientist challenges the whole community of competent inquirers. Yet, whatever the extent to which the scientist works in solitude, he is *always* in at least implicit attunement with his community. This attuning by no means necessarily entails agreement. Surely, it frequently consists in the formulating of radically dissident points of view regarding often fundamental issues.

However, philosophy is truly, by its intrinsic nature, the flowering of the individual: it is the consummate expression of his absolute uniqueness in the eternal order of things. For philosophy, "rational consciousness *is* its coming to know and take possession of *itself*."[5] Accordingly, as Bernard Lonergan has succinctly stated, philosophy cannot

> conform to the method, to the linguistic techniques, or to the group mentality of the scientist. The contribution of science and of scientific method to philosophy lies in a unique ability to supply philosophy with instances of the heuristic structures which a metaphysics integrates into a single view of the concrete universe.[6]

But, indebted as philosophers are to a powerful and compelling philosophic tradition, their vision, their styles of presentation, the immanently guiding directives toward philosophic truth they adopt, the procedures they employ in gathering evidence, the modes in which they effect synthesis to unified manifolds of publicly accessible but privately acquired insight—all these lie within the province of radically solitary thinkers. Though grateful for their predecessors' accomplishment and inspiration, philosophers—when all is said and done—are beholden only to conscience which shapes each one's own searching integrity.

C · THE ORGANICITY OF METHOD

(a) Meditation

When all is said and done, philosophic inquiry into the person is, in effect, a *re*meditating of that person. For it is a meditating anew, a meditating informed by various commitments: commitment to a philosophic theory, commitment to a substantive metaphysics, commitment to the wealth of personal experience, commitment to the results achieved by specialized disciplines. To meditate means to think, and insofar as one thinks authentically, one thinks as an integral being. As integral, one is centered. For, in that condition, the fragments of one's self are drawn into coherent unity. So understood, to meditate suggests both a being moved toward one's center by a dynamism which works from within one's own self and a being drawn toward that center by something external. Insofar as one is thus doubly drawn, one moves toward one's center through the mediation of something beyond one. Moreover, since to mediate derives from *metiri*, which means "to measure" or "to mete out," in its tropologic sense mediate implies that one estimates, sets a value upon a thing, judges one thing by another, or, in fine, thinks profoundly, resiliently, and durably.

Hence, in self-meditation, the diverse parts of a person are, so to speak, collected, drawn in, and concentrated upon his own essence: the "center" of his being, his transcendental core. Step by step, in his inmost being, a person who meditates awakens to the inward knowing of his own essentiality. An irradiating of his being, this inward knowing is the source of such interior luminosity as will ineluctably affect all who come into his presence. In meditating another, in *his* presence—as we shall see—one potentiates from that other *his own* self-meditating.

Etymologically,[7] "person" is related to *personare*, meaning "to sound through" or "to resound." The word derives from the Greek πρόσωπον, from πρός and ὄπα from ὄψ (or, πρός and ὦπα from ὦψ), literally, "a placing before the voice." What kind of placing? Looking to the origin of the term in the Greek theater, one discovers that, like the Latin cognate *persona*, πρόσωπον is a mask which is placed before the mouth for the purpose of amplifying the voice. Through this amplification, the spoken word becomes dramatic and resonant; it reverberates through the theater, the stage upon which the drama of man in his essential being is re-enacted. According to this interpretation, it is the presence of the inner being of the person which is thus dramatically called forth, hence awakened as though from slumber. When *person* and *mediation* are juxtaposed, they convey the sense of an awakening into radiant and dramatic presenting of what hitherto had been concealed but is now, through this awakening, disclosed. The veils of superficial being are torn asunder. The inmost person is e-voked. Literally, he is called forth, called forth in a double calling: first, by himself, as through the calling, or vocation, of his own being; secondly, by another who beckons to him.

I have stressed the significance of repetition in Method. Etymologically, I mean a re-*petitioning*; for, *re-petition* and *petition* are derived from the Latin, *petere*, meaning *to seek* or *to beg*, or, in effect, *to plead*; hence, repetition is both *seeking-ness* and *prayerfulness*. Combining the terms *person, repetition*, and *meditation*, I note first that a person is *one who fulfills the obligation of personhood by re-peated meditation*. Translating this expression into its etymological components, I arrive at this interpretation: an inner voice resounds within one and passes from him to another; this voice beckons to both that each might seek again and again; it enjoins both, self and other, to seek and, beyond that, to plead (as in a kind of prayer) that each might quietly be led to his own center. The state toward which each is led, I must now add, is one of radiant grace. To be in this state is to experience the redemptive ground of one's own being.

On the other hand, insofar as a person strives and struggles, as though ruled by his Ego—on a narrow construal of Ego—his authentic being is refracted through that Ego: in effect, through his masks, his persona. Because, becoming disoriented, the person now orients himself toward self and other in a fashion which is fragmented and dispersed rather than coordinated and unified, he experiences himself as de-formed. For, quite literally, he becomes diminished with respect to his veridical "form"—his $\varepsilon\tilde{\iota}\delta o\varsigma$, the image of his being: a symbol transparent to his inner core. Thereby, the person is transformed into such a state of inessential existence that he becomes weighty and obscure; for he has fallen away from the lightness, the luminosity, of centeredness. He passes from wakefulness to slumber. For not to exist in one's essentiality is to be displaced from, to be in $\H{\varepsilon}\kappa\sigma\tau\alpha\sigma\iota\varsigma$, i.e., the vibrancy of non-stasis. To be in stasis is to be statically equilibrated; it is to exist apart from one's dynamically equilibrated transcendentality. When a person is thus displaced, his perceptions and conceptions are distorted. Failing *to take thoroughly* (as in *per-capere*) the items of reality in their true character, he falls away from non-illusory perception. Failing *to take together* (as in *con-capere*) the items of reality in their coherent assemblage, he falls into inchoate conception.

What is the bearing of this etymological exercise on Method qua inherently organic? The organicity of Method consists in its power to unify the multitude of disparate approaches for illuminating the one sought; by its unity, Method causes his inmost being to shine forth. For the very locus of the unity of methodic approaches *is*, precisely, a meditative confrontation of the object of query —and the drawing from the person encountered of an impetus toward self-clarification which resides at the core of his being. With gathering momentum, that person so moves (in query) toward his own center that he reveals to the inquirer who he truly is. In self-disclosure, he—the sought one—irradiates the inquirer with his presence. On his part, the seeker must (likewise) meditate *himself*; he must seek his *own* inner reality. *This* meditating consists in calling forth from within himself, the very seeker, *his* essential being as, in these searching acts, entwined with the now luminous being of the one originally sought. By thus illuminating himself, and instituting such conditions as will aid the object of his quest reciprocally to illuminate *himself*, both seeker and sought are embraced in mutual irradiation. To call forth being, essentially, from oneself and to call forth being, essentially, from the one confronted in search are, in actuality, one and the same activity.

This activity is the very *esprit* of methodic inquiry into the person. From it, all other aspects of methodicity are derived; with respect to it, they are all perspectives. The *organism* of Method evolves in moments: empathy, indwelling, purification. As with previously designated phases and moments, a merely sequential interpretation of this unfolding violates the organic character of Method. As before, these moments (of Method as organic) are contemporaneously, though quite intricately, linked with one another.

Empathy, the first moment, concerns a profound identification of the seeker's experience of *his* essential being with the essential being of the one sought; conversely, when the one sought has revealed his *own* inmost being to the seeker, he too experiences an analogous identification. Hence, empathy refers to the binding together of seeker and sought in reciprocal dependency with respect to the unfolding processes of searching. From a philosophic point of view, an authentic mutuality prevails between seeker and sought. In general, the being of any person shares an identity with the being of every person in the searching community; and, by my earlier argument, the *entire* community of persons *is*, at bottom, a community of searchers.

(b) The Passage from Method to Ontology

Searching men direct their inquiries toward other searching men. Immanent within this directedness of man, yet transcending its every manifestation, is his potency from which the entire configuration of a man's *modus vivendi* shapes itself. Potency is never fully actualized. Nothing, as Tillich declares, "pours its power of being completely into its state of existence."[8] Previously, I suggested that a man may be wholly revealed in his every act; yet now I allude to unfulfilled potentialities. By this paradoxical formulation, I want to suggest that man's existence is constituted by mystery as well as by lucidity. Some general comments about the ontology of searching are in order.

To say, according to this view, that man is powerful means that he has a destiny and a distinctive style of life, that though the special qualities of his being may be similar to those of another—all must, after all, eat and sleep, experience terror, remorse, joy and peace—they nevertheless alloy themselves into something unique. It means, moreover, that he can through a free act of imagination comprehend this destiny, discern its impact upon others; and through a free act of will hasten or impede its fulfillment, or even by a miraculous feat of counter power alter and redirect it. Man, in short, is a creature capable of self-affirmation. His power and his will, in full coincidence, may illuminate to transparency all his movements.

Yet man is embedded in a vast and irretrievably mysterious universe, a universe only partly comprehensible by the ways of science. He derives his power of acting from his participation within an ever-expanding community of agencies. His being, on one level of its existence sharply contoured and delimited from other beings, on another level is defined by its connections with the wholly Other from which his creative ability, tapping immeasurable resources, draws sustenance. For though the individuality of things, inert and un–self-determining, rests upon exclusion, that of agents, of which people are examples, is enriched and, in the final analysis, constituted by mutuality.

Spinoza's analysis of "substance"—the substratum or constituent stuff of all being—distinguishes *natura naturans* (creating nature or *Deus*) from *natura naturata* (nature realized, or *Natura* proper) in the famous formula for expressing the totality of what is: *Deus sive Natura*.[9] A primordial, inexhaustible potency—ultimately unfathomable and mysterious—actualizes itself in an infinite texture of "modes." Jung's archetypes may, indeed, be interpreted as one attempt at formulating principles in accordance with which potency organizes itself into the specific psychic patterns of existence and relationship for the mode we call man. And Konrad Lorenz, working in the field of comparative behaviorology, discovers as a biologic parallel systems of rhythmical coordinated nervous impulses—the "autorhythmias"—indigenous to lower animals (e.g., the creeping tendency of the earthworm) which he feels form the basis (i.e., the potentiality) for the spontaneity of all instinctive activity.[10] The rules governing the formation of the complex of autorhythmias (as in musical experience) activated as the organism encounters its environment may, we might speculate, constitute an analogous interpretation.

Each mode, as derivative from the infinite sea of potency, reproduces by analogy (i.e., as a microcosm) both its autonomy and its inscrutability. But as privation of this cosmic potency, a crystallization out of the relational matrix which it constitutes, every mode must struggle in a world of partially hostile forces. All persons, accordingly, hover in status between *full* being (i.e., bodyhood) and, as they become alienated from their intrinsic potencies, mere thinghood—in effect, non-being. To experience both one's separateness, in loneliness and helplessness, and one's relatedness, in exuberance or serenity, is a necessary condition for attaining the human estate.

One's potency is activated only through authentic encounters with another (i.e., Martin Buber's I–thou relationships). The "other" may be an inanimate object, completely malleable to human creative impact, a natural object (e.g., a tree) with its own inherent dynamism or, in consummate encounter, another sentient being. In the act of communion in which full reciprocity prevails, each individual remains entirely "open" to the other, ready to experience, without sacrificing autonomy, *his* feelings and thoughts, *his* rhythms, the *Gestalt* of *his* being. Each communicant becomes truly an inquirer.

By "inquirer" I do not mean a person bewildered by veiled experience who gropes for clarity, for uniting what in lonely despair or depression is felt as fragmented and nebulous. (For the conditions under which clarity will occur must be *instituted*, not by one's solitary affirmation and seeking, but by a *coming together* with another.) The groping person is, in effect, engaged in "repetition compulsion," an obsessive puzzlement about his true but repressed feelings. Only when unobstructed channels of communication are established in which a person, in his essential "core," can get through to the other is the need to obscure a vital experience abolished.

By an "inquirer" I mean, therefore, a person whose experiences are *already* luminous, a person who wants, in solidarity with another, to grasp the potency of the other, to accept its mysterious depths, its ramifications, and its impingements, a person who is alive to what he sees, hears, smells, touches, one who is in the quiet excitement of contact. Only *he* can communicate with another in that sustained, committed, and searching way I call "inquiry." Only he can caress the texture of his experience, discern its hidden beauties and values, as in the inexhaustible novelty of shapes, rhythms, colors, and meanings of a great painting.

An encounter takes both communicants out of what Heidegger calls "concealment." [11] It joins them in intimacy to form a *new entity* which momentarily transcends its constituents. This metamorphosis shakes the encounterers. When we listen to a symphony, for example, our entire being, in its physiologic and psychic dimensions, reverberates. We feel the music *within* us, actually *becoming* the music, flowering and pulsating as *it* does. It is *not* an object which we, as subject, merely meet as *out there*. The rhythms strike chords in the "center" of our being, so that *we* can vibrate in the same pattern as the music vibrates.

Indeed, each sensory modality elicits a characteristic mode of interfusion. So when people encounter one another, where all the senses are called into play, a *mutual* identification and resonance takes place. Surely, within every man, as Fromm writes, is "the infant, the child, the adolescent, the criminal, the insane, the saint, the artist, the male *and* the female"; [12] and by the intrapsychic experience of these parts of one's being, joined to their experience as concretely exemplified and embodied in another, the bridging of the gap between psyches is achieved. Distinction between the realm of the intrapsychic and that of the interpersonal is obliterated as people are "fused" without sacrificing but, rather, intensifying, their separateness while enriching and extending their relatedness. Each person, thereby, enters into the being of the other and reconstitutes it, producing new variations on its life theme or even altering its basic rhythms. The transformation effected by a genuine encounter is, indeed, permanent. The individual is repotentiated; the scope and intensity of his subsequent encounterings increase; his world expands and deepens.

Every encounter comprises two interdependent moments: an approach by the Other, and a going toward the Other. The first moment expresses the impact in its shock, constraint, resistance and oddity, of the Other upon him who encounters: here what Freud calls the reality principle holds sway. The second moment expresses a shaping, a fantasizing, an interpretation, the imaginative rearrangement of elements composing the Other: this is the domain of the authentic operation of Freud's pleasure principle. In the perverse functioning of this principle, the "going toward" is degraded into narcissism: that alienation from the power to encounter which, fortified by previous failures to encounter, induces compensatory projections onto what in reality is encounterable but in deprived experience is a void—where one, in effect, encounters only a reflection of oneself.

Every creative "going toward" involves confrontation of the unknown. For whatever is confronted has uncanny depths which we, by encountering, seek to reveal in their emergent possibilities. Whether a blank canvas is to be shaped into a new living experience or, simply, a natural scene to be enjoyed, what is perceived entails activity and realignment, wonder at the miracle which might be born, dread lest it fail, a sense of compelling the hidden from concealment. Each focus within the perceptive act releases new energies for wider-ranging exploration; so every encounter potentiates, for both subjects, something new into activity from a limitless reservoir of power.

In the context of encounter so construed, seeker and sought alike become aware of each as *indwelling* within each—indwelling which (as second moment of organic Method), indeed, is constitutive of the essence of both. As this indwelling is reflected back and forth, from seeker to sought, understanding by either of the other is enriched and clarified. Acknowledgment of this mutual fructification constitutes *purification*—the final moment of organic Method. For, in this activity of reciprocal acknowledgment, each truly comes to know the other in himself and himself in the other. A harmony of dwelling ensues: each with each, each with himself. Accordingly, empathy, indwelling, and purification are profoundly intertwined as organic Method. From the methodological point of view, the perpetual interplay of seeker and sought entails an important ontologic consequence: every person is, at once, unity and plurality, subject and object, *relatum* and relationship.

At this point, Method completely passes over into Ontology. It is no longer possible to treat methodicity without systematically elaborating the ontologic import of the polarities, the injunctions, the norms, the principles set forth in this volume. What remains to be considered of Method, from the standpoint of query —sustained and systematic—into the essential person, must henceforth be extracted from the detailed working out of a philosophic theory of the person.

For, in this passage of method to ontology, the central theme of a methodic study of man will reveal itself as radically dissociated from themes pertaining to non-human topics of systematic inquiry. Alone among the "objects" of inquiry, man is a *self*—not a mere subject endowed with sentiency and capable of spontaneous action, but a reflecting self capable of self-conscious and autonomous action. To meditate the being of man is to dwell at the core of freedom: its purity and its ambiguity. Unique in the sphere of known phenomena, man is free and self-determining. True, higher biologic organisms prefigure these powers. But, not until nature has so denatured itself as to glow consistently with the element of the spiritual has the miraculous leap from organism to person been achieved. In succeeding books, the dialectic between freedom pristine and freedom tainted will disclose itself in its numberless subtleties and ramifications, in its origins and in its destiny. First, the natural ground for this transfiguration will be set forth. Then, myriad facets of the estate of man, insofar as they bear upon a generalized theory of the person, will prevail as sustained focus for this inquiry.

By man's freedom, in all its vicissitudes, as soon as man the object is known man the subject breaks through all causal schemes, as he fully presents himself; as soon as man the subject is experienced, man the object once more emerges as the causal patterning of this or that aspect of his subjectivity. Qua object, man is determined; his freedom vanishes. Qua subject, man is free; his determinism vanishes. Accordingly, the very procedures whereby his objectivity is articulated draw forth man's subjectivity. For every objectively human presence is a response, *freely* (self-)determined, to those procedures, and, hence, a modification of their applicability and, indeed, their content. Yet, conversely, the empathic relatedness in which context alone man's subjectivity is felt becomes dominated by his objectivity. For no sympathetic identification of man with man can eventually fail to elicit *each*, inquirer and the one investigated, in his recalcitrance to any quest to enter *into* his being. This resistance of man's being is his *non*–self-determined, therefore causally patterned, surd.

Surely, no other phenomenon exhibits this elusive and paradoxical character, this inherent ambiguity of human freedom. Moreover, the study of no other phenomenon entails a phenomenon phenomenologizing itself with respect to a like phenomenon, engaged in analogous activity, such as occurs at the heart of methodic inquiry. Indeed, a reciprocity of two (interwoven) phenomena phenomenologizing themselves with respect to one another pervades all human relations, hence all inquiry (a species of human relation) into human beings. In consequence of this profound mutuality, no clear distinction can be made, in the last analysis, between inquirer, object of inquiry, and method of inquiry: all three are inextricably enmeshed. In this sense, when applied to a systematic study of the person, Method draws forth from within its own content Ontology. The being together of human beings, with all the subtleties this relationship implies, *is* the ontologized method whereby human being reveals its essential character.

(c) Transcendental Method: Personal Transfiguration

Further to elucidate my inquiry into the conditions requisite for the methodic study of man as self-determining, I briefly comment on that quality by which man pre-eminently distinguishes himself from all that is not human. Alone among creatures, man is endowed with the power of speech; and, beyond that power, the power, through speech, to illumine the cosmos, and by the light cast by speech resolutely to shape his ever emergent character as nonetheless ineluctably unresolved. Two juxtaposed texts from Scripture will allow me to stress a hitherto undeveloped dimension of my problematic. One is drawn from The Gospel according to Saint John; the other, from The Book of Genesis.

"In the beginning," declares the Gospel, "was the Word," a beacon to all creation.

> and the Word was with God, and the Word was God. . . . In Him was life; and the life was the light of men. And the light shineth in darkness; and the darkness comprehended it not. There was a man sent from God, whose name was John. The same came for a witness, to bear witness of the Light, that all men through him might believe. He was not that Light, but was sent to bear witness of that Light. That [Word] was the true Light, which lighteth every man that cometh into the world. . . . And the Word was made flesh, and dwelt among us, . . . full of grace and truth. . . . And of his fulness we have all received, and grace for grace [John 1–2, 4–9, 14, 16].

By the Word of God will man know Him. But, not by the Word alone. By the Word illumined, by the Word irradiated by Light. Yet, not alone by the Word which glows by the Light of God will man know Him. Man will know God only by the Word incarnate. But, this Light must be pointed toward; it must be designated; and this by man who becomes the medium through whom the Word is spoken and who, accordingly, "bears witness of that Light." He, the witness, shows wherein consists "the true Light, which lighteth every man that cometh into the world." He reveals the effulgence of God become Flesh, His paradigm and symbol and living embodiment. Dwelling with this symbol, which is also substance, man utters words which *are* the Word of God. The representative of God on earth, man partakes, in his flesh, of the Fullness of God. For, in the beginning,

> God created man in His own image, in the image of God created He him; male and female He created them. . . . And every plant of the field before . . . the heavens . . . was in the earth, and every herb of the field before it grew; for the Lord God had not caused it to rain upon the earth, and there was not a man to till the ground. But there went up a mist from the earth, and watered the whole face of the ground. And the Lord God formed man of the dust of the ground, and breathed into his nostrils the breath of life; and man became a living soul [Gen. 1:27, 2:4–7].

"To till the ground," to cultivate the soil, to tend the plants, man was placed upon the earth. A "living soul... formed of the dust of the ground," and the breath of the Word of God, man hovers between the dust and the Light. Where dust becomes iridescent with light, and the Word effloresces, man reveals himself. For the Light suffuses the Word, and the Word is illuminated by the Light; and the two become one, one in flesh and one in spirit. Created in the image of God, and fructified by the Incarnate Archetype of that image, man echoes the Word of God; he reflects the Light of God; he is an emanation of the Fullness of God.

An emanation woven of Word and Light, man is the vehicle of the spirit of God. He dwells in a kingdom apart from beast and plant. His mission on earth is to reflect, in *his* word and in *his* light, the divine Center, mirroring with his finitude the infinite yet integral rhythms of God. Yet, "formed . . . of the dust of the ground," man dwells also in a kingdom wherein he participates with beast and plant. He joins his life, and his fate, to their lives, and to their fates; his finitude is fructified by their finitude. His mission on earth is, too, to be at one with the creatures of the earth, to tend them, and to bring them to fruition. For man dwells in two kingdoms; and two kingdoms dwell in man: the heavens and the earth. The medium wherein both heaven and earth glow, he is the region in whom they meet. By his speech illumined, man reveals his essential being; he lays bare the paradoxes of his union of finite and infinite, the ambiguities of his freedom.

Adapting the cited texts to my concept of method: the "center" of man is the Word of God passing through man; his "periphery" is the flesh which incorporates that Word. From "center" to "periphery," man is luminous in flesh and in word. In this context, how may men know man? This has been the problematic of my book. By freely interpreting the texts, I may now declare: man knows man by meditating the word which man speaks, for that word is the vehicle of the Word of God; man knows man by meditating the flesh which surrounds that word, for that flesh is the vehicle of the Light of God. And each, flesh and word, will cast its light upon the other; and each will cast its shadow upon the other. By knowing the movements of the light and the movements of the shadow, man will know man. For man dwells in the Word of God, and he partakes of the

Light of God. It is the manner of this dwelling, and it is the mode of this participation, which man seeks when man would know man. For the speech of man
transcribes the silent language of God; the conduct of man transmits the hidden
light of God. To be *with* man through his speech and his conduct, as these both
reveal him and conceal him, in the movements of the light and the shadow, is
to know man. Surely, truly to know man is to know how man stands in relationship to that which truly centers man; it is to know man as the medium wherein
God, communicating the eternal resonances of the cosmos, reveals Himself to man.

Man speaks; and his speaking is in many layers; and, each of these layers is
illumined by his conduct. His every subtle strand of comportment accompanies
and discloses the meaning of his speech; his every uttered word accompanies
and discloses the meaning of his comportment. For the two are joined as one.
Now, I set forth some guiding principles by which the texture of speech and the
texture of comportment, each pervading and illuminating the other, when properly heard and seen, for the hearing and the seeing are one, become the revelation
of the soul of one man to the soul of another man. For, only thus may it be that
man can "bear witness ... of grace and truth," and through "grace for grace" may
every man know each man. Yet, though man knows man through his speech, and
the meshing of his comportment with his speech, he does not know man through
what he says so much as through how he says it; nor through what he does so
much as through how he does it. For man's speech, the content of his utterance,
is illumined not only by the visibility of his comportment, but, more significantly, by the nuances which flicker upon his speech and the inflections which
play within his speech; and by the manner in which these nuances and these
inflections are woven to the variegated facets of his non-wordly conduct. Surely,
too, man's comportment, its manifest content, is only a symbol which, properly
deciphered, in the light and in the shadow of the speech to which it is joined,
shows the latent dynamism of man; hence, not by what is manifested but by
what is therein concealed, and now revealed, is man himself revealed. Thus, it is
more through knowing what man does *not* say or do than by knowing what he
does say or do that man may know man.

Alternatively, speech and comportment are each figure upon ground of the
other. At times, one emerges into experiential dominance, at times the other. In
either instance, both are multilaminated. In the former, its texture is thick with
layers of inflection, phonemic differentiation and distribution, tonal variations,
elisions, contrapuntal designs, designations of variable ambiguity, allusions half-
concealed and half-revealed, metonomy, style, accent, metaphor, simile, *lapsus
linguae,* and multitudinous additional nuances. Analogously, in the latter, the
texture is thick with layers of physiognomic subtlety, postural deflections, gestural
inconsistencies and incongruities, tremors coarse and fine, shifting hues of complexion, changing gait, mobile lineaments of feature etched roughly or delicately,
slowly changing and interchanging emaciation and fleshiness, musculature taut
or relaxed, and (again) numberless comportmental modulations. For both, methodic inquiry which would expose the person in his unique and idiosyncratic
nature must, layer by layer, strip away penumbral traits, each pregnant with
import, and, so to speak, detach and reify each layer, scrutinizing it and drawing
appropriate inferences. Each lamina must then be rejuxtaposed, in the tutored

imagination of the investigator, to those laminae adjacent to it, so that he may discern how previously aggregated meanings are now realigned to authentic coalescence and diffusion. Thus he proceeds until the total complexion of these laminae is discerned as an integral fabric of signifier and signified, all woven together, in meanings and vehicle by which meanings are communicated. Thus, he reveals the blending of all meaning to disclose the inner being, "the breath and finer spirit" of man.

For the inquirer into the person must place himself at the very center of his subject. He must experience within *himself* the rhythms of speech and comportment, their peculiarly effulgent orchestration. Then, he may perceive man as both freely making speech and constrainedly dwelling within an ambience of speech. Then, he discerns how the person inserts himself into the linguistic intricacies of a scheme of speech within a context which has already shaped him. Thrusting himself into language, he transcribes, into the peculiar idiom of his private fantasy, the numberless linguistic layers within which he from moment to moment, from birth to death, participates. Now, he may disclose the subtle interplay between a speech engraved upon man born into its shaping matrix and a matrix replete with fragile re-formations and delicately idiosyncratic resonances. And all that I have said of speech can *pari passu* be applied to comportment. For the two are synchronous aspects of the unitary, living presence of man. Structures of comportment are passed from generation to generation, from culture to culture, from species to species. Indeed, proto-human organisms are filled with the silence of speech which ever again, but ineluctably aborted, endeavors to break through comportment, to organize the latter about it as its unifying and illuminating focus. But organisms are doomed to failure. Yet the *person* emerges, by a miraculous leap, into *rendering* his comportment, hence his being, and ultimately his freedom, by his utterances, both those which are actual and those which are potential.

Accordingly, methodic inquiry into the person requires the investigator to place himself at the center of the speech of his subject and, therein placed, to work his way through the numberless caverns and recesses of its labyrinthine structure, to trace its contours and its manifold ramifications, and to perceive the patterned networks of confluence which these shape. In this way, but without renouncing a profound attunement to the source and ambience of speech—bringing the latter to focal awareness, then allowing it to recede into the penumbral aura of flesh which perpetually haunts every spoken word—this inquirer may be inspired to conceptualize what is unique in the person, his ambiguous freedom. I say "inspired," for, quite literally, the inquirer who would *know* the person must breathe words *with* the person. He must inhale and exhale the phonemic rhythms flowing forth from the latter. For by thus making himself *substantively* continuous with the object of his investigation, conjoining their respective vitalities, he may attain the objective of his quest: to show how, by method become ontology, the essential person is revealed.

The living presence of man is in perpetual transfiguration. The light which plays upon him is a light which glows within him. It is a light which is shaped by his own actions; and, quite as much, by his inaction. When I say "shaped," I imply man's autonomy. At the same time, I imply limits to his autonomy. For to shape is not to create *de novo*; it is to transform materials conferred for the purpose of shaping. Given by a donor other than man, the possibilities for shaping these materials are breathed into them by a creative force other than man. At first glance, nature provides both materials and possibilities. Ultimately, God is Donor and Provider; and man is His agent. A creature of nature and God, man's freedom is profoundly ambiguous. Indefeasibly spontaneous, and in a certain sense instinctual, man is more like infrapersonal organisms than he is like angels. Yet, authentically free, he is inspired by "the breath of life" by which he "became a living soul." As such, he aspires toward the latter; and, in his reaching, he touches the regions wherein they dwell.

For I proclaim this doctrine: man's spontaneity consists in his instinctual re-modeling of nature, the powers of which are implanted within it by a divine being; man's freedom consists in his quest to imprint into that nature the symbolic image, whatever its specific form, of the angels. Impelled by his inner freedom to engrave upon nature the ideal of his yearnings, man is therein enabled to perceive himself as he might be and, indeed, as he *would* be, were he not but clay molded by the hand of God. Hence, not so much in the actual deeds of his sculpting does man declare his free being; for these are the spontaneous outpouring of his human nature. Rather, he affirms his freedom through the incarnation of the spirit with which he is empowered to assign content to those deeds. For, however man has shaped nature to his own inclinations, he constitutes nature a sign of his *divine* nature. Surely, man is the welding of two to one, dust and soul. On the one hand, man *is* a nature. He cannot evade the obligations existentially imposed upon him by that nature. A physical event become a living organism, man cannot escape those obligations—whatever he accomplishes or strives toward. But he is also a producer of symbols; and, in symbols, he seeks to reincarnate himself as pure soul, to draw the scintillae of mere bodyhood into the effulgent unity of consummate personhood.

Accordingly, the method by which alone man may be known must, as its root supposition—the heuristic principle of its governance—acknowledge the twofold origin of man, and his twofold destiny. As dust, he participates in the privation of being; as soul, he participates in the plenitude of being. For man is a blend of *emanata* of non-being and pure being. Through the application of the tenets outlined in this book, the person will be studied (in subsequent books) in this double aspect. For man truly hovers between two realms. In touching one realm, he is alienated from the other. Yet at no moment in his life is he too remote from either realm. Alone among creatures, he dwells in intimacy with the natural and the spiritual.

The framing of an ontology of the person—the ultimate objective of my inquiry—requires methodic examination of this oscillation. In effect, the person will (in future books) be held before us, and, so to speak, gradually rotated as, one by one, "the stages of his life's way"[13] will systematically be set forth. Four major topics dominate my quest: man's natural status as inanimate woven with animate; the dialectical interplay of man's unconscious with his consciousness; man's metamorphoses and his symbolisms; man's status as seeker, the medium wherein the universe reveals, articulates, and brings to fruition its eternal rhythms. Finally, the Method herein proposed will be amplified. For, at the end, as the culmination of my quest, I shall gather together, in a systematic cosmology, the general metaphysical assumptions which progressively emerge in this evolving program. Therein, I shall point toward the cosmos itself as the crucible of man and, thereby, illuminate the quintessential person under a cosmic perspective.

NOTES

1. Alfred North Whitehead, *Modes of Thought* (New York: Capricorn, 1958), p. 196.

2. Ibid.

3. In this and the following two paragraphs I am strongly indebted to Justus Buchler's superb books *Toward a General Theory of Human Judgment* and *Nature and Judgment* (New York: Columbia University Press, 1955).

4. Lonergan, *Insight*, p. 429.

5. Ibid.

6. Ibid., p. 430.

7. My etymologic discussion is based on the origins of the relevant terms as found in Eric Partridge, *Origins: A Short Etymological Dictionary of Modern English* (London: Routledge & Kegan Paul, 1959).

8. Paul Tillich, *Systematic Theology*, 3 vols. (Chicago: The University of Chicago Press, 1951–1963), II 21.

9. "God or Nature"; see Spinoza, "Ethics," Part I.

10. Konrad Lorenz, "Comparative Behaviorology," in *Discussions on Child Development*, edd. J. M. Tanner and Bärbel Inhelder, 4 vols. (New York: International Universities Press, 1953), I 103–31.

11. *Introduction to Metaphysics*, p. 114.

12. "Psychoanalysis and Zen Buddhism," pp. 138–39.

13. Adapted from the title of Søren Kierkegaard, *Stages of Life's Way*, trans. W. Lowrie (Princeton: Princeton University Press, 1945).

EPILOGUE

TO RECAPITULATE SUCCINCTLY the deliberations regarding Method in which I have engaged would not be possible. Too many strands, facets, and dimensions are involved. However I can sketch and cursorily indicate the import of my approach. According to my position, but without again arguing on behalf of its main tenets, my method for studying the person may, to a first approximation, be stated quite simply. For it consists essentially in addressing questions, listening to responses, and framing interpretations. Beyond that, it involves the interpenetrations, transfigurations, and spiralings of those phases. For the interpretation of any set of responses entails a new set of questions; in turn, renewed listening is required, hence renewed interpreting.

In this methodic process, information is gathered about the nature of the person with respect to three kinds of peculiarities which distinguish him from the usual objects of inquiry, peculiarities set forth in my Prologue: namely, that dialogic makeup which identifies his very substance with the (dialogic) method for investigating that substance; the indefeasible uniqueness of his substance by which factor he constitutes himself a concrete universal; the unfathomable and ceaseless efflorescing, and the labyrinthine interiority, of his substance. Since in these profound ways the person differs from all other entities, a special method is needed for his study: a method appropriate to the complexities of his being, yet, at the same time, a method which includes, as a subordinate moment, the investigatory principles of natural science. Accordingly, a formula for expressing this *ontologized* method for inquiring into the person may be stated: orchestrated spiralings of questioning, listening, responding (interpretatively). Clearly, each of these phases is both intricately contrived and intensively executed.

With respect to questioning and listening, every facet of the person must be attended and drawn forth into full light of scrutiny. Yet never may the inquirer overlook the injunction that *contextuality must reign*. For, though he shifts his gaze from one facet to another, each facet, he should ceaselessly remind himself, is prescinded from a larger matrix of activities, the ferment which *is* the person. Nor may this extracting of parts ever be allowed to blind the inquirer to this configuration. True, one or another facet might perforce be brought into sharply contoured focus. For precision must not be sacrificed in formulating the links between variegated elements gathered in by intent and by comprehensive listening. Nonetheless, however vague, the contextual background haunts such formulatings; sensitivity to this enveloping aura must always prevail.

In effect, the unique individual is held before the investigator for systematic inspection. It is as though he were continually rotated, placed now in this perspective and now in that. Each set of conditions under which he is examined provides a special context within which a particular (evanescing) event appears: namely, *the person himself* held conceptually fixed as his diverse structures and functions are studied. From this point of view, *the* person may be regarded as a class of events; each member of the class is a momentary appearing of that person as gesture, vocal inflection, and physiognomomy are extracted from the "event," and their interconnections specified. Qua class of events, the singular person, the individual himself, may be studied in a naturalistically scientific manner. How, one may legitimately ask, are the constellations of comportment, and the inner spiritual or (more narrowly) psychic being of the person event they manifest, upon one "showing" of this "event," related to analogous constellations upon another "showing"? Further, as in any scientific investigation, specific exemplars may be chosen from this series as paradigmatic of the class as a whole. Considerable information about the person may thereby be adduced. By sufficiently attentive study of these paradigms, one may infer much regarding the recurrent factors in the class of events which represents, or corresponds to, *the* person. Nevertheless, this "class" of transient "events" is but a group of episodes in the life of one person. His self-identity, a continuous strand of human substance, binds these episodes together. How to study a unique self-identity! This is the root problem posed by methodic inquiry, within an ontologic context, into the irreplaceably singular person.

Accordingly, the ever-prevailing background to methodic listening is an acute perception of this ferment, the substantive process which is the person's self-identity; yet never may this perception be allowed to obfuscate what simultaneously must be kept in the foreground of attention: namely, sustained respect for fact and detail. Factors discriminated within fact! Neither element may be ignored. For one can never know in advance which facet might suddenly be illuminated by sharp contrasts emerging between it and the context of its functioning. Unpredictably, energies flowing from that context might, as it were, concentrate themselves upon one rather than another facet. Hence, though abstraction is always required, for interrogation is necessarily concerned with a particular aspect of the person, the essential datum, it must be borne in mind, is always integral and concrete. In responding to inquiry, no matter how focused a question, the person—actually no mere datum, but a *datio*—replies from his inmost being, and by his own self-determinations. Accordingly, responses must be heard in their veridical layerings, an interwoven matrix of foci enveloping foci, factors segregated and factors in confluence. Dominating the inquiry, the *problematic* status of the person sets in motion its manifold investigatory trajectories.

No matter which facet of the person is being inquired into, the questions, though stressing that facet, are invariably addressed to the person as a whole, and, in consequence, the person responds to those questions with his whole being. Accordingly, as I have emphasized, any interpretation of the import of those aspects of the response which bear upon that facet presupposes the entire context of the inquiry: namely, the person *in concreto* and *in toto*. From this fact, an important injunction to the inquirer follows: be prepared to modify, at rapidly fluctuant rates, every vision acquired concerning *who* the person is. For, in the spiraling interplay of the three phases of inquiry, novel intrusions from that person's problematic ferment may always occur. But, since Method itself springs from the inquirer's own searching proclivities, and these in turn manifest *his* problematic being, the tenets of Method must themselves inherit the same problematic character.

Disclosing those tenets through its own concrete application, Method becomes a self-corrective and a self-enriching process; it is the process by which two analogously constituted substantive contexts are interwoven: the context of Method applying itself, and the context of that to which Method applies itself. Though relatively autonomous activities, these substantive contexts (namely, inquiring acts and acts inquired into) nonetheless interpenetrate and interact. Thereby, in correlative and mutually dependent fashion, both are transformed. For Method is but the endeavor to formalize a ferment which, being the human ferment itself, perpetually eludes formalization. Seeking to fix in categories what unfolds in human beings—i.e., human activity, hence, interpersonal dialogue—Method, issuing from human beings, is itself interpersonal dialogue. True, the phases of interrogating, listening, and interpreting, phases indigenous to all dialogue (and all dialogue is searching), may be more or less sharply demarcated. In particular, in customary human intercourse, *formal* differentiations between and within those phases cannot be as precisely delineated as may that methodic dialogue which is inquiry; yet, in both instances, these phases are compresent and mutually transfiguring. For, as I announced in my Prologue, and reiterated throughout this book, with respect to the person method and ontology are, at bottom, one and the same.

Substantively speaking—and this theme I argue throughout my subsequent books—a person is, by essence, woven of mutuality. Accordingly, to define his nature, the inquirer must always presuppose another person and, ultimately, a community of persons in dialogic relatedness. Too, for *its* essential nature to be revealed, Method likewise presupposes a community of persons, and this in two senses: Method requires both the one inquired into and the inquirer himself; Method requires other inquirers to affirm, to test, and to confirm the tenets it methodically employs. In the latter case, a *community* of methodic dialogists is presumed; thus searching into the legitimacy of Method, this community necessarily exposes the substantive makeup of those who *use* Method. In the former case (and, by inference, in the latter as well), the one inquired into, whether or not he himself explicitly uses Method, is always, by nature, at least an implicit searcher. Accordingly, each individual, the one who frankly uses Method and the one who is the subject of inquiry, have parity with respect to their mutual activity of searching. Yet these mutual activities are not merely complementary. At bottom, they are one and the same. Hence, when in this book I sought to ascertain the nature of humanly employed Method into human ontology, I was, in actuality, implicitly setting forth the contours of a human ontology itself: Ontology under the perspective of Method.

Though for deeper understanding of this book, one must work through the concrete applications of Method in subsequent books, it can be read (as I stated in my Prologue) for its own sake as an independent and self-sufficient statement of an explicitly developed method and an implicitly anticipated ontology. In the books which follow, the person will successively be disclosed as pre-eminently the one who searches. In the present one, Method itself has been shown to be a searching into the person. Later, the person herein understood as requiring to be searched into is revealed as himself a searcher—i.e., as the one who employs Method, namely, the method set forth in this volume, though non-formally and not necessarily with explicit intent. In consequence, though the later books are explicitly concerned with ontology they, in effect, invert the orientation of the present book. For they are all implicitly framing Method. In the final book (and the titles of my proposed books were enumerated in the prologue), in which I systematically gather together the metaphysical principles which emerge as fragments throughout the series, and endeavor to locate the person as keystone of a general cosmology, the strands of Method herein pursued, being ultimately equated with the strands of Personal Ontology, will be incorporated as a fundamental component.

At present, however, and in epigrammatic conclusion to this book, I can only repeat the triadic formula which most succinctly expresses its theme, a formula stated on page 4 of my Prologue: Method *is* Ontology; (Human) Ontology *is* Freedom; Freedom *is* Ambiguous. From one or another perspective, all the books are concerned with the systematic expansion of this formula. The present volume, in effect, but outlines the main contours of this expansion.

Index

DATE DUE

6. 25. '81	

BRODART, INC.   Cat. No. 23-221

Lewis and Clark College - Watzek Library
BD331 .F427   wmain
Feldstein, Leonard/Homo quaerens, the se   LIBRARY
                                                97219

3 5209 00318 4526